A SPECIAL KIND OF COURAGE

A SPECIAL KIND OF COURAGE

Profiles of Young Americans

Geraldo Rivera

BANTAM BOOKS · TORONTO · NEW YORK · LONDON

*This low-priced Bantam Book
has been completely reset in a type face
designed for easy reading, and was printed
from new plates. It contains the complete
text of the original hard-cover edition.*
NOT ONE WORD HAS BEEN OMITTED.

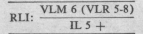

RLI: $\dfrac{\text{VLM 6 (VLR 5-8)}}{\text{IL 5 +}}$

A SPECIAL KIND OF COURAGE
*A Bantam Book / published by arrangement with
Simon and Schuster, Inc.*

PRINTING HISTORY
Simon and Schuster edition published March 1976
Serializations have appeared in GOOD HOUSEKEEPING, NEWSDAY
and the CHICAGO SUN TIMES
Bantam edition / May 1977

*Bantam Books are published by Bantam Books, Inc. Its trade-
mark, consisting of the words "Bantam Books" and the por-
trayal of a bantam, is registered in the United States Patent
Office and in other countries. Marca Registrada. Bantam
Books, Inc., 666 Fifth Avenue, New York, New York 10019.*

PRINTED IN THE UNITED STATES OF AMERICA

ACKNOWLEDGMENTS

To Edie for her illustrations, to Judi Beck for her loving patience and typing, to Patrick Hanson for his hours spent on the road and in the dusty research libraries, to Jonathan Dolger for his advice and consent, to Dee Ratterree for her telephone calls, and to the parents for their willingness to relive it all for me.

For the kids

The kid's name was Eddie Ramos. He was eleven years old and dying of leukemia. His parents had taken him to the best doctors and the best hospitals in Puerto Rico, but the case was hopeless. Eddie was dying, and nobody could help him. Using the little money they had managed to save over the years, Eddie's parents flew him up to New York City. He had never seen a big city before, and in the time he had left, Mr. and Mrs. Ramos wanted him to see and experience as many things as possible. When they got to the city, relatives gave Eddie a whirlwind tour of the Big Apple. In two days, he got to see the Statue of Liberty, the observation tower on top of the Empire State Building and even the big open-air market in East Harlem. Near the end of the visit, Eddie asked his parents if there was any chance of visiting Walt Disney World in Florida before they all returned to Puerto Rico. Most of their money was already gone, but Mr. Ramos managed to borrow just enough from their New York relatives to make a short stop in Orlando on the way home. But before they could leave, Eddie became ill again and had to be admitted to a New York hospital. During his stay there, his folks had to use the Disney World money for living expenses.

A social worker at the hospital heard about their plight and called my television station, asking if there was anything I could do to keep Eddie from being disappointed. I met him and his parents at the home of a relative the day he came out of the hospital. He was incredible—frail and weakened by the disease, he still had more dignity and self-respect than many grown-ups I'd met. I did an interview with him, and in the TV story explained his situation. The audience response was wonderful. In two hours, the station received hundreds of telephone calls pledging everything from cash donations to free airplane ticket and hotel accommodations at Disney World. Eddie and his folks left for Florida three days later, and before he went he made a special point of thanking everybody who had been nice to him. And when he did it, Eddie looked right at you with a serious and sincere set to his face that made you know for a certainty that he understood exactly what had been done for him and exactly what was happening to him. Everyone at my office went through the same series of emotions. First, chills at the eleven-year-old's maturity and understanding, then tears for his tragedy, and finally admiration and respect for his spunk and courage. He died less than a week after returning home from his Disney World trip.

At that point in my life, that is, before I met Eddie, I was steadily becoming infected by at least some of the cynicism and skepticism that has affected so many of my generation. I was becoming unwilling to believe anyone was what he seemed to be or said he was. That kid turned me around. Too inexperienced to be jaded, too powerless to be corrupted, too weak to oppress others, too young to lose hope, he was a hero to trust and admire without reservation.

When I first decided to write this book, it was with the intention of searching through the nation's history and reporting on the lives of other children (like Eddie) who had been extraordinarily brave or in some other way strong in character and heart. Happily for America, that selection proved to be impossible: our history is filled with stories of exemplary young people who have conducted themselves in inspirationally heroic ways. No random sample could do justice to the whole—the overwhelming amount of historical material made it impossible to choose. And so I turned to today. This book, then, is limited to contemporary young Americans whose courage has particularly moved me.

In a sense, it *is* a history, pieced together over a two-year period with the help of approximately two hundred interviews, public documents, and newspaper clippings. It is a history book of eleven modern kids whose stories clearly demonstrate the qualities of heroism that benefit not only themselves but their families, friends, and, by their example, society itself. It was, for me, a special book to write, and I dedicate it to the youths who have chosen to act on their own, with honor and dignity, at moments of individual crisis.

GERALDO RIVERA

New York
1975

In December of 1960 I was a punk and pimpled roughneck teen, sixteen years old and just beginning to work after school in my first legitimate job. I was an office boy/apprentice draftsman for the Winfield Sliding Door Company, of West Babylon, Long Island. Working at a real job was a radical departure for me. At the time, I had been spending most of my afternoons either hanging out with a street gang called the Corner Boys or terrorizing the corridors of the high school with fellow members of the wrestling team. For my friends and me, the only income-producing activity had traditionally been stealing other people's tires and hubcaps. But that pursuit was too erratic and the returns too uncertain to solve my present predicament.

I had reluctantly taken this, to me, degrading office-boy job to pay off a car accident I'd been involved in a few weeks earlier. While driving a friend's car one rainy evening, with neither license nor insurance, I had managed to caress the side of another car. The other driver had consented not to tell either my parents or the cops if I made good the damages to his car, which came to three hundred dollars—at that time a seemingly fantastic and virtually unobtainable amount. At a dollar an hour, and working each afternoon and all day Saturdays, that translated into the unpleasant prospect of at least a five-month career in the apprentice drafting business.

I hated it from the first day. First of all, it was boring, and second, I really resented having to spend so much time indoors and away from my friends. To kill time on the job, I used to hang out with Freddie, the porter, in the back room, where the copy machine was

1

located. A twenty-year-old high-school dropout from Long Island's black ghetto village of Wyandanch, he hated his job as much as I did mine. While pretending to be busy at work, him sweeping and me duplicating blueprints, Freddie and I used the time away from our respective supervisors to grab a clandestine smoke and listen to rock-'n'-roll music on his radio.

Just after lunch late one rainy Saturday, Freddie was fiddling with his weak old radio, trying to find a good music station. The unfinished-plywood room, furnished just with the copy machine and two stools, was dismally dark. The only light was from one small unshaded bulb. Normally, it wasn't even used, the big window usually providing enough light, but this early afternoon it seemed almost twilight outside because of the cold rain icing over banks of yesterday's snowfall.

After turning the knob from full right to full left and finding only static and chattering disc jokeys, Freddie started backtracking, turning his dial to the right again. The first station to come in clearly was WNBC. It sounded as if the news was on.

"This is Bill Ryan. Emphasis, the family of man. An epitaph for a small boy. . . . The boy, of course, is Stephen Baltz. He was eleven years old, and until Friday morning, just one of hundreds of thousands of eleven-year-olds in the world. Special only to those who knew and loved him . . ."

After pausing for a few seconds in his twisting of the dial, just to make sure that no music was in the offing from WNBC, Freddie renewed his nervous pursuit of rock-'n'-roll.

I grabbed his hand. "Hey! Wait a minute, man. I want to hear that."

"I don't want to listen to no news," he said, flicking my hand away.

"C'mon, Freddie," I said, now with rough insistence. "That's about that kid in the airplane crash . . . you heard about him, the 'miracle' boy. The one that lived through that big plane crash yesterday." Then, with impatience to end the dialogue, "Put it on, man."

Freddie reluctantly twisted the dial back to Bill

Ryan, but to show his displeasure he walked out of the back room, leaving me alone with what was being said.

". . . tossed into a snowbank, grievously injured, but alive, he suddenly became the subject of worldwide concern. The lad was rushed to a hospital, where nine doctors and five nurses pooled their skills in a massive effort to keep the spark of life in him from going out . . ."

The normally steady, straightforward announcer was speaking with uncharacteristic emotion.

"They worked for more than twenty-six hours at that task, but, finally, they failed."

"Damn . . . he died." I muttered that to the empty room.

"The lad," continued Mr. Ryan, "in the words of the head of the Methodist Hospital in Brooklyn, closed his eyes and went to sleep."

I shut the radio off abruptly. "He died . . ." I repeated to no one. I slowly got up off a stool where I had been sitting next to the copy machine. After a second's hesitation I started walking out toward the drawing table that served me as desk and office. Sleepwalking past Freddie on the way out, I heard him call after me.

"Hey, Geraldo. What's wrong wid chu?"

"He died . . ." I spoke it like somebody in a trance. It was the third time I had repeated that, but for the first time, somebody heard me.

"Who died?"

"The miracle boy."

"Oh, the kid . . . too bad," said Freddie sincerely, walking back into the room to retrieve his radio. Then, saying good-bye, "I'll catch you later. I got to get back to work."

"I have to write a letter," I responded, once again to no one.

He had been anonymous. Unknown, one eleven-year-old among millions, Stevie was special only to his family and friends before the horrible crash. But because he was somehow granted a reprieve while so many others had been killed instantly, and because of the pure, noble, and simple way he conducted himself in the hours before he died, Stevie would become a national symbol of flawless innocence and high courage in misfortune. In a nation preoccupied with preparations for the holiday season, his life and death would stir the hearts and minds of countless strangers throughout the country. For the time he survived, he reminded and reaffirmed the best in us, and left as a legacy an example of enduring faith and a stout heart.

I was one of the strangers touched by him. In the first consciously charitable act of my punk/bully adolescence, I took a pad and pencil and sat down to write a letter of sympathy and condolence to the parents of eleven-year-old Stevie Baltz, who for twenty-six hours had been the only survivor of what was the worst air disaster in history.

Two commercial airliners had collided in the clouds over New York harbor. One of them, a TWA Super Constellation flying from Columbus, Ohio, to New York's LaGuardia Airport, had exploded in midair. The graceful, four-engined, propeller-driven aircraft had been torn apart and had fallen in three huge fiery chunks on Staten Island. All thirty-nine of its passengers, including two infants, and its crew of five were certainly dead before it even hit the ground.

Stevie had been flying in the other plane, a United DC-8, bound from Los Angeles and Chicago to New York's largest airport, Idlewild. Unlike the Constellation, the big jet wasn't blown apart by the collision. With his plane crippled, a wing partially sheared off, on fire, and rapdily losing altitude, the pilot had made a last, desperate attempt to crash-land in Prospect Park, the only open space he had any chance of reaching as the jet plunged toward the densely populated borough of Brooklyn. But the DC-8 ran out of altitude before it got to the park and smashed, instead, into a quiet Brooklyn neighborhood, instantly killing seventy-six of its seventy-seven passengers, all of its seven-person crew, and five people on the ground, including an old man named Ben, who was selling Christmas trees on the corner of Sterling Place and Seventh Avenue.

Minutes before the big jet had come screaming and burning down through the overcast, the predominant sound around Ben's Christmas-tree stand had been the slurp of cars driving through the wet slush and melting ice left over from the week's snowfall. On the fringes of the once fashionable Park Slope area, the neighborhood was a run-down but still respectable residential section of brownstones and turn-of-the-century tenements. Just two blocks from the busy Flatbush Avenue commercial district, it was a neighborhood-in-transition, where poor people had begun moving into brownstones that had been converted into rooming houses and once spacious apartments that had been carved up into one-and two-room flats.

This morning, the neighborhood suffered the ultimate misfortune of being located just a half mile down the hill from Prospect Park, the only place the despairing pilot could find to try to set down his mortally wounded airplane.

Police officers Ralph Pica and Joseph Mannino were on the eight-to-four day shift that Friday. They had left the Bergen Street precinct a couple of hours before and had been patrolling their assigned area around Seventh Avenue since then. The intersection of Sterling and Seventh was basically indistinguishable from the other corners in the neighborhood. Its main landmarks were a grocery store, a little church, a meat market, and an apparently abandoned barber shop with a dusty and forlornly optimistic sign, "Closed for Renovation," in the window.

Across the street from the church, Joe spotted Ben opening up several bundles of recently arrived trees, so he told his partner to pull over.

"Let's check out some of Ben's new stock." It had been a quiet morning, and they had talked earlier about picking up a Christmas tree before the end of the day. The holiday was now just nine days away, and both had promised to bring a tree home.

Joe and Ralph had been partners patrolling this neighborhood together for the last three years. Aside from both being thirty-three-year-old family men, they were both Italian and had come on the job together. Their wives had since become best friends.

Ralph slowly pulled over. The slush and ice made driving treacherous, and he didn't want to skid. They got out of the car, greeted Ben, who had sold them their trees for the last couple of years, and started looking through his reasonably priced selections.

"They look pretty good this year . . . full," said Ralph, as he picked up several of the trees at random.

"A good crop this year," agreed the old man, who had started selling Christmas trees when he retired from his job in the garment center after fifty years. "A real good crop," he repeated, happy that two of his favorite customers were pleased.

He had almost single-handedly been responsible for brightening up the neighborhood. Christmas wreaths sold inexpensively by Ben were hanging in the church and in virtually every other window facing the intersection, and his trees were already the centerpieces in dozens of living rooms.

As he chatted with Joe and Ralph, pointing out the attributes of the various trees, Charlie Cooper came over. He was a thirty-four-year-old sanitation worker who had been shoveling snow and straightening up the overflowing trash cans waiting on the corner to be picked up by sanitation trucks diverted to the job of clearing snow for the last several days.

Charlie said hello to Ben and the cops as he leaned his shovel against a convenient trash can and started browsing through the trees for his own favorite. The city had already taken on the special tempo and good humor it sometimes adopts in anticipation of a major holiday, and particularly a white Christmas.

"C'mon, Joe," Ralph said after a few minutes. "We'd better get moving."

"We'll come back after work, at about four-thirty," Joe said to Ben, giving him a friendly pat on the back. "Save us two of the good ones."

"There'll be two of the best," assured old Ben.

"Two of the best," he repeated as he turned to find two "specials" to put aside for his friends.

Once inside the patrol car, both officers unbuttoned their heavy woolen uniform coats. Joe looked out the window to check the traffic behind them. A car was coming, but Ralph had plenty of time to pull out so Joe said, "Go ahead, you got it." Then, as he was turning around, he did a horrified double-take, as he saw and heard the screaming, outrageous roar of the plummeting, burning, gigantic airplane, level now with the top of the three-story buildings across the street and just behind them.

The DC-8 had been flying level, but just as Joe spotted it, its right wing dropped sickeningly and plowed into the top floor of a tenement, whipping the jet toward the street. It had become a building-sized torch, and it was right above the patrol car.

"*Hit it! Hit it!*" screamed Joe, urging Ralph to gun the car's engine before the plane was on them.

"Oh, Jesus!" was all Ralph said. He was already seen the careening specter and had jammed the gas pedal hard against the floor at almost the same instant.

For split seconds the officers remember as eternal, the patrol car fishtailed and slid on the slush, trying to run in its terrifying race against a dying airplane in the awesomely destructive last moments of life. Finally, the car tires found a dry spot of pavement, gripped and hurled them forward, out from under the DC-8, just as it smashed onto Sterling Place.

It landed right on top of Ben and his wonderful crop of Christmas trees. The car that had been behind the patrol car as it pulled out was also caught in the inferno. The sound of the crash was enormous. There were later reports that people heard it in Manhattan, across the river. What was left of the structure of the aircraft cracked apart as it hit, spewing huge burning pieces skidding along the icy pavement, as if in malicious pursuit of the fleeing police car. Charlie, the tree-shopping sanitation man, was horribly mutilated by an engine that tore loose on impact. The quiet intersection had become a mass of twisted metal, fire, and melting ice.

"Car 4 to base! Car 4 to base!" Joe was calling frantically for help. "A disaster. . . ! A crash—a plane crash—Sterling and Seventh—Sterling and Seventh. . . !" As his partner screamed into his radio, calling for all available units, Ralph made a sliding left turn at Sixth Avenue, another on Park Place, then another, bringing them back on Seventh Avenue, facing the still exploding wreckage of what had once been a jet airliner.

The corner was unrecognizable. Death and bedlam were everywhere. At least ten of the tenements were burning. The little church on the corner, ironically named Pillar of Fire, was completely gone except for its facade which had been soaked with jet fuel and now blazed as an independent torch. Wally Lewis, the ninety-year-old caretaker of the church, had died at precisely the same instant as his old friend Ben just across the street. The grocery store, the meat market, and the empty barber shop all rapidly followed the church into flames. As the officers approached the corner, people were beginning to run panic-stricken from their homes. At their doors, they paused only long enough to figure which direction took them away from the white-hot wreckage, before bolting.

To the cops, the fire was bad enough, but the real horror was the mangled bodies and bits of bodies scattered all around the intersection, now barricaded by the tall tail section of the airplane.

"Hey!" Ralph shouted. "That colored kid's alive!" On his knees, right alongside the airplane that had carried him from Chicago, was eleven-year-old Stevie Baltz. His life had been miraculously prolonged when the fuselage split open just at the point where he had been sitting. When Officer Pica spotted him, Stevie was on fire, and his arms were stretched out to either side of him. "He looked like a burning crucifix," Ralph remembers.

"C'mon!" Joe said as he grabbed for the fire extinguisher, kept under the glove compartment on the right side of the dash. In those first frantic moments, the air crash was a disaster of almost incomprehensible magnitude, but a kid in trouble was something the experienced officers knew how to deal with. Ralph twisted around and reached over to grab his heavy rubber service raincoat from the back seat. They leaped out of the car almost simultaneously, running toward the burning kid. They could hear him calling for help, as they ran. Stevie was already charred by the time they got there, and it wasn't until much later in the day that they found he wasn't a black kid after all.

Joe engaged the extinguisher as Ralph threw his coat around Stevie, both men trying desperately to smother the flames that now threatened to consume him. Stevie's clothing and his skin were still burning, fused together at this point, and the intense heat quickly began to melt Ralph's raincoat. At Brooklyn Methodist Hospital, where the eleven-year-old was later taken, they had a plaque hanging in the main lobby. Mounted on it are the nine coins that Stevie had in his pocket that day, five nickels and four dimes. All of them fused into one welded lump by the heat.

Finally Ralph picked Stevie up in his arms and ran, carrying him to one of the wet piles of gray snow that Charlie had been shoveling just a few minutes before. As he rolled Stevie around in the slush, the flames went out. The little "colored" boy was alive, and somehow still conscious.

"Am I going to die?" he asked his rescuer in the calm, matter-of-fact way you ask somebody if it's going to rain.

"No . . . of course you're not going to die," lied Officer Pica, wondering how the youngster had managed to live even this long. "What's your name, sonny?" Ralph asked, wondering why he hadn't seen this kid around the neighborhood before the crash.

"Stephen Baltz . . . I'm from Wilmette, Illinois . . . my mother is waiting for me . . . she's waiting . . ."

For a second, Ralph couldn't say anything. The kid wasn't from around here. He was from the airplane, and now he was asking for his mother, who had apparently been on the airplane with him.

"She'll be all right, Steve . . ." the officer gently lied again, looking over his shoulder at the flaming wreckage, positive that if the woman had been on the airplane, she was most certainly dead. "Don't worry . . . she'll be all right."

"She's waiting for me . . ." Stevie said again, ". . . with Dee, at the airport." Lying on his back in the snowbank, his burnt hands dangling limply in front of him, Stevie looked right up at Ralph and tried urgently to communicate the need for somebody to call his mother before she began to worry about him. "Please tell her where I am."

Realizing that Stevie wasn't confused, and that his mother had not been a passenger on the airplane, Ralph told him that he would have somebody call her right away. But the officer's major concern now, surrounded by carnage and the burning tenements, was the threat of further explosions.

Joe had run into the buildings to get whoever was left inside to safety, but Joe needed help.

Harry's Bowling Alley was a favorite hangout for the neighborhood's unemployed. It was on Park Place, a block over from Sterling, and just a few feet east of Seventh Avenue. When the men inside heard the huge explosion, many of them rushed outside to see what had happened. As they turned the corner of Seventh Avenue, they were confronted by the burning buildings and scattered corpses. Some of the bowlers just turned and ran away, but the more intrepid among them went cautiously toward Officer Pica, who was still kneeling over the grievously injured boy. Around that intersection they were the only living people in sight.

"Help us! Help us!" Ralph called out, excitedly urging the gaping group to come closer. He had a desolate image of the whole neighborhood exploding, adding the hundreds who hid frozen with fear in their apartments to the scores of dead people lying all around him.

Despite the intense heat pouring from the Pillar of

Fire Church, four or five men began to gather around
Stevie.

"Take care of him!" Ralph ordered. "I'll be back
as soon as I can," he said, dashing away, and up the
stairs of buildings that were still filled with people.

Gasps and shock waves rippled through the volunteers as they looked down at Stevie and realized that he
was a survivor of the plane crash.

"Call an ambulance!"

"Get the kid a priest!"

For a few seconds, frantic suggestions passed back
and forth through the semiparalyzed group. They sincerely wanted to help, but his condition seemed so desperate they didn't know what to do. The sound of sirens, distant but increasing, and the arrival of Father
Harry thankfully relieved them of the need to act decisively.

The Reverend Harry A. Sterling, of St. John's
Episcopal Church, just down the block, was already the
nearest thing to a legend in Park Slope. A wonderful
and compassionate priest, he was seventy years old,
wore wire-rim glasses on a round face that was unmis-
takably benevolent, and used to spend his afternoons
walking up and down the streets handing out candy
from his bulging pockets to the children of the neighborhood.

Caring for children was his special ministry, and
his heart broke when he saw how brutally Stevie had
been injured. He was thankful only that it was a week-
day, and with school in session, there hadn't been any
neighborhood children on the street when the plane
crashed.

He knelt immediately beside the boy sitting in the
slush and took him gently in his arms. "Oh, my son . . .
my son . . ."

"Am I going to die?" Steve asked again. There was
still no concern or urgency in his voice. He just wanted
to know.

"Oh, child!" the priest gasped softly, far more upset than Stevie. "I don't know . . . but I'm going to
ask God to visit you now . . . and take care of you."

Holding Stevie and rocking him slowly, gently, back and forth, the old priest gave him a conditional absolution. Stevie, who belonged to a Methodist church back home in Wilmette, said "Amen" with him.

"My mother is waiting for me at the airport. Please could you call her? I don't want her to worry. We came to visit my grandma."

"What's your name, son?" the priest asked.

"Stephen Baltz."

"Ahhh . . ." said Father Harry, as he introduced himself, trying not to show his shock at the boy's charred face and body. "Your namesake is Saint Stephen . . ." he continued, as he quickly told Stevie the story of Christendom's first martyr. All the while Father Harry was telling Stevie the story, he was looking around at the devastation and praying for the arrival of the ambulance that would take the boy to a hospital.

"I'm from Illinois," Stevie told him proudly. "And I was flying all by myself." When the old man congratulated him on being such a grown-up, Stevie showed him the new watch his father had just given him to mark the occasion. "But I broke it, I think," the eleven-year-old said apologetically as he held up his burnt right arm and looked sadly at the metal wrist band. It was twisted and smelled of jet fuel. The hands had stopped at 9:37, presumably Chicago time, and the sight of it was more than the priest could bear. He choked and started to cry.

A moment later, another police car arrived. Two cops came running toward him, picked Stevie up, laid him across the back seat, and sped away for the hospital. It was just 10:47. Less than ten minutes before, Ben had been selling Christmas trees on this corner.

Father Harry almost had to be picked up and carried away from the still-raging inferno. He never got over his chance meeting that morning with an eleven-year-old boy who wasn't afraid to die, but who worried about worrying his mother. When he heard the next day that the boy had died, he went into deep mourning. A broken old man after that, he stopped saying services and seldom left his room on the top floor of the rectory, refusing meals, and just staring out his window and smoking his pipe. When Uncle Harry (as the other priests at St. John's dubbed him) died two months later, he was buried on the grounds of his church, a block from the still burned-out intersection of Seventh Avenue and Sterling Place.

Stevie had lived with his mom and pop, ten-year-old sister, Dee, and kid brother, four-year-old Billy, in a big old stucco house in the Chicago suburb of Wilmette, Illinois. Built around the turn of the century, it was a solid, family-type home, with a big well-manicured lawn, typical of this prosperous North Shore community.

Even though the house had three floors and ten rooms, the kids never had any problem filling it up with their inexhaustible energy. Of course, they also had plenty of help. Dee's friends were constantly coming over to play, and so were Stevie's. He had been a Little Leaguer, a Boy Scout, a member of the youth choir at the First Methodist Church, and just a plain sixth-grader at Central School. And all these organizations and affiliations contributed friends, and friends of friends, to the constant ebb and flow of kids into and out of the big house on Broadway.

Late Thursday afternoon, the house had been relatively calm. It was drizzling outside, and little Billy was upstairs asleep. Stan, as William S. Baltz, Stevie's father, is called, was sitting half asleep in his favorite chair in the living room, dozing through the afternoon newspaper. The only real noise was coming from the kitchen, where "Lady Blue" was cheerfully clanking and humming her way through the dinner preparations.

Her real name is Pearl Belue (pronounced "blue"), and over the years families all along the North Shore had come to depend on her around the house. She was a good cook and a competent housekeeper, but most of all, Lady Blue was wonderful with the children. She was kind and friendly to them, but she was also an imposingly spunky lady who wouldn't tolerate sass or disrespectful backtalk.

When Mrs. Baltz, with her daughter, had gone to visit her parents in New York a few days before, she had confidently left Lady Blue in charge of the house. Phyllis knew from experience that Stan and little Billy would be well fed while she was away, and that Stephen would be properly packed and ready to join her in New York.

Up in his room, Stevie and his really one and only best friend, David, were talking quietly but excitedly. Stevie's trip was scheduled for the next day, and it was the boys' main topic of animated but subdued conversation. Between them, on Stevie's bed, was his open suitcase. Actually, it had already been carefully packed by his mother before she'd left, so they were just admiring its ready-willing-and-able-to-go look. Originally, Stevie, his mother and sister were all supposed to go to New York together to visit Mrs. Baltz's parents. But he'd developed a terrible sore throat the day before they were to leave. He kept insisting that he was well enough to make it, but the doctor had given a thumbs down to Stevie's suggestion. So the ladies had gone ahead, and Stevie would be joining them tomorrow.

Getting off his bed, he walked over to the glass cage he had put together for his hamsters. He was proud of it, because it was patterned after their natural habitat.

"Don't forget to feed and water the hamsters, David."

"Don't worry about it," answered Stevie's camping, fishing, and animal-raising companion. "I'll take good care of them."

"Are you going to the Scout meeting tomorrow night?" Stephen asked, suddenly remembering that he had neglected to tell his Troop 3 Scout leader that he'd be missing a meeting.

"Yeah. You want me to tell them you'll be there for the next meeting?"

"Ummm . . . I think Mom said we'd be back on the day before Christmas Eve."

"Whatta you getting me for Christmas?" asked David with playful curiosity.

"You tell me first."

When, a half hour later, Lady Blue realized it was

dark out, she stopped what she was doing in the kitchen, walked over to the bottom of the stairs, and called up to the boys, strongly suggesting that it was time for David to go home.

After she'd gotten David safely off, she seated Mr. Baltz and his boys around the dinner table. In between her urgings of extra portions, Lady Blue talked expansively of Stevie's pending trip. Whenever he tried excitedly to answer her, she sternly, albeit playfully, told him to stop talking with his mouth full.

Later, as Mr. Baltz sat, quietly reflective, across the dinner table from his elder son, he proudly sized Stevie up. His boy would be twelve years old in January. It was hard to believe, but Stevie was almost a teenager. Big for his age, he was already a solid five feet tall, and growing fast. Stevie was a good boy, mature and thoughtful, and could certainly handle the solo trip to New York, silently concluded his father.

"Looking forward to tomorrow, son?"

"I sure am . . . I can't wait!"

Early the next morning the dozing passengers on the big DC-8 jetliner were yawning and grumbling as the new flight crew came on board at O'Hare Airport. This two-hour intermediate stop in Chicago, which it was virtually impossible to sleep through, was the worst aspect of United's "red-eye" overnight flight between Los Angeles and New York's Idlewild Airport. It was just seven o'clock, and the cold winds swirling across the great open runways of O'Hare made the jet uncomfortably drafty.

Even the few experienced travelers who did manage to sleep through the bumpy flight into Chicago, the landing, and the almost two-hour layover were wakened when the Chicago contingent of passengers started coming on board, shortly before nine o'clock. Stewardess Mary Mahoney greeted passengers and checked tickets as they came up the steps. Augustine Ferrar seated the dozen or so first-class passengers, mostly business types, and Annie Brouthen and Patty Keller seated the people heading back toward the long coach section.

Patty, who somehow managed to be perky even

though she'd gotten up at five that morning, had the additional responsibility of supervising an unattended minor. He was an eleven-year-old boy who was coming on board in Chicago.

Stevie had been awake since five o'clock. As a matter of fact, he was so excited about the prospect of his first ride in a jetliner that he had hardly slept at all. He had made at least one surreptitious telephone call to David, and several times during the night had jumped up and frantically checked his watch, making sure that he and his father hadn't overslept.

Because he was so anxious to get on with the trip, already delayed three days by that sore throat, Stevie was up, dressed, and ready for the drive in from Wilmette to O'Hare a full hour before his dad. He was wearing a new gray suit his parents had bought especially for the trip. It was a neat outfit, smartly topped by a dapper gray hat that Stevie really liked because it had a feather in the band. He occupied his extra time either looking in the mirror in search of just the right tilt for his new hat or happily helping Lady Blue prepare breakfast. When it was finally time to go, she admonished him to behave himself. Stevie said good-bye to his drowsy brother, then ran out to the car where Mr. Baltz was waiting for him. For the whole ride he talked endlessly of airplanes and about spending time with his grandparents in New York. For the most part, Mr. Baltz was pleased to let Stevie do most of the talking, only occasionally contributing a comment of his own.

Aside from Stephen's maturity, there were other reasons he felt no apprehension at all about his son's trip. On the new jet, it would take only a couple of hours at most to get to New York, and the stewardesses had already been notified that Stevie would be flying alone. And once he got to Idlewild, Mrs. Baltz and Dee would be at the airport to greet him.

At the boarding gate, next to the sign that read,

UNITED AIR LINES
Flight 826
Passengers Only

Mr. Baltz was going to say good-bye to his son, but then decided to escort him on board. After all, it was Stevie's first trip by himself. They talked as they headed out toward the ramp.

"Be sure to give your grandparents a kiss for me, son."

"I sure will, Dad. And I'll wish them a Merry Christmas too."

"Thanks. And don't forget to tell them that I really wanted to come. I'm sure your mother has explained that I couldn't get away from the office, but you tell them as well. All right? And kiss your mother too."

As they reached the ramp, Mary Mahoney greeted Stevie.

"Hi." She smiled cheerfully. "My name is Mary."

"I'm Stephen Baltz," he answered with only a touch of shyness as they started up the steps. "And I'm pleased to meet you."

Mary and Mr. Baltz smiled a greeting as they watched Stevie check out the big airplane. Up the ramp, it seemed gigantic to him. Hesitating on the top step, and looking fore and aft, he marveled at the size of the jet's engines.

"Look at them Dad!"

Mary smiled again and asked Stevie if he liked airplanes. He told her about his big collection of model airplanes at home, explaining modestly that he had assembled them all by himself, but that, of course, there was just a little help from his father.

Once on board, Mr. Baltz walked Stevie back to his assigned seat. When they reached his row, Stevie sat down near the window.

"Fasten your seat belt, son," his father said. Then, just before saying good-bye, Stan asked the gentleman sitting next to Stevie if he'd mind keeping an eye on the eleven-year-old until they arrived in New York. Reassured, father and son manfully shook hands, and Mr. Baltz left the airplane.

Patty Keller came over, introduced herself, and checked Stevie's seat belt.

"Would you like a glass of milk or a Coca-Cola?"

Stevie reflected a moment. He really wanted a Coke, but he asked for a glass of milk because it was so early in the morning.

"I'll bring it to you as soon as we're airborne. Okay?"

"Sure."

Flight 826 was being flown that morning by a very experienced crew that had been over this same route many times before. The pilot, forty-six-year-old Captain Bob Sawyer, was the kind of sober and knowledgeable aviator to inspire confidence in even the most sweaty-palmed passenger. A flier since 1941, he had more than nineteen thousand air hours to his credit.

Sitting next to him that Friday morning, in the copilot's seat, was First Officer Robert Fiebling. He was crisply reading off the items on the long preflight check-list, pausing after each item so that the captain could scan the instrument panel and, once satisfied that all was well, respond, "Check."

Copilot Fiebling, although a few years younger than Captain Sawyer, was an experienced pilot in his own right. He had over eight thousand flying hours, more than four hundred of which had been logged in this relatively new type of jet.

Sitting directly behind the copilot was Dick Pruitt, the flight engineer and the "kid" of the crew. But at the age of thirty, Second Officer Pruitt had already been working for United Air Lines for five years, and had managed also to log more than eight thousand flying hours.

After the preflight ritual had been completed, the DC-8 was pushed away from the ramp area, and then taxied away from the terminal. Stevie was waving energetically to his father, who was standing and waving back from behind the big plate-glass windows of the terminal building.

As soon as the jet pulled away from the building, Patty came over to Stevie to make sure everything was all right. She had been working as a stewardess for only six months, and he was her first unescorted minor.

Stevie, for his part, was tremendously pleased, not so much with her eager attention, which was sort of embarrassing, but mostly with the fact that they'd soon be airborne. He kept his nose almost against the window and envisioned himself flying airplanes.

"Prepare for departure."

When Captain Sawyer's voice came over the public-address system, Patty excused herself, telling Stevie she'd be back in a minute with his milk, and hurried to her jump seat. He looked away from the window for a moment, said "Okay," and quickly looked back out. Patty buckled in, just as the skipper gunned the four powerful Pratt and Whitney turbojet engines, and the plane charged down the runway.

The DC-8 was "wheels off," or airborne, by eleven minutes after nine o'clock.

As soon as they were up, many of the Los Angeles passengers determinedly attempted to go back to sleep, their uncomfortable two-hour interruption finally over.

Flying time into New York was scheduled to take one hour, twenty-nine minutes. It's impossible to be sure, but knowing Patty's vivacious personality and Stevie's excitement and curiosity, an estimate of their in-flight conversations can reasonably be made.

"Here's your milk, Stevie. How do you like it so far?"

"Thank you." He was really a polite kid. "I like it fine! . . . Can I ask you a question?"

"Sure. I hope I can answer it."

"How fast are we going?"

"Well . . ." She wasn't really positive. "Hold on a second. I'll ask Annie."

She walked down the aisle, asked her colleague, then came back to Stevie with the answer.

"She says we're going about five hundred and fifty miles per hour."

"No kidding!" he exclaimed, looking back out at the cloud cover racing by.

Cruising at 27,000 feet, the records show they encountered some turbulence, but the flight into the New York area was otherwise normal. The undercast visually confirmed the reports of bad weather in the metropolitan area that the crew had received before leaving Chicago.

At twelve minutes past ten, and in position to begin the gradual descent toward Idlewild, Captain Sawyer radioed the New York Air Route Traffic Control Center.

The center quickly answered: "United 826, New York Center, roger, have your progress, radar service not available, descend to and maintain flight level 25,000, over."

Captain Sawyer reported leaving 27,000 feet. He was in the process of leveling off at his newly assigned altitude when New York Center advised him to maintain 25,000 feet and follow an approach course first over Allentown, Pennsylvania, and then Robbinsville, New Jersey. The instructions called for a series of relatively rapid course changes, but with the sophisticated navigational equipment carried on board the jet, such changes were usually accomplished with minimal difficulty. Flight 826 acknowledged receipt of New York Center's instructions.

The first hint of trouble came just a few minutes later. As Copilot Fiebling, who under these circumstances would be handling the navigation, tuned his instruments to calculate their new heading, he discovered that one wasn't working properly.

"Hey, Bob," he said calmly to Captain Sawyer, "one of the VOR receivers is out."

"You sure?" responded the captain, looking at the instrument console in front of them. "Check it again."

The copilot again tuned the two radio navigational receivers, but one of them was still not working.

"Nope. It's out."

"I'm going to advise ARINC," responded the captain, pronouncing the abbreviation of the Aeronautical Radio, Inc., as "ah-re-neck." It was the company that operated and maintained the aeronautical communications system for United Air Lines.

After setting his radio on the appropriate frequency, Captain Sawyer advised the maintenance company in a slightly annoyed voice, "Number-two navigational receiver accessory unit inoperative."

The man at the ARINC office radio first made a note to have some repairmen check out the equipment as soon as the plane landed; then he advised the United office at Idlewild that one of its planes had an equipment malfunction. What everyone forgot to do, including Captain Sawyer and Copilot Fiebling, was to inform New York Center that anything was wrong with their airplane's equipment. So the air-traffic controllers on the ground kept relaying instructions to the DC-8 on the assumption that everything was normal. It turned out to be a fatal omission.

Since that time, the Civil Aeronautics Board has issued a special regulation requiring pilots flying with the assistance of instruments to report immediately any in-flight malfunction of navigation or communication equipment. But on Friday, December 16, 1960, no such regulation existed.

The two radio navigational receivers on board Flight 826 were used to get a cross-bearing, or "fix," on specific landmarks. Thus, even when flying through or over dense cloud cover, like that day's, the flight crew could rapidly determine exactly where they were. With only one unit working, they could still figure out where they were, but it was a more complicated process, involving much more time and rapid mental calculation and interpretation. For one reason or another, the crew of Stevie's airplane wasn't up to it.

New York Center radioed them again at twenty-one minutes after ten, clearing Flight 826 to descend to 13,000 feet. Captain Sawyer, flying just above the dense clouds and conscious of the fact that he'd be needing more time than usual to navigate the aircraft, replied, "We'd rather hold upstairs." At least until the center made radar contact with the plane.

A minute later, the center called again, "United 826, New York Center, radar contact."

Captain Sawyer answered quickly. "Roger, we're cleared to 13,000. If we're going to have a delay, we would still rather hold upstairs than down. Do you have a weather report handy?"

The center replied, "No. But I'll get it. There have been no delays until now."

Just after Flight 826 reported passing over Allentown, the center advised that the weather at Idlewild was rain and fog, with visibility down to just a half-mile. A few seconds later, Captain Sawyer radioed, "We're starting down."

When the "Fasten seat belts" sign flashed on, the four stewardesses, with their own areas of responsibility, began cheerfully to check the seat belts of their seventy-six passengers.

"It looks pretty icky down there," said Patty to her young charge. "We'll be landing on instruments, I think."

"I wonder if it's raining or snowing," Stevie responded. "My mother and sister are meeting me at the airport, and I hope they're not out in the cold."

"Oh, don't worry about that." As Patty was describing the huge facilities at the airport terminal, the plane shook in the rough air. "Ohhh . . ." she groaned cheerfully. "We're into the clouds."

"Gosh. I can't see a thing," said Stevie, resuming his favorite position of nose-to-window. He said later that when he first saw the snow-covered city of New York from the airplane window, it looked like "a fairyland."

Down at the airport, Mrs. Baltz and her daughter were already waiting expectantly, and in Stevie's mother's case, apprehensively. The weather was really rotten—an unattractive combination of rain, sleet, light snow, and fog. As an experienced traveler, she understood that the risk was minimal, but still she'd be a lot happier when her son was on the ground.

At 10:25 A.M., the center radioed Flight 826 and amended its clearance: "826 cleared to proceed on Victor 30 until interception Victor 123. It'll be a little quicker." The new instructions shortened the distance to the airport approach by eleven miles. Ordinarily, a schedule-minded pilot would welcome the shortcut. But on Flight 826, with one of its VOR receivers out, the new course imposed an increased burden on the already hard-pressed navigator.

Five minutes later, United 826 was cleared to "descend to and maintain 5,000 feet." Captain Sawyer acknowledged, put the nose of the DC-8 down, and reported leaving 13,000 feet.

He turned toward his copilot and asked, "You okay?"

"Yes," replied First Officer Fiebling, without looking up from his instruments. "But this is a pain in the neck."

TWA Flight 266 had departed the airport at Columbia, Ohio, at nine o'clock. As the flight passed over Linden, New Jersey, an hour and a half after takeoff, the LaGuardia Approach Control began vectoring it by radar to a final course for landing on runway four. A minute later, the Constellation was cleared to descend to 5,000 feet and was twice advised of air traffic in the vicinity.

At 10:33, New York Center advised United 826 that radar service was terminated. "826 . . . contact Idlewild Approach Control." Responsibility for guiding the airplane through the clouds was passed from the air traffic controllers to the airport tower.

With the courtesy that universally prevails in the aviation profession, Captain Sawyer responded, "Roger, New York Center. Thank you and good day."

Thirty seconds after tuning the radio to the appropriate new frequency, Flight 826 called, "Idlewild Approach Control, United 826, approaching Preston [a navigational landmark] at 5,000." They were due to arrive at Idlewild in 4½ minutes.

It was the last radio transmission from Stevie's airplane.

An examination of the DC-8's flight recorder after the crash indicated that at the time Captain Sawyer was reporting his aircraft approaching the Preston landmark, it was actually already nine miles past that point.

With his nose to the window, Stevie could have

been one of the few witnesses to the whole terrible drama. From his seat in the rear-left-hand section of the jet, he could see the converging Constellation moments before even the pilot of his own airplane. The TWA flight was heading east over Staten Island at 176 miles an hour. Stevie's DC-8 came on them from behind and to the right. At the instant of collision, the jet was charging blindly through the clouds at about 330 miles an hour.

The Constellation was visible to Captain Sawyer for perhaps one or two seconds. Even in that hopelessly brief time, his vast flying experience triggered an instinctive survival response. He managed to avoid a direct impact by heaving up on his control column and turning it roughly to the left. He was trying to get over and behind the aircraft ahead of him. He almost made it.

The left wing of the DC-8 did not quite manage to clear the Constellation. Half of it was sheared off. But not before it had acted as a deadly knife, cutting off half the right wing and most of the tall tail assembly of the other aircraft.

At an altitude later computed to be between 5,175 and 5,250 feet above sea level, the TWA flight burst into flames. Totally out of control, it began the graceful downward spiral of a giant bird fatally wounded. The wreckage exploded when it hit and was strewn over a half-mile of the Miller Air Field, near the village of New Dorp on Staten Island.

Stevie's plane was crippled, but not burning. It continued flying across Staten Island, limping in a northeasterly direction toward Brooklyn.

The Idlewild approach controllers, still not aware of the aerial trauma, called normally: "United 826, this is Idlewild Approach Control. Maintain 5,000. Little or no delay. Visibility 600 feet, scattered; estimated ceiling, 1,500 feet; visibility half-mile, light rain and fog."

The only response to the call was the sound of an open microphone. Captain Sawyer apparently, in the very process of answering, had realized there was nothing anyone on the ground could do to help them. After a momentary hesitation, he decided instead to concentrate on crash-landing his disabled airplane.

The passenger compartment was probably filled with screams as shocked people came to the realization that they had smashed into another airplane. There was only a tattered half-wing left on Stevie's side, and one of the big engines he had so admired when he boarded, just over an hour before, was gone.

The plane was being shaken again and again with sickening and violent tremors.

Captain Sawyer and Copilot Fiebling wasted neither speech, nor thought on recriminations. Both held tightly to the control columns in front of them, fighting heroically to keep their stricken craft on level flight. At an altitude of 1,500 feet, they burst through the undercast. They had made it across the Narrows. Brooklyn was below them.

The park! Prospect Park was less than two miles away. They were losing altitude rapidly; there was absolutely no chance of making any airport. Brooklyn's biggest park was the only open ground they had any hope of reaching. Striving mightily with their sluggish and unresponsive controls, Sawyer and Fiebling managed to point the DC-8 in the right direction.

They ran out of sky about a half-mile down the hill from the park, over Ben's Christmas-tree stand.

The fuselage broke in half upon impact. The forward half, including the flight deck, was immediately consumed by fire and explosions. If Captain Sawyer, Copilot Fiebling and Engineer Pruitt survived the initial impact, they were almost instantly burned to death.

About ten minutes later, Stevie was in the back seat of a speeding police car, racing the short distance to the nearest hospital.

"What happened to Patty?" he asked, quietly looking up at the officer who was holding him in the seat.

"Who's Patty, kid?" The big cop talked in a soft voice that he was obviously unaccustomed to using.

"From the airplane . . ." Stevie added.

"Ohh . . . she's fine, kid. She's fine," the officer

assured him understandingly, exchanging a momentary glance with his partner, who was driving the speeding patrol car.

"Where are we going now?" Stevie asked, as he looked past the officer at the buildings swishing past.

"We're going to Methodist Hospital, kid." It was painful, even for this veteran cop, to look at Stevie, and somehow more so because the boy suffered with such quiet dignity. "Don't worry. We'll be there in a minute. It's just a few blocks away."

"I'm a Methodist," Stevie informed him, happy with the coincidence and making an impossible attempt to smile. "I'm a Sunday-school boy."

"How about that!" the officer exclaimed, feigning enthusiasm. "That's really nice," he added, desperate to arrive at the emergency room entrance.

Dr. Aldo Mazzarino, just twenty-six years old, had been working in Methodist Hospital for only six months. A recent graduate of the medical school of Bologna University in Italy, he was serving his residency at this Brooklyn hospital. That December he was assigned to the orthopedic service.

At the time of the crash, Dr. Mazzarino was on the second floor of the hospital, in the X-ray department, going through the complete physical examination required each year of the hospital staff.

The attending technician had just completed the comprehensive gastrointestinal series on the doctor, and the two men were talking. The radio was playing on the technician's desk. It was just background sound until they heard the first bulletin about the crash.

"Isn't that close to here?" asked Dr. Mazzarino, in his soft Italian accent.

"Right down the block!" replied the stunned technician.

"I wonder if anyone lived . . ." asked the doctor. Then, as if in response to his own question, "I better get downstairs!"

Just as the doctor ran out into the corridor, he heard his name being called by the tinny voice of the PA system.

"Dr. Mazzarino. Dr. Mazzarino. Please report to the emergency room immediately."

Stevie had already been admitted. Singed from head to toe, he really did look like a black child. A young intern was attaching an intravenous unit to Stevie's arm when Dr. Mazzarino hurried into the room. He had run down the steps, fearing the elevator would be too slow. The boy lay face-up on a stretcher, screened from the rest of the emergency room by cloth partitions.

His right arm and leg were broken, but despite all the pain that must have been coming from his multiple injuries and severe burns, Stevie was still conscious. He politely answered all the doctors' questions.

He told them about the other airplane, and about the noise. He didn't remember much after that except that he had clutched his seat tightly as the airplane went down.

"I'm from Wilmette . . . I was coming to see my grandmother. My mom is waiting for me at the airport. I'm afraid she's going to be worried. Could you please tell her where I am? My name is Stephen Baltz."

Stevie's identification, together with most of his clothes, had been charred. But the boy told the doctors his name, and even where to contact his father in Illinois. He had just been flung from an inferno, but what continued to preoccupy him most was his parents' anxiety.

Dr. Mazzarino kept asking Stevie if he felt any pain. He was ready with morphine and other anesthetics, but . . . "He never complained about the pain. Stephen didn't want to worry us," said Dr. Mazzarino, afterwards.

After his arm and leg had been splinted and his body bandaged, Stephen was taken up to the fourth floor. He had to be isolated, both to prevent infection of his wounds and to protect him from harassment by the hordes of newsmen who, within the hour, were converging on the hospital to catch a glimpse of the eleven-year-old they were already calling the "miracle boy."

Aside from the host of reporters based in the city, the American Press Institute's City Editors' Seminar for twenty-nine out-of-town papers happened to be going on at the time. So the crush of newsmen was even greater than usual.

The fourth floor of Brooklyn Methodist wasn't in use at the time. It had been cleared in preparation for renovation work still to be started. Stevie, who still hadn't cried despite his terrible ordeal, was placed in a room that had been hurriedly and specially fitted out as an intensive-care unit. He didn't seem to be having any trouble breathing, but all the attending physicians were extremely worried about the extent of internal burns. Stevie's throat had been badly burned, and preliminary chest X-rays indicated that his lungs had also been badly charred by the intense heat of the flaming jet fuel.

Although they didn't have one of the advanced burn units that are now being activated in hospitals across the country, the medical staff of Brooklyn Methodist mobilized as best they could to save Stevie. Arterial lines were connected to measure the oxygen level in his blood, and he was given large doses of cortisone to suppress the secretion pouring out from the burnt linings of his lungs, threatening to choke him.

In a healthy person, the oxygen, or pO_2, level in the blood is usually around 95. When Stevie was first admitted, it was around 85 and dropping fast. Below 60, brain damage and coma set in; and if it drops below that, death soon becomes inevitable.

They started him on oxygen in an attempt to keep the pO_2 level from dropping below that life-sustaining level.

The airplane was almost forty minutes late when the people waiting at the airport for Flight 826 got the first ominous indication of disaster. United Air Lines officials, wearing their neat blazers, circulated through the area, asking people awaiting the arrival of the flight from Los Angeles via Chicago to follow them into another room. Apprehensive glances were exchanged, but most of the fifty or so people, fearing what they might hear, were reluctant to ask many questions.

Up on the illuminated arrival/departure board, the flight listing was removed.

On the long and virtually silent processional from the waiting area to the specially designated room, somebody said something about the flight having been diverted to Baltimore. Relief flooded through the crowd as one person after another noisily assured himself and whoever else was listening that, of course, that was what they were going to be told by the stern-faced officials as soon as they got where they were going. It was as if they thought confident repetition would convert the Baltimore rumor into fact.

Just behind a young airline representative, Phyllis Baltz was walking silently near the head of the line, tightly holding the hand of her ten-year-old daughter. When the word of the diversion reached their section of the long line, she smiled in relief, but the smile quickly faded. She had seen no change in the troubled face of the airline official ahead of her when he looked back to hear what was being said.

Her apprehension rapidly turned to shock and then almost to panic when she entered the room. It was swarming with news people and glaring with the bright lights of their cameras.

Appalled, Mrs. Baltz led Dee into a relatively quiet corner of the room. Reporters were interviewing people as soon as they walked in, successfully capturing bursts of anguish as they informed their interviewees that Flight 826 had crashed.

"What am I going to do . . . what am I going to do?" asked one woman, rhetorically, as tears streamed down her cheeks. She had been waiting for her husband, to whom she had been married for less than a month. When others in the group tried to comfort her by assuring her that her husband was still alive, she sobbed, "No, no, there's only one survivor."

Phyllis sat frozen in the corner.

"What's the matter, Mommy? Where's Stevie?" asked ten-year-old Randee.

"I don't know, yet, darling." Too shocked even to

cry, Mrs. Baltz took comfort in comforting her daughter. "We just have to wait here until somebody tells us something."

It seemed an excruciatingly long wait, but finally an airline representative came over to them and asked Mrs. Baltz to follow him. She and Dee walked into a small anteroom, where she was told what she already knew.

"Something terrible has happened, Mrs. Baltz. There's been a crash."

"Is Stevie . . . ?"

"No. He's alive, but badly hurt. We have a car here to take you to him."

Before leaving for the hospital, Mrs. Baltz called her brother, Howard, who lived in the New York suburb of Westchester County, near their parents. Mrs. Baltz told him what had happened and asked him to meet her at the hospital. Then she and her daughter quietly walked out through the grief-stricken larger room.

The ride in from the airport seemed interminable. After explaining to Dee, as best she could, what had happened, Phyllis lapsed into shock.

Howard was already waiting for them at the hospital, just inside one of the side entrances. Hospital officials were using it so Mrs. Baltz could avoid the reporters attracted by their biggest story in months: the world's worst air disaster had happened right in their own backyard. To make matters even more newsworthy, a precocious, polite eleven-year-old kid had apparently survived the holocaust.

Howard and Phyllis had a hurried conversation; then Mrs. Baltz spoke with her daughter.

"Randee, I'm going up to see Stephen. You're going to go home with Uncle Howard . . . and you wait for me at his house. Okay?"

"Can't I see Stevie too?"

"No, darling. He's very sick. You can see him as soon as he's well."

Until this point, Phyllis had been inwardly calming herself by thinking that her son was alive and that he was going to be all right. It was that thought that pounded in her brain as she hurried off the elevator and followed a nurse toward Stevie's room on the fourth floor. Her calm facade lasted just until she went through the door.

Her son was so horribly burned he was almost unrecognizable. The sight of him lying there made her gasp and swallow the greeting she had prepared. Stevie spoke first.

"Hi, Mom. My plane crashed."

"Oh, Stevie . . . I know."

Mrs. Baltz wanted desperately to touch her son, but he looked so painfully fragile, lying there swathed in bandages.

After seeing Stevie off at the airport, Mr. Baltz had driven to his office in downtown Chicago. He was general counsel for a large electronics firm, and he was sitting at his desk when his secretary buzzed to say the Chairman of the Board was on the phone.

"Hello. To what do I owe the pleasure of your call?"

"Stan. Could you come into my office right away?" The chairman's voice was so burdened with the weight of some portentous development, it precluded any further discussion. Mr. Baltz just quietly said, "Sure," and walked quickly out of his office.

"He'll see you right away," said the chairman's secretary as soon as Stan walked into the outer office. He had been politely smiling a greeting when he opened the door, but the secretary seemed to avert her eyes, pretending to be busily working with the papers on her desk.

He walked past, knocked on the chairman's door, and went in. His boss had his hands clasped behind his back and was looking out the window.

"Hello, Stan," he said quietly as he turned toward Mr. Baltz. "Please sit down." He gestured to a chair, walked out from behind his desk, and pulled another chair over to where Stan was sitting down.

"There's been a crash . . ." he said suddenly. Mr.

Baltz shuddered. It was a brief, involuntary movement. Mr. Siragusa reached across quickly to reassure him. "But a miracle has happened . . . Stevie is alive. He's in a hospital in New York. He's young and strong; he'll be all right."

"I've got to get to New York!" Mr. Baltz said with the desperation of a loving parent whose child is hurt or threatened.

"I've already checked. Get your coat. We have forty-five minutes to get you on the next flight out."

Driven out to the airport, Stan managed to catch the two o'clock American Airlines flight into LaGuardia. He was reunited with his wife and son two hours later.

Actually, he saw Phyllis first. She was dejectedly walking out of Stevie's room when she looked up to see her husband hurrying toward her. They embraced. "How is he?" asked Mr. Baltz.

"Not well," she answered, desperately. "He's been badly burned."

"Is he going to be all right?"

"They don't know. . . ."

"Can we see him? Is he awake?"

"Yes, he is."

They went into the room. Phyllis stayed near the door as Stan walked to the head of the bed. His son was apparently dozing, but when his father gently called his name, Stevie was quickly awake.

"Hi, Dad."

"Hello, son," he said, reaching out to his horribly scorched boy, but not knowing where to put his hand. "How are you feeling?" he asked finally.

Stevie assured his father that he was not feeling too bad. Mr. Baltz told him that as soon as he was well again, they would take that trip they'd been planning to Yellowstone Park.

"Yes, Dad. Sure we will. . . ."

Twenty-two-year-old Sheila Connors had just been appointed head nurse in the Emergency Room. She competently dominated, and had brought at least minimal order to the usually chaotic facility, despite her relative youth. She had just gotten off work when she heard the news of the plane crash and hurried back to the hospital.

Sheila arrived there shortly after Mr. Baltz. The parents of the boy had already been inside to see their son, so both were still wearing the hospital gowns and masks required when a patient is in intensive care. They were outside the entrance to his room, conferring in hushed, concerned tones with a group of doctors. Sheila's offer of help, which she had telephoned ahead, had been gratefully accepted by the hospital administration. She had been assigned to stay with Stevie from four until midnight.

Sheila stood discreetly outside the circle of doctors until it was clear that the parents had finished their troubled questioning. She introduced herself. Stevie's mother started politely to thank Sheila for coming in, but before she could add anything to the greeting, she swayed.

Her husband put his arm around her for support. "Don't worry, dear. He'll make it." Then he looked up at Sheila and added his thanks in a quiet voice. "We'll be in and out of the room all night, I guess."

The nurse walked into the room, briefly checked the intravenous connections on her young charge, then took up her action station, on a chair near the foot of the bed. Stevie was floating near the surface of consciousness. From time to time, he would break through and speak. When he did, he seemed a totally normal, albeit sick child. His voice gave no hint of the extent to which his body had been ravaged by the flames.

"Hello."

"Hello, Stevie."

"What's your name?"

"Sheila."

"Are you taking care of me now?"

"Yes, Stevie. Do you want anything?"

"No, thank you. . . . I don't feel so good though."

"I know . . ." was all she could manage.

He was still conscious when his mother came back into the room an hour later.

"Mom. Will you remind me to call and ask Lady Blue or David to feed the hamsters?"

"I'm sure they're already on the job, Stephen." She smiled, but it was a painful action that almost brought tears. "You can talk to them tomorrow, but why don't you try to sleep now?" she added.

At that, Sheila stood up and walked toward the head of the bed. Putting a supporting arm around Mrs. Baltz's shoulder, she looked down at Stephen.

"That's a good idea your mother's got there, Stevie," she said, as she reached to gently cover his bandaged body with the light blanket that had been folded near the bed. "Come on. It's already dark out. You're not going to miss anything."

Stephen either fell asleep or lapsed into unconsciousness. For the next several hours, Dr. Mazzarino and a rotating group of eight other physicians and five nurses kept coming into the room to check on his condition and do what they could. Their findings were discouraging. In burn cases, the first forty-eight hours are critical. If a patient can survive that period, his chances for recovery are greatly enhanced. But far from recovering, Stevie was fading. His pO_2 was near 60 and still falling. The internal injuries were undoubtedly as critical as Dr. Mazzarino had initially feared. The boy had apparently inhaled massive quantities of jet fuel and flames.

His parents could see Stevie fading also. The hospital administration had set up two beds in the room next door to their son's, so they stayed in the hospital. But they couldn't sleep. Every hour, sometimes more frequently, they came in to see Stevie. All evening he had been asleep, but increasingly, it was a restless, tossing, nightmare-laden sleep.

At about three in the morning, he regained consciousness for the last time. He was deeply in pain and almost delirious. He tried to speak, but at first could not. Mr. Baltz hurried into the hallway and called out to a doctor. Once in the room, the physician saw that the boy was obviously in distress and gave him a sedative. In a few minutes, he was calmer.

"Dad, you know my boxcars . . ." Stevie said, referring to his heavy, cast-iron model-train set.

"Yes, son," his father answered softly. "What about them?"

"It feels like there's a hundred of them . . . right here . . ." he managed to say, pointing vaguely to his chest before he drifted again into semi-consciousness. ". . . boxcars . . ." he said several more times, and was asleep.

He died at one o'clock Saturday afternoon. After taking an hour to compose themselves in their grief, Mr. and Mrs. Baltz agreed reluctantly to say something about their son to the dozens of reporters waiting downstairs. The news people had maintained the vigil with them, and through the media had made millions aware of Stevie's fight for life. In recognition of their efforts, Officers Pica and Mannino were present at the grim announcement.

Worn out from the long night and day, Mr. and Mrs. Baltz looked emotionally crushed and physically fragile as they stepped behind a battery of microphones that had been set up in the hospital auditorium.

"Well," Stan started, almost in a whisper, "Our Stevie passed away at one o'clock . . . Stevie tried hard. He tried awfully hard . . ." He choked and grasped his wife's hand tightly. "He was a wonderful boy. Not because he was my son, but because he was—" he searched for an appropriate word—"he was Stevie," he said finally.

On Tuesday the members of Boy Scout Troop 3 held a Court of Honor in the troop room of the Wilmette Methodist Church. On that night Stephen's friends showed what they thought of him by posthumously awarding him his first-class badge.

Thousands of people took time during that busy holiday season to send, first, gifts and letters of encouragement and then, after Stevie died, messages of sympathy and condolence. Throughout the country, people who had been following his dramatic fight for life were asking how Stevie had come to be spared and why, after all that, he had had to die.

Shortly after his death, an elderly lady sent an anonymous gift of a thousand dollars. With it and the many smaller cash gifts received, a memorial room was established on the children's floor of Methodist Hospital.

The Baltzes, after living quietly through the heartbreaking time immediately after Stevie died, sought to thank the people who had sent gifts and the children who had written them about their son.

I remember getting a Valentine's Day card from the family. I kept it for years, looking at it occasionally and drawing some private inspiration from the spunky kid who almost made it through the famous Brooklyn plane crash.

"**W**ake up, child. You don't want to be late on your first day in a new school!" In the historic seaport city of New Orleans, November is often a damp and chilly time, and Gail's mother was compounding the little girl's discomfort by waking her up much too early, even for a schoolday. "Come on, honey." Mrs. Etienne gently patted her six-year-old on the behind as she coaxed her awake. "You got to get out of bed."

It was Monday, and a big day for Gail. The first-grader had been told over the weekend that she'd be transferring to a new school. Both her old school, McCarty, and the new school she'd be going to, John McDonogh No. 19, were just a block or so from home. As a matter of fact, you can see them both from the front porch of the Etiennes' neat little frame house, but McDonogh was much more modern and well-equipped.

Even that advantage, though, hadn't made the child enthusiastic about the transfer. She was bewildered and unhappy. The school year was going on three months old, and Gail had lots of friends at McCarty. For the last two days she had been complaining, to her mother especially, that she'd be lonely if she had to leave them behind.

But her parents kept insisting that Gail had to make the transfer. Her daddy kept telling her about "greater opportunities for a better life." Besides, they both reassured her, she'd make new friends in her new school.

Everyone at the breakfast table ate quietly. It was as if some solemn ceremony were taking place. Except for Gail. Once she'd gotten up and rubbed the sleep from her eyes, the six-year-old was the most animated person in the house. She was also the only one with no idea of what was really happening. To her, this first historic step toward compliance with federal-court desegregation rulings in the hard-core-resistance area of the Deep South was just an unusual and unhappy change in schools.

Later, after the sun had a chance to burn the chilly morning haze from the Mississippi River, Gail was to be integrated. Deputy federal marshals were going to attempt to enroll her and three other black children in two previously all-white public elementary schools.

A few minutes after the family had finished breakfast, Mr. Etienne broke out of a thoughtful reverie. Hitting both hands down hard on the kitchen table, he stood up. It was the firm gesture of a now determined man.

The tall, stately black man was in his early thirties. And he had the impeccable dignity that used to be associated with railroad porters during the days when trains had class. He walked over to his daughter and told her gently to hurry inside and get ready.

"Come on, little lady. You got to hurry and get dressed. This is a pretty special day."

"Yes, sir." She smiled up at her daddy and hurried into her room.

Her mother, also smiling for the first time that day, followed after her.

Outside their house, on busy St. Claude Street, dozens of the shiny black patrol cars of the New Orleans Police Department were already cruising up and down the block, in anticipation of trouble. Because the racially mixed neighborhood, with its narrow streets and modest white houses, still looked so lazy and peaceful, the squad cars seemed entirely out of place.

There were no crowds yet in front of McDonogh No. 19, the white school, and the only sounds came from the hundreds of birds spending the cool early morning among the palms and fragrant myrtles that lined the quiet streets of the lower ninth ward.

As Gail and her mother admired her white-lace dress, carefully laid out across the six-year-old's bed, patrolmen in gold-striped blue uniforms, black boots, and white helmets were dismounting from their motorcycles and grimly taking up positions outside the McDonogh School.

Gail's pretty white dress was new. It was the kind little girls get for a special party or for Easter Sunday. Mrs. Etienne picked it up and held it against her daughter.

"My, my. How pretty you are going to look today!"

But as she carefully put the dress over one arm so she wouldn't wrinkle it, Mrs. Etienne was very nervous. She tightly shut her eyes and sighed deeply as she helped her daughter off with her bathrobe.

Five girls had originally been accepted for transfer to white schools under a federally approved grade-a-year desegregation plan. But one family, worried over the physical danger to their child, had decided against allowing the move. The thought had occurred to Gail's parents many times, but now they were committed. It was only hours before the start of school.

"Come, child. It's getting late," Mrs. Etienne said, pulling herself back from the edge of uncertainty.

As her mother helped her to slip the dress over her head, Gail asked, "Mamma, why am I wearing my new dress to school?"

Mrs. Etienne started softly to cry as she answered, "Because, like your daddy said, child, this is a pretty special day."

An hour before the scheduled start of classes, scores of uniformed city policemen and plainclothes detectives had already stationed themselves around the two elementary schools that had been targeted for integration. Federal men were also there. They were tall, stern-faced deputy marshals wearing somber gray suits, obviously official even without their bright-yellow armbands.

After Gail and her mother had been in the bedroom for ten minutes or so, Mr. Etienne was called inside by his wife.

"Well, Daddy. What do you think of your big girl

now?" As she spoke, Gail's mother was putting the finishing touch on her daughter's outfit. It was a white ribbon that Mrs. Etienne expertly tied into a bow and put into Gail's hair at a jaunty angle.

Her father walked over to Gail, bent, and kissed her forehead.

"I have a surprise for you, honey."

She looked like a flower girl in a wedding, and the combination of her new dress and the anticipation of her daddy's surprise made her smile shyly.

"What is it, Daddy? Can you tell me now?"

Gail's father sat down on the bed.

"We're going to drive you to school," he said. She was delighted, but slightly confused. After all, her new school was only a block and a half from home.

Her father continued, explaining that some men were going to drive them in a special government car. They were like policemen. United States marshals, he called them, and they were coming along to make sure nothing bad happened to Daddy's little girl.

"What could happen?"

"Nothing, darling. Probably nothing at all," he said, looking up at his wife with silent reassurance.

Gail remembers only a sense of excitement. She was going on an adventure.

As she was getting ready for her big day, thousands of others all across the sultry river city were preparing for it in their own ways.

Federal District Court Judge J. Skelly Wright was holding an extraordinary meeting in his chambers. It was his final briefing for the federal marshals supervising the first integrated schoolday in the history of Louisiana.

It was a job for which the jurist had neither preference nor experience. Normally a judge orders a particular result, then leaves it to others to execute or enforce. This was different.

In a historic move, the federal court had ordered desegregation. But state officials had refused to comply. The marshals had been called in to protect the black children, not only against angry white parents, but also against state officials sworn to keep them out of white schools.

The Louisiana State Legislature had met all the night before in the last of a long series of attempts to frustrate legislatively the desegregation order of Judge Wright's court. Encouraged and fully supported by Jimmy H. Davis, the singing governor of Louisiana best known for impromptu renditions of "You Are My Sunshine," the legislature had been holding special sessions for the last three months.

Meeting on an almost daily basis, they passed over one hundred would-be state laws designed to maintain the state's centuries-old policy of strictly segregated schools. The night before, for instance, the legislature had voted to remove four of the five members of the Orleans Parish School Board, because those officials had agreed to abide by the court's desegregation order. It was the first time in state-government history that an attempt had been made to remove an elected city official.

And they went further. The legislature also passed a resolution directing Richard A. Dowling, the New Orleans district attorney, to indict as criminals the four members of the school board for their refusal to comply with the legislature's orders.

As he had been called on to do a hundred times before over the last three months, Judge Wright issued restraining orders forbidding both desperate attempts to challenge the will of the court. He had copies of his latest order distributed to all the marshals.

Judge Wright was very nearly a target of the state legislature himself. State Representative Wellborn Jack told his fellow members that he questioned whether the judge was "mentally right." And another representative, Julian S. Garrett, called for the judge's arrest by state officials. But no formal action was taken on Mr. Garrett's proposal.

Judge Wright also had the advantage of knowing exactly what was going on in the capital, Baton Rouge, almost as soon as it happened. Just a few blocks from where Gail lived, in the home of NAACP counsel Daniel Byrd, a group of lawyers was monitoring the radio news broadcasts.

Whenever the Louisiana legislature passed one of its anti-integration "laws," the gentlemen in Mr. Byrd's house would draw up a petition restraining the state from enforcing it. The petitions would then be rushed to the courthouse for Judge Wright's signature.

The lawyer coordinating the effort was the NAACP's chief counsel, Thurgood Marshall, now a justice on the United States Supreme Court.

In the half-hour left before the schoolday began, the legislature passed still another putative law to prevent the enrollment of the four black children. The law purported to transfer control of the entire city school system to the state government and to proclaim the day a school holiday. Orders to close down were carried by unarmed plainclothes state policemen to each of New Orleans' forty-eight elementary schools.

The troopers were met at the school entrances by principals, escorted by more federal marshals. The school officials refused the written demands delivered by the troopers, who had been sworn in as special sergeants-at-arms. Instead, the principals carried out the directions of the school board to try to conduct classes as usual.

In his paneled and stately office in the federal-court building, the judge used these last few minutes to speak to his marshals in a quiet, anxious voice. He warned them still again of the potential for violence. With the level of emotions running so high, there was a real possibility that the special state "sergeants-at-arms" might try to prevent the children from entering the schools.

Hundreds had been sworn in over the weekend in Baton Rouge. Their announced and specific responsibility was physically to oppose integration.

"Your job is to get the children safely into the schoolhouse buildings," said the judge as he paced his chambers, nervously wringing his hands. He was a short, almost elfish man, about fifty years old. Raised in Louisiana, he had the elegant drawl and precise manners associated with Old South aristocracy. Yet he was more decisively responsible than any other man for bringing about the most monumental change in the history of the state's educational system.

"The crowds will probably be angry," he continued, "but I don't expect they'll be very large at first." He looked around at the serious, businesslike faces of his marshals, a formidable, mechanically competent group. "The parents don't know which schools we've chosen. They'll find out, as sure as I'm standing here. But they don't know yet."

In an effort to prevent large crowds from gathering in front of the two schools about to be integrated, their identities had been withheld.

But the heavy concentrations of police officers in front of both McDonogh and the other school, William Franz, several miles away, soon started to draw dozens, then finally hundreds of spectators.

At one point, the judge's clerk hurried into the gloomy chambers with an obviously important message. He handed it to Judge Wright, then waited expectantly as he read it. After a few seconds the elegant judge looked up at the marshals gathered around him and smiled.

"I have just been informed that Secretary of State Rogers, speaking for President Eisenhower, has warned Governor Davis that he will permit no more interference from the state with the integration process."

Even the marshals smiled reluctantly. The small force of federal officials at Judge Wright's disposal would, if necessary, be supplemented by federal troops to accomplish the court-ordered desegregation. Of course, the troops could never be mobilized in time to protect the students going into the schools on this first day. Still, the statement of unequivocal support from Washington was a tremendous morale booster to the pro-integration forces.

Buoyed by the message from Eisenhower, Judge Wright's final instruction to his marshals was to make their best efforts to achieve their objective. Only if guns were drawn were the federal officials to turn back.

After a telephone call from the courthouse, the marshals designated as escorts made a final check of preparations at the two schools, then drove off to the homes of the four pupils chosen to participate in the drama unfolding. Like the names of the schools, the identities of the children had been kept secret to prevent retaliation by militant opponents to desegregation.

Gail, as an individual, hadn't really counted for much in the strategy sessions of either side, up to this point. To the adult decision-makers, she was a description on the motions and the countermotions, more symbolic than real. Now all the legal papers were coming alive. In a few minutes, Gail and three other children would be used to demonstrate the determination of the courts of the United States that the public schools of New Orleans become color blind.

On the other side of the city, miles from the French elegance of the court district, the white people were calling the day "Black Monday." In the working-class district of Saint Bernard Parish, a community-minded man named Leander Perez had organized an expedition unprecedented in academic history.

Staunchly, totally opposed to desegregation, he had announced to his followers that they should force the entire public-school system to shut down for good rather than watch even one white elementary school admit even one black child. And because so many elected officials had announced a similar viewpoint, few people expected that things would get as far as they had. But now the fight was lost. Black Monday had come.

Recognizing defeat, Perez had vowed to make the day as unpleasant as possible for the blacks reckless enough to challenge history.

He had recruited several thousand white parents, mostly women with young children, from Saint Bernard Parish. At their rendezvous point that morning, he had busily reorganized them into smaller groups, directing them to a waiting fleet of cars and buses.

Since Lloyd Rittiner, the brave, determined president of the Orleans Parish School Board, had insisted that only the board, the superintendent of schools, and the federal officials know which schools had been chosen, Perez decided to place a contingent of demonstrators in front of each of the city's forty-eight elementary schools. With thousands of eager, angry followers, it was easily accomplished. Hundreds made their way to McDonogh No. 19, swelling the crowds already attracted by the police activity.

Emotions outside the school were an accurate reflection of the way the majority of white people in the city were reacting to the forced integration of their public schools. The crowd milling around in the parking lot in front of the school was mad, and it was afraid. Their century-old tradition of racial separation was about to be abolished, and leaders like Mr. Perez had fanned resentment and an understandable fear of the unknown into rabid hostility, bordering on hatred.

The ancient caste system of the Deep South was about to be changed by the federal government in Washington. It was the ultimate enemy, trying to change the way people had always lived. But the government wasn't enrolling that morning in either McDonogh No. 19 or the William Franz elementary school. Four black children were, and they became the targets of an outraged white citizenry.

The city of New Orleans, French and Catholic, has historically been an illogical place. With more in common with Paris than Baton Rouge, it had the reputation of being Dixie's most progressive and swinging city. Even given that cosmopolitan veneer, however, it was still a town where niggers knew their place.

Much of the city's famous French quarter is noted for its elegant French colonial town houses with their graceful old-world balconies and elaborate wrought-iron gates. With the oleanders and palms and the air filled with the soulful sound of original jazz, a visitor half-expects to see a streetcar named "Desire" rolling past.

But at the foot of Canal Street, one of the main thoroughfares, there is also a monument commemorating an 1871 uprising against the reconstructionists of the post–Civil War era. Erected during the 1930's, it is a tall pillar with a brass plate riveted to its side. The message inscribed there praises and immortalizes the idea of white supremacy.

The monument is an offensive anachronism, but in 1960 there was functional evidence of bigotry. There were screens, for instance, to divide racially all city buses, and even the city's legendary night life abounded with "Whites Only" restaurants and hotels, and rest rooms clearly marked "White" or "Colored."

The most grievous, and in the long run most adversely effective, of all racial divisions, however, was in the public-school system. "Separate but equal" facilities for white and black children was theoretically the guiding principle for the Orleans Parish School Board, as it was for most of the rest of the South. But it was a principle honored only in the breach. The facilities were separate, but they were not equal.

While those elementary schools designated as white were frequently modern and underutilized, black facilities, like Gail's old school, were rundown fire traps. McCarty Elementary, the only school in the lower ninth ward set aside for black children, was an ancient, rickety wooden building dating back to the nineteenth century. It was overcrowded, had double sessions, and used only those out-of-date textbooks discarded as obsolete by one of the parish's white schools.

To understand how institutionalized, traditional, and absolute the separation of the races was in New Orleans in 1960 is to understand more clearly the courage demonstrated by Gail, the other black children, and their families. When she set foot inside a previously all-white school later that morning, she would be breaking dramatic new ground, as significant in its way as any exploration of Mount Everest or the moon.

The court ruling that ordered McDonogh No. 19 to open its doors to six-year-old Gail Etienne was ten years in the making. Originally the case had been brought by a man named Oliver Bush, at the urging of Daniel Byrd, the eloquent local representative of the National Association for the Advancement of Colored People.

Bush was the father of thirteen children and the

president of the McCarty Elementary School PTA. With the help of the NAACP, he sued the Orleans Parish School Board to force them to enroll his son Earl in a half-empty all-white school located just across the street from the Bush home.

The case came before Judge Wright, an activist liberal judge, long the champion of civil rights. At the time, the U.S. Supreme Court was hearing arguments in the landmark case of *Brown v. The Board of Education of Topeka,* so Judge Wright postponed his ruling until the high court could hand down its decision.

On May 17, 1954, Chief Justice Earl Warren, speaking for a unanimous court, said, "We conclude that in the field of public education, the doctrine of 'separate but equal' has no place. Separate educational facilities are inherently unequal."

Two years later, ruling in the case of *Bush v. The Orleans Parish School Board,* Judge Wright struck down an 1877 Louisiana law that required separate schools for white and black children. Still, the outraged city fathers continued to fight and delay the enforcement of the court's ruling for four more years, until 1960. By that time, Earl Bush had already graduated from high school.

The superintendent of schools, faced with a federal court order to desegregate with "all deliberate speed," chose five first-graders from McCarty Elementary as integration fodder. When the family of one little girl decided not to go along because of the threat of violence, that left four. Gail was one of them.

As she and her daddy walked out of their front door that Black Monday morning, Gail was introduced to the four federal marshals who were waiting on the porch. She gave a little curtsy and said with rehearsed formality, "How do you do, sir," as she turned to face each man.

To the six-year-old they seemed mountainous, friendly giants. It was the first time she had ever spoken to white people.

Gail remembers the ride to school as curiously somber. It was quiet in the car, and the ride was short.

She sat up front, dwarfed by the marshal on either side of her. Her father sat in the back seat, also sandwiched between two marshals.

When the car turned slowly into the school parking lot, the quiet on St. Claude Street was shattered by hundreds of screaming, shouting demonstrators. They ran angrily toward the car and began pounding on the roof and hood. Spit smacked against the car windows, then oozed down in little rivulets, gathering in the cracks where the windows met the doors. There were more white people than Gail had ever seen in one place.

"Daddy, what's the matter?"

Her father reached across the front seat and tightly held his daughter's hand.

"Never you mind, child. Everything is going to be all right."

Gail was more curious than afraid. She wasn't even crying. She just stared wide-eyed, without fully understanding why all those people were mad at her.

"Kill them niggers!" shouted one red-faced man in the crowd.

"Two, four, six, eight, we don't want to integrate," several of the young people in the crowd started chanting.

". . . six, four, two, we don't want no chigeroo!"

Leander Perez had done a fine job mobilizing his forces. The several hundred he had managed to concentrate outside McDonogh No. 19 were more than enough to disrupt, frighten, and ensure that even if the black children got inside, no classroom activity could possibly take place.

The mob of onlookers consisted mostly of young mothers, many of whom had their children with them. One of the Black Monday's most popular slogans was "I'd rather have my kids dead than going to school with niggers!"

This frenzy and hysteria had been building for almost three months. It had started in September, a week before the scheduled opening day of classes, the original deadline set by the court for integration.

When it had become apparent that the legal battle

against integration had been lost, Lloyd Rittiner, who had been a fiery segregationist as president of the school board, appeared in Judge Wright's chambers. The big, portly man explained to the judge that while he had always opposed desegregation, he was also a man who always obeyed the law. Rittiner promised the judge he would do everything in his power, now that legal means were exhausted, to comply with the court's order. It was a moral decision that Rittiner suffered dearly for. Ultimately, he had to leave New Orleans, his engineering business bankrupt and his family living under the constant threat of violence.

The one concession Rittiner asked the judge to grant was a sixty-day delay in executing the federal integration order. The school-board president had ordered a poll taken, and it was eloquent testimony to how intensely emotions were running. The board had sent out a questionnaire to all white parents with children in public schools. Eighty-nine percent responded. Ninety-six percent of those responding had said they would rather see all the public schools permanently shut down than allow a single one to be integrated.

In the vain hope that a delay would cool things off, the judge agreed to the postponement. However, not wanting the New Orleans school situation to become a national political issue, the judge postponed the deadline for ten weeks. It was put off until November 14, the Monday following the Kennedy-Nixon presidential-election battle. Black Monday.

So Gail began the year in her old school instead of in McDonogh No. 19, as originally planned. Her father wonders now if things would have gone quite so badly if she had been permitted to start in the new school with everybody else in September.

As Gail and her father stepped out of the car, the marshals steadfastly formed a protective circle around them. At her appearance, the shouts of the crowd swelled to a deafening, ugly roar. For the first time it looked as if it would all explode into violence. But as the crowd swayed and tightened around the six-year-old and her escorts, the city policemen aggressively moved in, fifty of them, including men on horseback. They started driving the crowd out of the lot and across the street.

Mayor de Lesseps Morrison had been careful not to participate in the divisive and ancient debate over integration, but he had vowed to keep the peace in his city regardless of the outcome of the court contest. The fact that desegregation took place without violence was a tribute to his resolve to keep order.

All the shouting and movement began to really frighten the six-year-old. Gail tightened her grip on her daddy's hand and looked around uncomprehendingly. Finally the marshals formed a flying wedge and began driving their way through the scores of people remaining in front of the schoolhouse door. The closer they got, the more threateningly the crowd jeered. The moment of truth was approaching. They could see the special state sergeants-at-arms standing astride the doorway.

But as the federal marshals and their little charges approached, the state officials hesitated, but after a moment of high drama, stepped aside. Judge Wright's most immediate fear was not realized.

Once inside the school, with the door shut safely behind them, the noise level dropped sharply. What had been frenzied was now merely chaotic. Since none of the personnel had known that McDonogh was one of the schools chosen for integration, the day had begun relatively normally, at least when compared with what was going on outside. Of the 460 students assigned to the school, fully ninety-four had shown up for classes that morning. By the standards of Black Monday, that was as nearly normal as anything else in New Orleans that day.

As the federal caravan carrying Gail and the two other girls had pulled into McDonogh's parking lot, however, even that circumscribed normality began to deteriorate. The students lined the windows, while teachers and staff congregated in the hallways.

"Why us?"

The rhetorical question dominated the conversation inside the three-story building.

The marshals, armed with Judge Wright's admonition to get the children quickly into their classrooms, walked past the staring teachers, scarcely seeming to notice them. Gail, still holding tightly to her father's hand, was almost oblivious to the people also, but for much different reasons. She had never been inside a building as fancy or as modern as this one.

The long, polished hallways colorfully decorated with the children's artwork, and the arrow-straight rows of sturdy new desks were of far greater interest.

"How do you like it, child?"

As Gail's wonderment and appreciation grew, her father began feeling more confident that his decision to send her here had been the right one.

"I like it."

She giggled softly, burying her face in her daddy's big hand. The difference between this place and the school she had left behind was so vast that even a six-year-old could begin to understand why her parents had insisted she transfer here.

Her father brought Gail into her classroom, and after speaking briefly with the flustered teacher there, walked his daughter down an aisle to her assigned seat.

"I got to go now, honey. I'm late for work."

Mr. Etienne was a proud but plainspoken young man who had spent all his working life as a clerk in the New Orleans Post Office. There was nothing militant or activist or even political about him; he was just doing what he thought was best for his family.

The bond between father and daughter was powerful, and the look of panic she gave him when he announced that it was time for him to leave almost broke his heart.

"I'll see you after school. All right, child?"

With that, Mr. Etienne gently removed his hand from his daughter's worried grip, touched her face, smiled, turned, and walked out of the room on his way to the post office downtown.

Frantically Gail looked around the room for a familiar face. She recognized only the two marshals, who had stayed with her. Grim, watchful, and unsmiling, one had taken up a position near the door, while the other walked behind the teacher's desk to peer outside at the crowds through the venetian blinds.

It was her moment of truth. All the decisions up to this point had been made by someone else, her parents or the marshals. But they had left her one option. She could cry or be brave. Gail was very lonesome and afraid, but that morning she didn't cry.

Within half an hour, word spread through the city that two elementary schools had been integrated. Outraged white parents, hearing the news through word-of-mouth or on the local radio bulletins, immediately began converging on both schools. At first they swelled the crowds outside. Then they demanded entrance.

Once inside, parents with children in either McDonogh No. 19 or William Franz angrily asked why their children's school had been chosen. When it became apparent that school officials were powerless to reverse the court's decision, the parents began taking their kids out.

Sitting quietly at her desk near the back of the room, Gail watched as frenzied parents burst into her classroom. Ignoring both the teacher and the marshals, they shouted rough orders at their own bewildered children to leave, or physically yanked them from the room.

Although greatly rushed, many of them took a moment to hurl insult or invective at Gail, the immediate source of their displeasure.

Years later, she would again recall her bewilderment. "At the time, I just couldn't understand why they were all so mad at me."

The exodus took less than three hours. Before the noon recess, fewer than thirty of the ninety-four students who had shown up for classes remained at their desks at McDonogh. Across town, at William Franz, which had a normal enrollment of 575 pupils, only 105 had started the schoolday. By noon, fewer than fifty were left.

Shortly after noon, large groups of about thirty-five high-school boys marched past both schools singing "Glory, glory, hallelujah, the South will rise again."

Leading both gala processions was another boy carrying a roughly assembled wooden cross with the word "segregation" crudely hand-painted across it in bright-red letters.

For the rest of the day Gail sat at her desk in the virtually empty classroom. With her teacher, three white students whose parents had somehow not gotten the word, and the two federal marshals, Gail played out the charade of a student in an integrated school.

When finally the closing bell echoed through the nearly deserted corridors of McDonogh No. 19, she and the two other black children were ecorted outside to the same cars they had come in. The crowds in the schoolyard and around the yellow stucco building were bigger than the morning's, their deep-seated anger unabated. Only another phalanx of marshals and city policemen kept them from hurting Gail and her companions as they made their way through the crowds to the cars.

For the entire walk, they were barraged with threatening shouts of "Don't come back tomorrow. . . . You better not come back at all!"

The short ride home down familiar St. Claude Street began the end of a long, frightening, and very confusing day for Gail. She was too shy and too shaken to ask the officers what had happened, but when she saw her mother waiting anxiously outside their home, her confusion finally dissolved into tears.

When her father came home from work, the family sat down to dinner at the same table where they had begun the incredible day. Gail demonstrated the hardy resilience of six-year-olds. After she had changed out of her pretty white-lace dress, she was smiling and had become curious again, asking her father about the things she had seen and heard that day.

As he would try to do until she was old enough to understand it all by herself, Mr. Etienne tried patiently to explain the significance of what had happened.

He told her that sometimes people had to do things they didn't like doing. Gail had gone to this new school, and now she had to stay there, he explained, because if she did, other children from McCarty would also be able to go there.

So she stayed at McDonogh No. 19. As the school year progressed from its tumultuous beginning, more and more white students dropped out of school, until the entire student body numbered fewer than a dozen children. Every day the unrelenting crowds waiting for her in front of the schoolhouse would greet Gail with shouts and jeers that became increasingly more venomous as time and frustration aggravated their bitterness. Ironically, she almost got used to it. As her father had told her, people can get used to anything.

Actually, her studies went well. In a school where teachers outnumbered students by four to one, she received much more attention than she would have at McCarty. Most of the teachers were gentle, kind, and competent, intent on making Gail's bravery worth the effort. The teachers were also the first white people to teach black children in the public-school history of Louisiana.

They were heroes as much as the children. The state legislature, as part of its continuing mischief, had impounded the funds of the Orleans Parish School Board. None of the teachers were being paid. It had been the hope of the politicians in Baton Rouge that none of the staff would stay on if there was no money for salaries.

But they had grossly underestimated the quality and commitment of the teachers. The overwhelming majority stayed on. Both William Franz and John McDonogh No. 19 remained open. And Gail finished the first grade.

Reflecting on that first year, Gail's father said years later, "I had no idea what would happen. But when it did, I certainly didn't think it would be so bad or go on for as long as it did. I tell you, I couldn't believe human beings, whatever their color, could act the way they did. For Mrs. Etienne and myself, getting Gail into the McDonogh school wasn't politically or racially motivated. We just knew the level of education was so much higher in the white system. That's all we thought about. Getting her into that good school."

There were white families and children in New Orleans also made to suffer that first year. A woman named Mary Sand had established a group called "Save Our Schools." Consisting of white parents with public-school children, SOS was pro-integration, and on Black Monday conducted a vigorous city-wide campaign with leaflets and loudspeakers, trying to persuade other white parents to keep their children in school. Except for a tiny handful, the effort failed totally.

The white children who stayed in either Franz or McDonogh after November 14 were frequently subjected to harassment and abuse similar to that heaped on the black children. They had to be driven to school every day for months by parents belonging to SOS. During that time the cars were sometimes forced off the road by carelessly driven trucks, and were frequently stoned by high-school punks who playfully thought that on this issue, at least, anything was fair.

The children's parents were socially ostracized, and many found themselves suddenly and hopelessly out of work. Under that relentless pressure, white enrollment dropped steadily until it was almost to zero by the end of the year.

Mary Sand had become a special target, receiving at least two or three anonymous threatening phone calls each night. One call was obviously placed by a small child. When Mary picked up the telephone, the excited little girl on the other end apparently couldn't think of anything appropriate to say, so she asked her mother for advice.

"What should I say, Ma?"

"Oh, say anything nasty," answered the woman loudly enough for Mary to hear.

There was a pause. Finally the child whispered, "Nigger lover," and hung up giggling.

Gail's second year at McDonogh was only slightly less extraordinary than her first had been. Almost all the white parents continued to picket, demonstrate, and keep their children out of school. The few whites who trickled back, presumably because their parents grew weary of having them home all year, became a new minority. Because a large number of black children had been transferred to McDonogh to fill the places left vacant by the boycotting whites, the school became overwhelmingly black.

The idea of an all-black school, however, was just as unacceptable to Judge Wright as an all-white school had been. In order to achieve racial balance, he ordered Gail and several other black children transferred to some of the other schools within the district.

Gail was assigned to the Simmes school. She was in the vanguard again, the first black child in a previously all-white institution. This time, however, there were none of the massive upheavals that marked her first sortie into the world of the whites. But in many ways, this move was more difficult. For one thing, she was older and, at eight, already a veteran of two years' concentrated education in racial hatred.

None of the white students left Simmes when Gail entered their school. Boycotting had failed to break the resolve of the Orleans Parish School Board. Its only effect had been adverse, depriving the white children of a year's education. So all stayed, a few with the apparent motive of making the little girl's life miserable.

For the next four years she fought a running battle with children who had learned to say "nigger" before they could ride bicycles. At one point, the situation became so intolerable that Daniel Byrd of the local NAACP brought a court action to remove the principal of the Simmes school.

It was charged that he wasn't doing enough to protect Gail from the verbal and physical abuse she was getting from her schoolmates. The legal action was unsuccessful, but it had the effect of partially taking the heat off her anyway. She stayed with it.

"As I got older and things still didn't change, I started thinking it was a losing battle," she says when she thinks now of her experience during the early 1960's. "But I didn't want to give up."

She never did. With the encouragement and support of her family and friends, and those members of the school staff and student body who managed to rise above the old ways, Gail finished elementary school, went on to graduate from high school in 1972, and then went on to college, attending Southern University in New Orleans.

"The experience taught me that all whites weren't bad or prejudiced," Gail said, looking back on that time, fifteen years later. "We got a lot of encouragement from white people all over the world. I remember one letter even came from Mrs. Eleanor Roosevelt."

Despite a childhood marred by hatred, she became a surprisingly unembittered adult. That's perhaps the best indicator of her courage. In the face of overwhelming provocation, she grew up untainted.

The scene at the institution had been horrible and revolting. In three years as a newsman in New York City, I had seen poverty, hunger, and people dead from fire, drug overdoses, and gunshot wounds. They were things that seemed the absolute pits of human misery and despair. But this had been worse. Willowbrook. It was such an ironically lyrical name, much more befitting a pastoral painting than a foul and overcrowded human warehouse. It was the world's largest and one of the nation's worst institutions for the mentally retarded.

Filled to overflowing with almost six thousand children, the air in the place had been heavy with the stink of feces and neglect. The two dozen buildings were all divided into four wards, each haphazardly littered with naked or barely dressed boys and girls. The wards are large rooms, maybe thirty feet square. Into that space were jammed between sixty and eighty children. Most were severely or profoundly retarded. They had either never learned to speak or had lost the ability, but their nightmarish moaning echoed from the hard cinder-block walls.

Concentration was necessary to perceive them even as human children. They were so filthy, and frighteningly out of control.

The kids who weren't groping toward our camera lights were just sitting on one of the four wooden benches strategically placed in the corners of the otherwise furnitureless space. These rocked back and forth, oblivious to everything and everyone around them.

There was virtually no supervision, just one hopelessly overburdened attendant. She was a heavyset black lady, who held a squirming child under each chubby

59

arm, while patiently trying to talk with a third retarded child who was pulling insistently at her uniform skirt. I tried to listen in on what she was saying, but the undulating moans in the background, like the sounds of a crashing sea, made it impossible to hear.

With that sound, and the nauseating smell, the institution would have been more at home in Dante's *Inferno* than on Staten Island, in the supposedly cosmopolitan and sophisticated city of New York.

When our unauthorized filming was completed, we dashed out the back door of B ward in Building 6 and into our waiting car. I was driving. To avoid trouble from the institution guards, we were off the grounds of the huge facility in less than sixty seconds. We drove with the windows open to purge our clothing of the wretched smell. Nobody spoke. For a long time the only sound was the rush of the wind and the screech of the tires.

"It's hopeless. Isn't it?" I finally asked Dr. Mike Wilkins, who was sitting alongside me in the front seat. He was the staff physician who had asked me to bring my cameras into Willowbrook. "I mean . . . nothing can really be done to help those kids . . . can it?"

"Geraldo, you'd be surprised at what can be done—if people care." When Dr. Wilkins spoke, even about an issue he was so deeply and emotionally involved in, it was always in a quiet, scholarly way. He was the teacher. I was the student, made willing to learn by the frightening spectacle he had just shown me. "Those kids weren't freaks," he continued. "They just have brains that are damaged or retarded. Some more than others." He gestured, pointing to me and then back to himself. "They have the same feelings we do, and if you give them half a chance, they respond the same as normal children do to things. They get happy. They get sad. And they need love and attention."

Dr. Wilkins was a young man, bespectacled and slightly built. But as with Gandhi, the strength of his convictions more than compensated for his physical frailty. He went on carefully, conscious of the fact that I had been deeply shocked and needed to be convinced that things didn't have to be the way they were.

"Willowbrook represents the worst possible care for the mentally retarded. That institution just holds them until they die. There is no attempt at education or rehabilitation. Nothing. Just abuse and neglect." He paused for a second. Taking his glasses off, he rubbed his forehead, as if trying to ease the pain of a bad headache. He shook his head. "You know something? The largest single cause of death at Willowbrook is pneumonia. You know how the children get it? They gag on the slop they're fed, because there's nobody around to teach them how to use utensils. Food particles get into their lungs, and it causes an infection. The infection eventually causes the pneumonia, and that causes death."

As we drove, Mike interrupted himself to give me directions. There was one other place where he wanted us to film before going back to the newsroom. It was only about fifteen minutes away from the institution.

"But the ultimate tragedy at Willowbrook," he explained, picking up where he had left off, "is the children who never should have been there at all."

"What do you mean?" I asked, hoping I had heard him wrong. I hadn't.

"Many of the residents aren't even mildly retarded."

"Don't tell me that," I said, almost pleading. The thought that some of the kids in that dreadful place might be there unnecessarily was appalling.

"I know it's terrible even to think about, but we have to think about it, because it's true." Mike went on regretfully, "There was a bad diagnosis when they were very young, or they have some kind of physical disability. Because there was no other, more appropriate place to put them, they get dumped in Willowbrook. . . . Well, after a couple of years spent on one of those wards, they get to seem retarded." Always the professor, Mike spared me none of the unhappy details. "Environment can retard a person almost as much as physical brain damage."

"That must really kill you—to see kids who aren't even retarded, rotting away on those wards."

"Let me answer it this way." He paused for a second, trying to find words. "I think this thing is going to change. As soon as we bring this story to the American people, they are going to be angry, and they are going to demand that that place and others like it be cleaned up."

The three other members of my film crew were sitting in the back seat of the car. Usually when this type of job-related conversation was going on in the front seat, these hard-nosed photo-journalists would be completely tuned out—looking out the windows, or napping, or reading the New York *Daily News*. Their personal involvement in a story usually ended when they left the scene, but this was obviously different.

They had been as deeply affected by what we'd seen as I was, and as Mike spoke, they listened intently.

"But the most frustrating aspect of the whole thing is that change doesn't happen overnight," Mike continued. "It's going to take time. Years, probably. And in that time, people who never should have been in that place are going to grow up, grow old, and die there."

I stammered, "But . . . I mean . . . can't we do something to get some of them out in the meantime?"

"We're getting some of them out."

"How are they doing?"

"Not badly. Considering where they've been. You know, it's not easy to adjust to life outside a hellhole like that one. Especially if it's the only life you've ever known."

"Can I meet some of the kids who've gotten out?"

"That's where I'm taking you now. I want you to meet Bernard."

"Who's Bernard?"

"He's twenty-one years old. And he just got out of Willowbrook."

"How long was he in there?"

"Sixteen years."

"And he's not retarded?"

"No. He's not retarded."

"Goddamnit."

"This is where we get off."

We turned off the highway, and I pulled the crew car into the driveway of an old house. It was about three in the afternoon. It was biting cold out, and the January sky was already getting dark. The house was sort of run-down, but at least it had a big yard, filled with trees and shrubbery, which in the summer, especially, would lend a real country feeling, not uncommon in the relatively suburban borough of Staten Island.

The house belonged to Bill Bronston, another young activist doctor from Willowbrook. We walked up to the porch. Mike was leading me; Bob Alis, the cameraman; Davey Weingold, the sound man; and Ronnie Paul, who did the lighting. Hustling in the cold with our portable TV equipment, we went in the front door and into a warm old living room crowded with people.

They all knew we had planned to go into Willowbrook earlier that afternoon to film the conditions there. Since that was expressly forbidden by the Department of Mental Hygiene, everyone had been anxiously awaiting word of our expedition.

"How did you make out?" Dr. Bronston nervously asked before we had even set the equipment down.

"All right, I guess," cautiously answered Dr. Wilkins.

"Great!" I put it more emphatically. (A word of explanation: In the news business, with some exceptions, there is a direct relationship between the importance of the story and the grimness it portrays; so if a cameraman has successfully filmed something that is horrible, a newsman can classify his story as "great.")

"You mean you got the cameras inside?"

"Yeah. We sure did."

"Fantastic!"

Bernard was sitting on the couch. As a living, breathing example of all that was wrong with Willowbrook, he was the star of the show, lavished from both sides with solicitous attention. It was a pleasant but unsettling change of pace for the young man who had spent most of his life living a grotesque nightmare.

I walked toward him, Mike and Bill guiding me through the crowded room.

"Bernard. I'd like you to meet Geraldo Rivera." Then, looking to me, Mike completed the introduction. "Geraldo, this is the friend I've been telling you about. Bernard Carabello."

"How ya doin', pal?" I asked him, energetically flashing what passes for a warm, friendly smile in embarrassing public situations. I extended my hand, and he tried to do the same. Bernard wanted to shake hands, but his arm and his thought processes seemed badly connected. Finally, after an embarrassing moment, he grabbed for his semiextended right arm and guided it toward me with his more controlled left. It was shaking as I reached for it, pretending not to notice anything extraordinary.

"So what's new, partner?" I asked. He struggled to answer.

Bernard's affliction is cerebral palsy, not mental retardation. His mind is perfect; it's just badly packaged, and that afternoon his handicap was painfully obvious. His speech is severely distorted during the best of times, and that day his physical handicap was compounded by his nervousness. After sixteen anonymous years in the ward, he was unaccustomed to being the center of attention.

"Nnnahot Mmmuch." He painfully forced speech out as I released his hand. Holding it had been unpleasant. Even though I had already done some stories about the physically handicapped, I still wasn't entirely at ease with them. It would have been difficult to estimate which of us, Bernard or me, for our different reasons, was more uneasy.

Although he had greatly improved his ability to control his movements since leaving the institution, this high-pressured situation caused him to relapse temporarily. Much to the dismay of the people sitting next to him, Bernard's arms flailed about in involuntary perpetual motion as he sat there on the old couch. Only with great effort did he manage to get both hands underneath himself, stopping their movement by sitting on them.

Bill asked the eager kids next to Bernard to get up so we could talk with him. As soon as I sat down next to Bernard, Mike skillfully avoided an awkward lapse in our fledgling conversation by telling me the story of how this twenty-one-year-old young man had come to spend most of his life in an institution worse than the worst prison.

Things were bad for Bernard from minute one of his life. There were complications. He had been badly positioned in his mother's womb, so doctors at New York's Bellevue Hospital had to struggle for hours to deliver him. When he came out, it was elbow-first, and his mother, Pedra, was left exhausted and sick from the experience. For five days she was listed in critical condition.

Bernard was the fifth child born to her and Louis Carabello, the janitor of a six-floor walk-up on Broome Street on the Lower East Side of Manhattan. So desperate was the family's financial situation that things would have been impossible for the Carabellos even if Bernard had been a normal child, born without complications. In return for maintaining the tenement building they lived in, Louis was given a three-room apartment, rent-free, and $120 a month. Two adults and five children crowded into a one-bedroom apartment, trying to get by on less than thirty dollars a week.

Mr. and Mrs. Carabello slept on the fold-out couch in what served as the living, dining, and utility room. Bernard slept next to them, in the same cheap crib that had served his brothers, Louie, Tony, and Howard, and his sister, Beverly.

The children, including Bernard, had been born with depressing regularity—one a year for the past five years. Each one made the situation more untenable. Bernard had escalated the deteriorating situation by having been born abnormal.

The week after she got out of the hospital, Pedra went to work. Still weak from her ordeal, she got a job for eighty dollars a week packing underwear at a rundown old factory near their home. The task of watching the children was shared by Mr. Carabello, when his duties around the building permitted, and by Louis junior, age 5½, the oldest of the kids.

Since Mr. Carabello disliked the domestic work, Louis had to diaper and feed his infant brother, whose handicap was already becoming apparent. Pedra would relieve him of his premature and arduous responsibility when she came home from work about six in the evening. She would be exhausted, but before resting she had to make dinner for everyone, including her husband, who was beginning to drink too much. The menu was almost always the same: rice and beans, and once a week, either dried fish or stringy beef.

After the meal, she would put the kids to bed. The four oldest, ranging from 5½ to 1½, all slept on the same big bed that had originally been shared by Pedra and Louis senior when they had first gotten married. The kids' room was sparsely decorated with cheap, shiny furniture. The bed itself was fringed in red pompons and nestled under a plaster-of-paris statue of Jesus.

With Mrs. Carabello bringing a few extra dollars in each week, things started marginally to improve. Then, as often happens in ghetto families with neither the recreation of television nor the protection of birth control, she got pregnant again. Pedra worked until the last minute, because she had to.

Jenny was born almost exactly one year after Bernard, who demanded increasing attention and care as his handicap became more and more pronounced. The house was impoverished and chaotic. The family was held together only by the patience and grim determination of the inexhaustible Pedra.

With relentless timing, David followed Jenny, and Margarita followed David. When there were eight children, all born within less than ten years, Louis Carabello left home.

In a knavish but, in the slums, common maneuver, he left Mrs. Carabello to make the best of the impossible situation by herself, with some public assistance.

Bernard was five years old. He still couldn't walk or talk, and he was not toilet-trained. Pedra had to diaper and change this normal-size five-year-old several times each day.

Concerned about Bernard's lack of development, Mrs. Carabello began taking him every two or three weeks to the public-health clinic at Bellevue Hospital. Doctors there had told her that Bernard's only hope for even seminormality was constant physical therapy.

In the beginning, getting her nonambulatory son to the clinic on East Twenty-fifth Street was a difficult but manageable proposition from her relatively nearby home on Broome Street. But because their old apartment there was far too small for all nine of them, Pedra had to move her brood to Brooklyn.

She had applied for and was granted a large two-bedroom apartment in the Scholes Street City housing projects in the Williamsburg section of Brooklyn. As a neighborhood, Williamsburg is neither better nor worse than the Lower East Side. Like the Carabellos' old neighborhood, this new one was predominantly Puerto Rican, with a substantial minority of Eastern European Jews, the two ethnic groups joined by their common poverty.

The projects were located within sight and sound of the old Broadway elevated subway train, which cut a rumbling swath through the area every fifteen minutes or so.

The new apartment was far larger than the one the Carabellos had left behind, but it was still far too small. Another and ultimately more important disadvantage was its distance from the clinic at Bellevue Hospital. Now, not only did Pedra have to struggle to dress and carry the deadweight of her growing son, but they also had to endure a combined subway and bus voyage of an hour and a quarter each way, every two weeks.

At the time, Pedra spoke no English, and since none of the young doctors at the public-health clinic spoke Spanish, an interpreter was always needed. Sometimes Pedra would just find somebody who happened to be at the hospital on the afternoon she brought in Bernard. Other times, she would bring a neighbor along to translate.

In the rushed, harried atmosphere of the clinic, the overworked interns sympathized with Mrs. Carabello's misfortune. But they still avoided serving her and her child whenever possible. She was a brash woman, given to concerned but noisy outbursts at doctors who were patiently trying to explain Bernard's lack of progress. Even when she was docile, it was an inconvenience dealing with Mrs. Carabello. Since she spoke no English, talking with her took twice as long, conversations having to be translated by a middleman, sometimes a stranger.

Finally, one afternoon when Pedra came in complaining loudly, as she usually did, about the slowness of the Broadway train, she quieted abruptly when she saw the head of the clinic somberly walking toward her. With him was the stern-faced Spanish-speaking officer of the hospital's community-relations department. Neither of these exalted gentlemen had ever waited on her and Bernard before.

With the help of a girlfriend, Pedra had plopped Bernard onto one of the waiting-area benches and was in the process of taking off his outer coat when they came up to her.

She awkwardly stopped what she was doing. At the doctor's request, translated into Spanish by the community-relations man, Pedra anxiously and with uncharacteristic quiet followed them into the head man's glass-partitioned clinic office. Before walking off, Pedra had nodded to a friend and then at her son. The body language was easily understood; the neighbor walked over and finished taking Bernard's coat off and kept a protective hand on him.

Inside the glass walls, all the hyperactivity was still visible outside; only the crying and the clanking noises of the busy clinic seemed abated. The community-relations official was a shorter, darker, more active man than his pale and properly professional colleague. He carried the conversation; the doctor just listened. Looking at whoever was talking, the clinic doctor seemed to be following the intense emotional conversation. Even though he couldn't understand Spanish, he could easily approximate what was happening, because he had instructed the other man what to say.

"Señora, these trips all the way in to Manhattan are difficult. Are they not?"

"Yes. Of course, they're a pain in the neck," answered Mrs. Carabello, quickly recovering from her initial uneasiness at being called into the office. "You think it's easy to drag that kid in from Brooklyn all the time?"

"We know you're having a tough time. That's why we called you in here today."

"Why? You got a better way?"

"Yes, Señora, we think we do."

"What? Can you get the city to give me some more money? . . . How do they expect me to feed eight kids with $230 a month?"

"That's not what we have in mind."

"What, then?"

"Bernard should be placed in an institution."

"What institution?" she asked, softly now, as if recovering from a punch in the stomach.

"One close to where you live. A place where he could get the kind of help he needs." Mrs. Carabello's brashness was completely gone. Her eyes were beginning to shine wetly. Recognizing the danger signs of a potentially embarrassing emotional outburst, the official started patting her arm smoothly. "It will be much better for everybody this way," he continued, buttressing his honey-coated presentation still further. "You can't really take care of him at home. Not with all the other children."

Pedra knew he was only saying what was more true than she wished to admit. Recognizing his advantage, the community-relations man pressed home his most convincing argument. Nodding to the silent man sitting next to them, he said, "The doctor thinks it would be much better for Bernard. He knows that you try very hard to care for your son, but you have your hands more than filled." Then the coup de grace: "Think what's best for your son."

"Where will he go?" Pedra's question was phrased in the defeated syntax of a mother whose natural resistance toward giving up her child had been overcome.

"There's a place on Staten Island. You could take the ferry to see him there."

"What's it called?"

"Willowbrook."

"That's a nice name." It was the only thing she could think of to say.

Bernard was only one of thousands of children who grew up almost completely within the institution. At the time he was admitted, at the age of five, there was only a perfunctory screening of prospective residents. So the fact that Bernard was not actually retarded understandably went unnoticed. He had some handicap, and that was more than enough to qualify him for admission.

At the age of 5½ Bernard was placed in Building 25 at Willowbrook. Half of it was used for teenage girls, and at the time, the other half was occupied by younger boys and girls. Until his tenth birthday, Bernard's routine was established, harsh and unrelenting.

At five o'clock each morning, the last official act of the nightshift attendant was to walk through the crowded dormitory area, switching on the lights as she went, shouting, "Wake up! . . . Wake up!" The sixty children were expected to be out of bed before the vigilant attendant made her return trip through the ward. For some of the kids, like Bernard, getting out of bed was a difficult and time-consuming project, because they couldn't walk. But after incurring the painful prodding and pushing of tired and impatient attendants, Bernard soon developed a technique to get him out of bed and onto the floor within the requisite time period.

Lying on his back, he would start rocking back and forth, picking up momentum until he had rolled almost onto his side. At the farthest point in his motion, he would reach out and grab for the metal frame of the bed. Sometimes he would miss and have to start the rocking movement all over again. When he had finally taken hold of the frame, Bernard would pull himself over to the side of the bed. Poised there, he would make one final roll, off the bed, down onto the hard tile floor, maintaining his hold on the frame as he fell. Bernard did that so that the bottom half of his body, not his head, would hit first, absorbing the punishment of the impact.

Once out of bed and lying on the floor, Bernard had successfully fulfilled the requirements of reveille, but he still had the problem of navigating the one hundred feet to the bathroom. He still hadn't learned to crawl, and the attendant, even if she wanted to help Bernard, couldn't. For one thing, he was too heavy for her to carry. And besides, with sixty children under her supervision, there was simply no time for personalized attention.

Bernard had to use the only method of movement available to him. Rolling. Like normal children at play in a heavy snowfall, he would squirm until his body was pointed in the right direction, and then start flopping over and over. He would frequently have to stop, either from dizziness or to correct his direction. And the trip was fraught with other dangers. In the sleepy, early-morning hours, he wasn't easy to spot on the floor, and would often be stepped on accidentally or tripped over by the attendants or other residents hurrying to do whatever they had to do.

The bathrooms of Willowbrook are the single most unpleasant aspect of life in that institution. They are filthy, and they stink. Many of the residents aren't fully toilet-trained, but they realize that defecation is more acceptable in certain areas than in others. In the long, old-fashioned nightshirts worn by all the children, Bernard would have to roll around, or over, the feces of his co-residents as as he made the long trip to the toilet. There, he would have to grab the rim of the bowl and struggle to pull himself onto the toilet seat. The only help he got was from the iron-stomached attendant who wiped him and the others and then lifted him off and back onto the floor. There to endure the three-hundred-foot odyssey into the dining area for breakfast.

The morning meal consisted of an oatmeallike substance. Once Bernard had successfully pulled himself into one of the chairs at the long dining table, an attendant would feed him with a shoveling motion: scoop, force open his mouth, drop, then scoop again. Bernard quickly learned that the secret to not gagging and choking on the rapid-fire feeding was to swallow as soon as a mouthful was placed on his tongue, whether he wanted to or not. Delay meant that the next spoonful would be dumped on top of the lump already in his mouth, parlaying it into an unmanageably large mass in his throat. According to Bernard, this forced feeding wasn't the work of sadists.

"Naaahot all the aahtendants are baaad peeeople," he explained. "Ttthhere wwwaahsan't enough help." The newly arrived morning shift, two people for sixty children, had to rush if they were to feed everyone and get them ready for the day. Some of the attendants were more caring and compassionate than others, although kindness under those circumstances is really remarkable, considering that they took home less than a hundred dollars a week to work in a cesspool.

"Theyyy had it rough . . . really rough," said the young man who had every reason to hate them. "I don't know why theyyy woooorked in that place."

After surviving the ordeal of breakfast, Bernard would roll back into the "dayroom." It was the large and virtually empty space adjacent to the dormitory area. When all the children had assembled there, the attendants would dump the clean laundry into a large pile near the center of the room. The hill of clothing would be a haphazard collection of garments: gray shirts, pants, and nightshirts provided by the state, mixed in with more colorful and diverse garments donated by the Benevolent Society or some other charitable organization.

The ambulatory, high-functioning residents would select their own clothing from the pile, often with tragicomic results. Little boys would often select brightly col-

ored old ladies' dresses, while the little girls would frequently end up wearing a man's work shirt. The
costumes just added to the insane, surrealistic nightmare
quality of life in the building.

Bernard could only roll himself into reasonable
proximity with the clothing distribution point; he
couldn't make the selection by himself. The attendants
dressed him, almost always selecting an open hospital
gown. He usually didn't get underpants. That way, he
could go to the bathroom and manage most of that
process without their help—help that would have been
needed if the hard-pressed attendants had given him a
pair of pants to wear.

Willowbrook, until 1974, was called a state school,
even though very little formal education went on there.
It's now called a developmental center—a much less
ambitious and more realistic label. But there was a half-
day of classes, even in Bernard's day, for those children
who could make it to the classroom. For him, that
meant more rolling, and more struggling once he got
there, to get himself into his assigned seat. Because
these young and very handicapped kids could neither
read nor write and would have needed a tremendous
amount of individual attention to obtain those skills, the
classes consisted primarily of supervised play with educational toys: fitting the circle into the appropriate
place on the board, the square into the square, and so
on.

"Yaahhou noo whhat ahheye liked best?" asked
Bernard. "The readin'." He answered his own question.

The teacher would read fairy tales to the ten children in his class. Most of the time, Bernard had no idea
of what was being said. But the gentle, friendly voice
was in dramatic and refreshing contrast to the din of the
wards. For him, that was enough to make the long roll
from the dayroom to the classes, located on the other
side of Building 25, worth the trip.

The most unbearable aspect of his early years in
the institution was the summers. First of all, there were
no classes to relieve the plodding monotony of the dayroom. Then, there was the heat. New York's summers

are naturally hot and sticky, and the constant hosing in the bathrooms, much like the keeper's hosing of the animal cages in the zoo, added dampness to the already oppressive humidity in the wards. There was no air-conditioning, and no screens on the small windows near the top of the walls. Mosquitoes and flies shared all Bernard's meals in Willowbrook.

Some of the ambulatory children were occasionally permitted to play outside the building. But only occasionally, since there weren't sufficient attendants to supervise them and still watch for the inevitable crises among the children left inside the building. So the grounds of the huge institution—green, open spaces dotted with big old trees—always seemed deserted. From the outside it still looks like an abandoned, haunted suburban college campus. In any case, Bernard never got out. To him, outdoors was the small, enclosed concrete patio adjacent to the dayroom.

Bernard's day always ended with a shower. The administration had decreed this mandatory—a daily shower for everybody. It was an effort to cut down the incidence of infectious hepatitis, which at the time was striking 100 percent of Willowbrook's residents, being transmitted by the human feces lying in piles everywhere.

In order to comply with this requirement, Bernard had to roll into a shower stall. The water would already be running. Once inside, to prevent himself from drowning, he would be careful not to lie on his stomach. Eventually, years later, he learned to pull himself up off the bottom and onto his knees. It was a milestone, and it led finally to his first heroic breakthrough. When he was about nine years old, he learned to crawl. Imagine his wonder at finally being able to point himself in a direction, and then move without undergoing the disorientation of rolling over and over again to get there. He had learned how to crawl by watching the babies and the very young children living around him. What had come naturally to them was mastered out of necessity by Bernard in just under four years. Even so, he was a very inefficient crawler. His poor coordination caused exaggerated movements in his arms and legs. When he moved, he looked like an old-fashioned steam engine spinning furiously but slowly up an icy grade.

But his newfound skill was important as more than just a means of locomotion. When the physical therapist on one of her weekly visits to the building noticed him crawling, he was implicitly taken off the list of the totally hopeless cases. It ultimately led to a big change in his life. Within a short time he was tranferred out of Building 25 and into Building 2, the big building that also housed the hospital.

Everything was better for him in his new home. There were fewer kids in each ward, and a much more comprehensive educational program. The 2½ hours of classes were supplemented by an hour or two of speech therapy or physical rehabilitation. But for Bernard the happiest thing about the whole move was that his best friend, Joey, was transferred along with him.

Joseph Cucchiara is the same age as Bernard, and, like him, is a victim of cerebral palsy, not mental retardation. Even before these boys learned how to speak, Bernard and Joey seemed somehow to understand each other, to take comfort in the other's presence.

They were constant and mutually entertaining companions. Cowboys and Indians was their favorite game. Bernard was usually the Indian bad guy. They didn't have any of the usual trappings—no cap guns, cowboy hats, or anything like that. But pointing their cocked fingers at each other and ducking behind the benches or under their beds, they did manage to pass the time.

The boys taught each other also. They struggled together to verbalize, one of them learning a new word, then teaching it to his friend as they crawled along the floor.

Joey was the first one to walk. He took his first faltering steps at the age of eleven. Bernard, with the inspiration and guidance of his friend, learned shortly afterward. He would pull himself erect, holding onto his bed, or the back of a bench, or Joey's arm. Once he was standing, he would lurch forward, sometimes taking two or three or four awkward steps before careening back down to the floor. But he always got up. When the surface is slippery, Bernard still sometimes loses his balance. But he'd rather risk injury than resort to a wheelchair.

When they were about twelve years old, Bernard and Joey were transferred to Building 6. The prevailing feeling among the staff of the hospital building they had been living in, apparently, was that all that reasonably could have been done to rehabilitate the youngsters had been done. Besides, the space was needed for other, younger children who didn't even know how to walk.

Number 6 is the building I had seen on that first trip to Willowbrook. It was filled with older, bigger boys, some of them prone to violent, unreasoned outbursts; Joey and Bernard were terrorized there. Constant harassment and physical abuse became part of their daily regimen. The attendants, with some glowing exceptions, also seemed a more cold-blooded bunch. Perhaps it's understandable. In Building 25, at least, some of the children had been cute, or anyway smaller and easier to handle.

As Bernard's vocabulary grew, so too did his problems with the attendants. He would often complain to the building physician when one of them had been unnecessarily cruel to this or that resident. He and Joey were also becoming more doggedly independent. They would, for instance, sneak out of their beds after the official seven-o'clock lights-out. Sitting in a corner of the crowded dormitory or in the dark, empty dayroom, they would often talk for hours.

Their favorite conversation was about what they were going to do when they got out of Willowbrook. After a hundred evenings spent in grand speculation, they decided on a mansion in California. Since they had never consciously been off the grounds of the institution, it was a magnificent triumph of their collective imagination. With just the limited knowledge of the outside world gained from the old television set in the dayroom, they constructed an ideal future for themselves. Bernard was even thoughtful enough to provide them with a made-up maid and conjured butler to help with the housework.

Late one night, as Joey and Bernard whispered and giggled about their blissful futures, an attendant caught them. While most of his co-workers would have either overlooked or dealt mildly with this minor rules infraction, this man exploded. It was as if the boys had been conspiring to humiliate him.

"What the hell is going on here?" he shouted upon discovering them sitting on one of the benches in the half-lit dayroom. "You again, Bernard? This time I'm going to teach you to stay in bed when you're put in bed!" Whap. He slapped Bernard across the face.

"Yyyyuuu kah . . . kahrayzee," was all Bernard could manage as he uncoordinatedly lifted his hands to protect his face.

The attendant pulled Bernard off the bench by his ankles, slamming him to the ground. Joey reached toward him to help. "You want some too?" asked the attendant menacingly.

"Leeeave himmm alone!" cried Bernard as he squirmed on the floor to free his ankles.

Distracted by Bernard's surprisingly vigorous struggle, the attendant started dragging him toward the dormitory, taunting him as they went. "You ain't going to get out of bed anymore. Are you, big boy?"

When they finally reached the sleeping area, he roughly tossed Bernard into a pile at the foot of his bed. With the skirmish over, the attendant walked out of the dormitory, laughing softly at his small victory.

Sticking to the shadows, Joey, who walked with the same awkward gait as Bernard, did his best to make his way to his friend's bed without being noticed. When he got there, he helped Bernard to straighten out. Since they were both so poorly coordinated, the effort caused them to jerk sideways and up and down like two dancers in an amateur puppet show. Finally, after a struggle, they were sitting alongside each other on Bernard's bed.

"You okay?" asked Joey.

"Yeah," answered Bernard. "You okay?"

"Yeah. I'mmm goin' to bed."

"Gaanite, Joey."

" 'Night, Bernard."

When Bernard was nineteen, he was transferred to Building 7. Similar in most respects to Building 6, it was located about a quarter of a mile away. By this time Bernard had learned how to dress himself fairly well, although he could not tie his shoes and had difficulty buttoning his shirts. But this achievement, however limited, added an extra dimension to his life. Since he could dress himself and was basically ambulatory, Bernard was permitted to walk outside his building. That meant he could still see Joey, either on the grounds or by visiting him in Building 6, where he still lived.

It went that way for a while, until Joey told Bernard the big news. He was leaving the institution. His family had signed the consent forms, and Joey was moving into an apartment on Staten Island. Bernard greeted the momentous tidings with an understandably mixed reaction. He knew that Joey, like himself, wanted desperately to be out of Willowbrook, but he was afraid he wouldn't see his friend anymore. Joey made everything right when he told Bernard that he would still be coming to the institution every day. The adminstration had given him a paying job as a janitor.

Joey's freedom was an inspiration and a goal for Bernard. Whenever he saw his old friend, Bernard would eagerly ply him with questions about what his apartment was like, and the buses, and the movies, and everything else. Now that Joey was experiencing what life on the outside was really like, they didn't talk about their California mansion anymore.

Bernard was still going to school. He wasn't as advanced as Joey, and still had problems with his reading. So for two and a half hours a day he went to his classes. Until he reached his twenty-first birthday. When he passed that milestone, Bernard was no longer permitted to go to school. He was too old. The fact that he still was in dire need of more instruction was irrelevant. The rules were the rules, and Bernard was out.

When he had first been placed in the institution,

his family had paid Bernard frequent visits. But these had gradually tapered off, until he saw his mother and brothers and sisters only occasionally. When he was informed that he could no longer go to school, Bernard did something he rarely did: he called his mother at home. He asked her to sign him out of Willowbrook. It was a dead-end street for him now, he explained; he couldn't even get an education.

Concerned and confused, Pedra came out to Staten Island to see her son and to talk with the staff social workers. They told her what she expected to hear. Bernard was ill-prepared to survive in the rough, tough world outside the institution's gates. So he stayed in Willowbrook, his first real attempt at getting himself out ending in failure.

Despite his disappointment, Bernard chose to follow Joey's example, at least in part. He also got a job as a janitor. But while his friend qualified for the minimum wage, Bernard, as a resident of the institution, did not. He worked three hours each afternoon, cleaning the slop in the bathrooms of Building 7, and for that he was paid two dollars a month. If you break it down, it comes to less than fifty cents a week.

At the time, Bernard was living in a twilight zone. As a working and relatively high-functioning person, he was in a social stratum above most of the residents, many of whom were severely and profoundly retarded. But he was also far below the exalted level of the attendants. This ambiguity, coupled with his intense disappointment at not being able to get out of the institution, caused Bernard great loneliness. The only person he could talk with was Joey—that is, until he met some of the new breed of committed young social workers who had started working in Willowbrook after the public outrage over conditions there generated by Senator Robert Kennedy's visit in 1965. The kids were different from those usually attracted to positions that not only are low-paying but have the additional fringe detriment of atrocious working conditions.

These social workers worked hard to change Willowbrook from the inside. They knew they couldn't change the crusty administration, but they felt they could meaningfully affect the lives of some of the residents. A group of them spotted Bernard one afternoon hard at work with his mop and his pail in the bathroom of Building 7. One of them started complimenting Bernard on his thoroughness, speaking in the simple, flattering sentences grown-ups use when they talk to babies or house pets.

Bernard's response, after he got going, was, to them, surprisingly intelligent. Shocked, almost as if a friendly dog had started suddenly to speak to them, the social workers began to perceive him as a person of some potential. They offered Bernard a job as a messenger, at a heady new salary. Taking up a collection among themselves, the social workers were able to pay Bernard five dollars a week, which qualified him, by Willowbrook's standards, as a member of the nouveau riche.

More important than the money, Bernard, for the first time in his life, was spending time with people who had grown up outside a mental institution. Elizabeth Lee, Tim Casey, and Ira Fischer were all in their mid-twenties, and all were militantly committed to improving conditions at Willowbrook. They were political activists who had decided to channel their activism into something socially beneficial. Bernard became their resident expert on just how bad the quality of life was inside.

He angered and frustrated the social workers with the hapless story of his own experience, and curiously, these conversations had exactly the same effect on Bernard. It was as if he were also hearing the story for the first time. All his life he had seen and lived amid the crap, but the crap was always the norm. It didn't make him angry, because he had nothing with which to compare it. Watching Liz and Tim and Ira reacting to his descriptions, Bernard came to realize a bitter, central truth. He'd been duped. All the pain and most of the unpleasantness in his life had been unnecessary. Willowbrook was not the best that society could reasonably offer the mentally or physically handicapped. It was the worst.

To fill the time when he was picking up the pieces of his emotional life, Bernard began getting more involved in the extracurricular activities of the institution, such as they were. The sewing class had scheduled a show of fashions made by some of the residents. The teacher, to stir up interest, had offered a prize of a new pair of shoes to the resident who sold the most tickets. While Bernard was too old to attend the class, there was no age discrimination against ticket sellers, so he energetically began canvassing the grounds. He needed a new pair of shoes, and besides, he didn't have anything better to do.

After work, late one afternoon, Bernard decided to go over to Building 6 in his search for potential customers. The social workers had told him that the staff physician there might be interested in a ticket or two.

Walking into his old home, the B ward, Bernard greeted Thomas, a mildly retarded young man who had been one of his closest wardmates. They talked for a while, their conversation interrupted occasionally as Bernard said "hello" and "how are you?" to passing attendants and residents he recognized from his tenancy in the building. Finally Thomas pointed out the doctor Bernard had been looking for. As he walked past, Bernard called after him, and with Thomas' help got quickly off the bench to talk with the white-coated young doctor.

"Excuse me . . ." he said. "Mmmy name is Bernard."

"Well, Bernard. It's a pleasure meeting you finally," answered the young man, smiling. "Elizabeth Lee has been telling me all about you. My name is Mike Wilkins."

"Helllo, Dr. Wilkins . . ."

"Just call me Mike."

Bernard, put competely at ease by the friendly manner of Dr. Wilkins, so unlike most of the other staff doctors, felt no embarrassment at making a pitch for ticket sales. The doctor, while explaining that he would probably not be able to attend the fashion show, did say he would take a few tickets anyway. Mike asked Bernard to bring them over the next day, which was pay-day.

Bernard was there first thing in the morning. Mike laughed at his promptness. "What did you think—that I was going to skip town?" Bernard laughed with him, explaining, tongue-in-cheek, that he knew the doctor was very busy, and he didn't want him to forget. Mike decided that he wanted six of the tickets, which were selling for $3.50. The purchase was a big boost in Bernard's sales campaign, and helped him, eventually, to win the pair of shoes, with total sales of fifty tickets. But more important, Bernard had made a friend. With their business dealings over, Mike told Bernard that they should get together. Bernard, thinking the doctor was just being polite, said sure, thanked him warmly, and walked back to Building 7.

The next day, Bernard had to make a phone call. It was his sister Jenny's birthday, and he had promised he would call her. She probably had no idea how great a sacrifice that promise was for Bernard. In order to make a phone call, he had to walk in his careening shuffle the half-mile that separated Building 21 from his home in Building 7. The phone outside 21 was the closest to his ward. After he had made his call, Bernard was resting outside the phone booth in anticipation of the long trek back home. Just as he was about to take his reluctant first step, he heard a familiar voice. "Hey, Bernard!" He turned. It was Dr. Wilkins.

Mike asked Bernard what he was doing, then asked if he would like to join him and another friend for lunch at Palermo's an Italian restàurant out on Victory Boulevard.

"Nooo thank youuu, Mike," answered Bernard calmly, the tone of his voice giving no clue to what he was feeling inside "I'mmm not dressed propurrly."

"That's okay. What about tomorrow?"

"All right." Bernard's heart was racing as he and Mike ironed out the details of time and where they'd meet. Bernard had never been off the grounds of Willowbrook before, aside from several short rides with his family when he was very young. Mike was offering a real-life view of a world Bernard had seen only second-hand.

The removal of a resident from the grounds, even if it was by a doctor, and even if it was only for a short time, was a discouraging project requiring compliance with a mile of red tape. First Mike would have had to fill out a volunteer form, because he was spending his own time on a resident. Then he would have had to ask the supervisor of Bernard's building for permission to remove him from the grounds, stating their prospective destination and expected time of return. Bernard, it should be recalled, was twenty-one at the time, and perfectly capable of making his own decisions about whom he was going to lunch with. This procedure was just another of the countless minor outrages at the institution.

To avoid the bureaucracy, Bernard met Mike outside, about twenty feet down from Building 7, and climbed into his car. Liz the social worker, was already there, sitting alongside Mike in the front seat. In a happy mood, they drove to the Italian restaurant and sat down at a table for three. Although Palermo's can best be described as modest, it was full of wonders for Bernard. There were colorful prints of Italy on the walls, glittery goldlike little chandeliers that brightly lit the red-vinyl decor, and a menu filled with scenic shots of the Mediterranean.

After Bernard had been scanning the menu for a few times, Mike asked him what he wanted to order. Since Bernard was still having trouble with his reading, but was a bit embarrassed saying so, he said, "Roast beef." It was the first thing that came into his mind, and while it wasn't exactly the house specialty, it was, luckily, on the menu.

After the meal, which Bernard describes as "fantastic," he began telling Dr. Wilkins the story of why he was in Willowbrook, and what it was like for him. Mike listened, not with anger so much as with anguish.

When one of the assistant directors of Willowbrook later reprimanded Dr. Wilkins for taking Bernard off the grounds without permission, the almost always composed young man experienced a rare outburst. "I had

Bernard's permission. And, sir . . . so far as I'm concerned, that's the only permission I needed."

A month after that, in late December 1971, with Bernard as the catalyst and Dr. Wilkins and Elizabeth Lee as the leaders, many of the professional employees staged a low-keyed protest over living conditions at Willowbrook. The protest took the form, finally, of a list of grievances submitted to the administration, specifying the most glaring deficiencies. The official response was to terminate the employment of Mike and Liz, while temporarily suspending some of the other, and presumably less guilty, "troublemakers."

If the administration had calculated that the firings would end this infant upheaval, they had guessed very wrong. The protesting employees were joined on the newly established picket lines by hundreds of parents with children in those wards being cared for by Dr. Wilkins. He was a good doctor, they said, who only wanted to make things better for the children. It was the beginning of the first large-scale protest in the institution's history. When the administration refused to back down, more and more parents and employees joined in what was essentially a spontaneous expression of revulsion at conditions that for years had seemed inevitable. "We can do better . . . we must do better" became their unspoken slogan.

I was called to do the story, just a week after Mike had been fired; to be exact, it was January 5, 1972. I had met Dr. Wilkins a year or so before while covering a different story at the Public Health Service Hospital, where Mike had been working at the time as an intern. I was probably the only newsman he could think of when things started happenings at Willowbrook, so he telephoned me with the information.

"Geraldo. You have to see this place."

"Tell me a little about it." I was frequently called with tips about supposedly "hot" stories, but after a couple of years in the news business I was more cautious and slower to excite than I had been in the beginning.

"It's awful here."

"How is it awful, Mike?" I was polite but slightly impatient.

"Well . . . " There was so much to say, I know now, that Mike's frustration was at having to select which of the many horrible realities to talk about. "The children . . ." he chose. "You should see the way they treat the children."

"Oh?"

"There are sixty or seventy retarded kids to a ward. And most of them are naked and smeared with their own mess."

"Can I get my cameras inside the place?" Children being abused had always been a "favorite" story of mine —the word "favorite" being used in the inverted news sense I spoke of earlier.

"I think so," Mike answered, and we set to planning how we could secretly get inside to film the conditions he had started to describe.

The next day, by the time Dr. Wilkins and Bernard had finished telling me some of the details of the time he'd spent in the institution, it was already four o'clock and dark outside. I looked at my watch, realized how late it was, and jumped up.

"I've got to split, or I'll miss the deadline."

The early edition of the local news goes on at six in the evenings. We hurried, so we made it into Manhattan in forty-five minutes, with another forty-five minutes once we got in for developing the film; there was less than a half-hour to write the script and edit the film and get to the studio.

In the beginning of the report, I was fairly calm in my delivery. But as I talked about the conditions I had seen that day, calm exploded into fury. When I got to the part about Bernard, my voice cracked with pain and slurred with sorrow.

It was the start of one of the most massive local-news exposés in recent history. Within a few days every local newspaper, television news program, and national news magazine was reporting the obscene story of Willowbrook. When the story was first breaking and the public was learning the full magnitude of the horrors within the institution, I interviewed Bernard no less than four times. Although his speech was strained and difficult to follow, nobody, not even my news director, complained. Bernard was the undisputed expert, and he had earned the patience of the viewing audience by spending sixteen unnecessary years in what Senator Robert Kennedy had earlier labeled a "snakepit."

At first, the reaction of the State Department of Mental Hygiene was scandalously to resist the demands that Willowbrook be cleaned up. They claimed initially that the press reports were overstated and that conditions were not nearly as bad as we were telling people they were. But finally, in late February 1972, with extra millions appropriated by the state legislature on an emergency basis, the department dropped all pretense of denying the reality of the institution, and the painfully slow process of change began.

A month later, in March, Bernard's family signed him out of Willowbrook for the last time. He got an apartment on Staten Island, near his friend Joey, whom he stills sees all the time. On the outside, Bernard didn't become Pollyanna. It was an extremely difficult time for him; nothing came easy, and there were times when he wondered whether he hadn't been better off inside the institution. Willowbrook had been grim, but at least it was predictable, not like the mile-a-minute, dazzlingly uncertain outside world.

Finally, with help from his friends, things started to work for Bernard. He took additional speech therapy, improved his reading, and eventually got a job with One to One, a charity we had established to fund humane alternatives to institutional life for the mentally retarded. Now he's sort of the goodwill ambassador/public-relations man, giving speeches at high schools and colleges in the New York metropolitan area, drumming up support for the movement to improve the plight of the retarded.

On April 22, 1975, after more than three years of relentless pressure from the media and the federal courts, the Department of Mental Hygiene capitulated. The commissioner resigned, and the newly elected governor, Hugh Carey, announced that he was signing a consent judgment settling a federal lawsuit that had been filed on behalf of the residents of Willowbrook, shortly after Mike and Liz had been fired.

The federal court commanded that "straitjackets never be used again in Willowbrook, nor shall any resident be tied spread-eagled to a bed, or subjected to either corporal punishment, or degradation, or seclusion." It went on to prohibit "Physically intrusive, chemical or biomedical research or experimentation," and to demand that "health and safety hazards be corrected, radiators and steam pipes covered to protect residents, windows repaired and screened, lead paint removed, buildings air-conditioned, and cockroaches and vermin be eradicated."

The major sections of the agreement stipulated that the population of Willowbrook, which had been more than six thousand, be reduced to no more than two hundred and fifty residents. It further stipulated that training programs be immediately instituted to prepare more than three thousand residents for their return to society. And finally, the agreement called for the funding of more than two hundred small, community-based residences for the retarded, each housing no more than ten people.

Bruce Ennis, the counsel for the New York Civil Liberties Union, who had argued the case on the residents' behalf, said that the agreement "recognizes that retarded persons are capable of physical, emotional, and social growth." It was a historic agreement that stated, essentially, that there would be no more Willowbrooks in New York State.

The next day, I helped Bernard send off a telegram to Governor Carey, thanking him for his great humanity. We were all pleased, Bernard most of all.

The Temple City station house is one of those big, ugly, architecturally nondescript stucco buildings that mar the natural beauty of the Southern California countryside. In that pleasant subtropical climate the station-house landscaping consists of an asphalt parking lot in front of the building, and another, larger one behind it.

Richard Filbin got there at about half past eleven on a Saturday night in March 1973. The deputy had the midnight-to-eight-in-the-morning shift and didn't like to cut it too close.

He drove his car up the driveway and through the double-gate Cyclone fence with the "Authorized Personnel Only" sign on it. Once in the back, he drove slowly past the long straight rows of black-and-white patrol cars, highly polished and shining even in the dim light of the lot. The deputy parked in an appropriate spot, locked his car, and walked in through the back door of the station house, the same door used to bring in prisoners.

"Hey, Rich." One of the deputies sitting around in the bare, garishly lighted room that served the officers as a lounge grumbled a greeting as Deputy Filbin walked in.

"How are you doing?" Richard replied mechanically. He had been on this overnight shift for only a couple of weeks, and his system still hadn't quite adjusted to sleeping in the daytime and going to work at midnight.

The coffee room was sparsely furnished with two vending machines, a Formica table sticky with spilled coffee and wet sugar, and three chairs that looked like Salvation Army rejects. It was a seedy little room, typi-

89

cally institutional in the way that waiting rooms are in
small stations run by commuter railroads.

Three or four deputies were already there, also
waiting around to begin the midnight shift. Richard acknowledged them with a half-wave, then continued
walking through to the locker room.

The one assigned to him was number twenty-one,
but since all five rows of gray-metal lockers looked exactly the same, he often spent a frustrating few minutes
trying unsuccessfully to open his locker, only to dis-
cover he was in the wrong row.

Tonight he was more successful and tried the right
locker the first time.

Deputy Filbin was changing into his uniform when
Bob Hernandez walked over.

"How are you doing, Richard?" asked the sixteen-
year-old Explorer Scout.

"I'll be better after a cup of coffee," anwered the
twenty-six-year-old deputy good-naturedly, despite his
slight case of midnight grogginess.

He liked Bob and had gone on patrol with him
many times before. The youngster was one of the
police-officer trainees who serve in various branches of
the Los Angeles County Sheriff's Department as unpaid
volunteers. It's a program run by the Explorer Scouts,
and the hope is that the participants will eventually go
on to become full-fledged deputy sheriffs.

Bob had already been at it for a year, and right
from the beginning had fitted well into the station-house
life. All the deputies treated him with admiration and
good fellowship. Bob respected their profession, and to
the deputies he represented its next generation.

Of all the officers assigned to Temple City, Bob
preferred riding with Richard Filbin. The deputy was a
friendly and helpful teacher, and even more important
to Bob, he was a good cop.

"How are you doing tonight, Bob?" Deputy Filbin
was a lot taller than his protégé, and as the two of them
walked out of the locker room and into the lounge, they
made what in police jargon is called a Mutt-and-Jeff
team.

Richard got a container of coffee from the machine and walked out of the lounge area with the fifteen or so other deputies working the overnight shift. Bob walked alongside him to the briefing room—past the front desk, on the other side of the station house.

"Can I ride with you tonight?" Bob asked Richard as the sleepy group meandered down the long fluorescent-lit hallway.

"Sure, partner," the deputy answered with a smile, giving his young companion the kind of gentle pat on the back that means something like "Need you even ask!"

Once in the briefing room, the men of the midnight to eight all sat at one of the long tables facing the sergeant's podium. They sipped their coffees or told dirty jokes until the superior officer called for attention.

The sergeant gave them a briefing that outlined the major crimes or other extraordinary situations currently affecting their assigned area. Unless he had some truly shocking information, like a riot or a homicide, they usually paid only limited attention.

Except for Bob, who took everything about the business of police work extremely seriously. To him these briefings were hugely important, and he took copious notes on almost everything the sergeant said. As a result, he had already filled several notebooks with station-house trivia. His young partner's enthusiasm was amusing to Richard, but the deputy was sensitive enough never to put him down for it.

The kid had wanted to be a policeman from the time he was in grade school. A vague childhood desire to be a policeman "when I grow up" had been crystallized when a friend's father, a highway patrolman, had been killed in the line of duty. Bob was thirteen at the time, and he had been hanging around police stations ever since. On the precise day he turned fifteen and one-half, the rock-bottom minimum age, he had become an Explorer Scout in the sheriff's special program.

After a rigorous training period, similar in most respects to the training of rookie officers, the boys in the program were allowed to function almost as deputies. They went out on patrol, used the two-way radios, took complaints, and issued traffic tickets. Their uniforms were virtually the same as the deputies', and the only real difference was that the Scouts weren't permitted to carry any weapons.

The briefing lasted fifteen minutes. When it was over, the deputies all walked back toward the front desk to grab their helmets and the large tin boxes they carried with them on patrol. The boxes were filled with things like the forms needed to make out the various reports, extra ammunition, and a couple of alerts containing the pictures and descriptions of certain fugitives.

The box is fairly heavy, and as one of the prerogatives of rank, the junior man always carries it out to the car.

Richard and Bob had been assigned car 55B. Like the other patrol cars in the line, it was a new Plymouth, black with white doors, bearing the shield of the L.A. County Sheriff's Department. The deputies like the cars, because even though they were light, they packed the big four hundred-cubic-inch engines, effective for pursuit.

When they got to the car, Bob put the tin box on the front seat, then did the "walkaround" with his partner. In the same way that the pilots of small planes walk around and inspect their aircraft before takeoff, deputies are required to carefully check out their cars before going out on patrol.

They started at the trunk, ensuring that the oxygen, the blankets, and all the other emergency equipment was in there.

Next came the back seat. They checked it out with their flashlights. Prisoners are kept back there, and after being apprehended, suspects would frequently try to dump their contraband, usually drugs, in the car, hoping it wouldn't be discovered.

The deputies have to be able to testify that they were absolutely sure the back seat was empty before the prisoner was put into the car. If they can't, the contraband, even if it is discovered, will be useless as evidence.

After making sure about the back seat, the shotgun kept in the front seat, the lights, and all the rest of the special equipment, Deputy Filbin and Scout Hernandez pulled their car out of the parking lot and drove slowly out through the same double gate Richard had entered a half-hour before.

They had been assigned to patrol the city of South El Monte. Like the adjacent community of San Gabriel, Bob's home town, South El Monte is a small city within the county of Los Angeles. Both are essentially Mexican-American "enclaves"—the word "ghetto" would be misleading. While the income levels range from poor to lower-middle, the residential sections of these mini-cities are neat, suburban and well-maintained, dominated by small stucco one- and two-family homes.

On this side of the county, within the Chicano community, wanting to be a policeman is a surprising and unpopular choice of future professions. In 1969, the nearby town of East Los Angeles had been torn by a violent antipolice riot. Since then the relations between the community and the Sheriff's Department had been strained.

Many of the young people, especially, began thinking of the department as a foreign army of occupation rather than a force to safeguard their neighborhoods.

When it became generally known around San Gabriel High School that Bob had joined the Explorer program, he was subjected to a steady stream of abuse and invective from many of his classmates. To the angriest among them, he had sold out and become a pig, a traitor, and a coconut (brown and apparently Chicano on the outside, but white, indicating his real sympathies, on the inside).

One typical morning when Bob was sitting at the long work bench in his electronics class, the subject of his career was raised. The thirty boys in the class were all in the process of assembling hand-built radios, when

the kid sitting to Bob's right leaned over in front of him
and shouted to the three or four fellows working over
on the left side of the bench. "Hey! You guys hear Bob
wants to be a sheriff?"

"You fucking crazy?" demanded the guy sitting to
Bob's immediate left. "Why you want to be a pig for?"

"None of your business." Bob glared back at him.
All work had stopped in the shop. Everybody began
watching the action.

"Show us your badge," said the kid on the right,
who had started the whole thing.

"I don't have a badge," Bob answered angrily. It
was true. Although the uniforms of the Explorers were
similar in most respects to those of the deputies, one
important difference was the lack of a badge. Instead of
the six-pointed star of the county sheriff's office, the
Explorers had a patch sewn on their jackets.

"C'mon, sheriff, show us your badge," taunted the
bully-boy on the left. As he said it, he gave Bob a stiff
shove on the chest.

"Don't do that again," Bob warned.

"Why? . . . Big bad sheriff gonna kick my ass?"
He had a slick smile on his face, daring Bob to respond.
He shoved him again. "Come on, Hernandez, where's
the badge?"

"That's it!" Bob shouted as he leaped out at the
wise guy.

He grabbed him in a headlock, both of them falling onto the work bench, scattering radios and parts of
radios all over the floor. The teacher came running
over, and with the help of several students separated
them.

When it was over, Bob turned to the kid who had
been sitting on his right, the instigator who had started
it all.

"Thanks a lot, asshole," Bob said, his voice edged
with fury as he stormed out of the room.

From then on, in terms of popularity and acceptance, it was downhill for Bob at San Gabriel High.

"I had to fight my way through high school because of this thing."

It's a melancholy admission, but despite the harassment and the frequent fights it led to, Bob was still determined to become a cop. And his family supported him.

He's the youngest of eight children. Most of his brothers and sisters were married and had families of their own. Still, they were exceptionally close, and every Sunday afternoon they'd all get together at their mother's house.

Their father had died when Bob was only nine years old, so these Sunday-afternoon dinners weren't just devoted to the good times. Family problems and all major decisions were always openly and fully discussed.

Even though they knew Bob's decision to become a deputy would generate an adverse reaction from many of their neighbors, the Hernandez family still supported it. His mother, especially, took a proud and active interest in Bob's job, even inviting other deputies over to the house to have a cup of coffee and tell her how well her son was doing.

Over the last six months, the deputy who had come over most frequently was Rich Filbin. He and Bob had developed a close and friendly relationship. Bob had met his family, while the deputy had reciprocated, visiting Bob's home several times.

On those social calls, Richard spent most of the time assuring Mrs. Hernandez that he'd watch out for the sixteen-year-old if the two of them ever got into any sticky situations.

Saturday-night patrols always had more than their share of sticky situations. This one started with a call to check on a large drunk-and-disorderly party.

Dozens of drunken teens were whooping it up with reckless abandon, running up and down an otherwise quiet residential street. The appearance of the slowly cruising patrol car had the desired calming effect, though, and car 55B's first assignment was accomplished painlessly. Bob and Rich didn't even have to get out of their car.

The next incident happened when they were patrolling behind some factories in the big industrial section of the town. At night the area is covered with shadows and is virtually deserted. Anyone walking around behind those factories after dark is almost certainly up to no good. As the car's high beams pierced that blackness, Bob spotted some kids ducking behind the big garbage container in back of the chemical factory.

Filbin responded quickly, closing the distance and pinning the teenagers against the factory wall with the car's powerful spotlights.

When they turned out to be very young neighborhood boys, the deputy decided to let them off with the warning that if he saw them behind the buildings at night again he'd run them in for loitering.

A heart-attack emergency shortly followed. An elderly man in South El Monte had collapsed, and his frantic wife had called the police. The Temple City dispatcher alerted an ambulance, then called car 55B to assist, if necessary. The ambulance had arrived quickly, however, and had rushed the man away to the hospital without further complications.

"It's been a busy hour," the deputy said to Bob after they had resumed their patrolling.

"Yeah . . . but we don't have much to show for it," complained the jealous sixteen-year-old.

Whenever they patrolled together, Richard would act as a tutor, discussing hypothetical police problems with his receptive protégé. Once Bob had finished describing what he would do in certain imaginary situations, the deputy would point out the flaws, if any, in Bob's answer.

Tonight's lesson was simply to be patient.

"You know," Richard continued, "sometimes the busiest nights, and the nights you do your best police work, are the ones when you don't make a single arrest. . . . What's this?" The deputy suddenly interrupted himself.

A car overfilled with young people had just swerved onto the street just in front of them. It was weaving drunkenly back and forth across the road, and it was moving much too fast.

Richard accelerated in pursuit and turned on the red flashing lights. Bob strapped on his helmet, anticipating action.

Obviously seeing the patrol car coming up fast behind him, the driver of the other car slowed down to the legal speed limit. He was making an effort to get the car under control, but he wasn't pulling over.

"Hit 'em with your spotlight!" the deputy ordered.

The sixteen-year-old grabbed the handle of the spotlight mounted on his door and aimed it at the back window of the car they were chasing. It still didn't stop, and it looked as if there was going to be a chase.

Just then the car turned off the main street and pulled over in front of a house. The driver and his passengers started bailing out of their car, heading for the house, and still pretending they didn't see the patrol car now parked right behind them.

"Hold it right there!"

They froze when Richard roughly ordered them back into the car. As he had told Bob many times, stopping a car that's probably filled with drunks is a potentially dangerous situation. The best way to handle it is by keeping its occupants inside.

The sixteen-year-old took up a position, as he'd been taught, near the right-rear side of the stopped car. Richard cautiously approached the driver's window, his right hand resting on his still-holstered revolver.

"What's the matter, Speedy Gonzalez?" the deputy asked as sarcastically as he could manage. "Don't tell me. You couldn't see our lights. Right? Give me your license!" He didn't get angry easily, but Filbin was steaming right now.

He snatched the license offered up through the window, and was looking it over as he walked grimly back to the patrol car to write up the tickets.

Just then the radio burst alive. Deputy Donald Bear in car 55A was requesting assistance. It wasn't an immediate emergency. The deputy was in the process of arresting somebody when an angry crowd started gathering around him.

"Bob!" Deputy Filbin called the Explorer over to the patrol car. "Here. Give this back to that lucky bastard. We've gotta get moving!"

Bob ran up to the other car, flung the license into the driver's window, and sprinted back to the patrol car. Richard took off before Bob had even slammed his door shut.

"What's up?" Bob asked after getting the door closed.

The deputy held his hand up, indicating that he'd explain it as soon as he could. He had the microphone in his hand.

"This is car 55B . . . car 55B, please advise car 55A that our ETA is in two minutes. Repeating, car 55B responding. Our estimated time of arrival, Parlin Street, is two minutes."

When he'd finished the transmission, the deputy hurriedly told Bob that another officer had requested assistance.

As Richard power-skidded around corners and charged toward Deputy Bear's location, they heard a third car responding to the call for assistance. That car, which had been patrolling the nearby community of Rosemead, also gave an ETA of two minutes.

Deputy Bear had been patrolling Parlin Street when he noticed a group of about six noisy young men standing on the lawn in front of a house, passing around what looked like marijuana cigarettes. The deputy pulled over to question the group, but just as he was getting out of the patrol car, they broke and ran, most of them disappearing into the house.

Chasing the others on foot, Bear had managed to grab one of the guys he'd allegedly seen with the marijuana. Grass possession was a much more serious offense in 1973 than it is now in California, and the deputy decided to make what may now be thought of as a marginal arrest.

In any case, as he was excorting the guy back toward the patrol car, the others came back out of the house and followed menacingly behind him. A couple of very angry older men had joined them, and the new additions were obviously drunk.

"Where're you takin' him? You pig!"

"You ain't goin' nowhere with Jimmy, pig!"

When Bear got to the car, he pushed his prisoner against the car and ordered him to put his hands on the roof. But the rest of the group formed a tightening semi-circle around the deputy, continuing to shout their insulting challenges and seemingly just waiting to spring out at him.

That was when Bear had radioed for a backup unit, making sure he didn't turn his back on the crowd when he was doing it.

He recognized others from the original group and decided to grab them also when help finally arrived.

Car 55B slowed down as soon as it entered Parlin Street. Deputy Filbin had gotten there as quickly as he could, but the last thing he wanted to do now was upset a potentially explosive situation with a dramatic arrival.

Driving casually down the street, he and Bob could see the other deputy's car parked farther up on the left-hand side. Parlin is a fairly nice residential street that dead-ends into a complex of small factories about fifty feet beyond where Deputy Bear's car was parked.

At 1:30 in the morning the street was almost totally dark, except for a few porch lights and the rotating red flashers on Bear's car.

Richard parked behind that car and started walking toward the standoff; Bob was alongside him.

"Hey, Bob," the deputy said softly. "This doesn't look all that good . . . you better call for some more help."

"Right," the sixteen-year-old answered as he hurried back to the patrol car. Richard continued on, until he was close enough to ask Depty Bear about what was happening. When Bear had finished his quick whispered explanation, Richard gave the group a hard look. Bear had pointed out the others who'd been involved in the marijuana incident, and the two deputies started walking toward them. But as they approached, the boisterous group just started backing up toward the house again.

Those who'd been involved in the original group had already gone inside the house by the time the deputies got up to the porch. The older man were blocking the door.

"Step aside, sir," ordered Deputy Bear.

"Step aside, shit!" slurred the drunk who was evidently the owner of the house. He was about forty-five years old and completely disheveled, wearing a bathrobe. His eyes were bloodshot, and every time the sweep of the red lights on Bear's car illuminated his face, he looked positively demonic.

"Where's your search warrant, pig?" he continued, drawing moral support from the half-dozen men of various sizes and ages who were now gathered around him in the doorway.

Filbin was on the porch, standing on the right; Bear was alongside, to the left, and Bob, who had rejoined them after sending the call for help, was at the foot of the steps between the two of them. .

"We're in the process of making a felony arrest, sir," explained Filbin. The provocation was getting to him. "We don't need a warrant."

At this point the deputies were just trying to bide their time. Rich had told Bear that another car was on the way, so they were just keeping the group at the door, and in sight, until additional help arrived. Bear actually had his foot in the door. When he forced it momentarily open, he could see one of the suspects. He pointed at him, telling Filbin that he was the guy they really wanted.

"C'mon out," Deputy Filbin ordered.

The young man just walked into the center of the living room, crossed his arms, smiled, and said, "Come and take me."

The owner of the house spotted Bob and yelled at him in Spanish, "Hey, Chicano. Tell your friends to leave my family alone and get the hell out of here!"

"Sir . . ." Bob replied embarrassedly, "all we want is our prisoner. . . . Don't get involved in this."

The man spat out the words "whore" and "sellout" before giving Bear a stiff shove, trying to get the door closed.

Filbin began pushing against the door, helping Deputy Bear keep it open. Then the fighting really started. The group at the door started kicking and shoving. Somebody grabbed for Bear's holster and almost got it unstrapped. But Bob, standing just behind him, had managed to knock the hand away.

The outnumbered deputies were definitely getting the worst of it. Bear had been kicked in the groin, and both Bob and Richard had taken several blows to the face.

Filbin and Bear both pulled out their saps. They're like leather blackjacks, the short, heavy little clubs that became so controversial during the antiwar movement. Using them, the deputies started driving their attackers back inside the house.

When the door opened again, Filbin could see a woman holding a small child standing just a few feet from the door.

"Stop it before somebody really gets hurt!" he shouted inside the house at the men, who only increased the pitch of the fighting.

At this point they'd been at the doorway for six or seven minutes, but the expected help had still not arrived.

Then the first shot was fired. Depty Filbin described it as "a flashcube going off from the middle of the crowd." The sound of it was deafening, drowning out the memory of the shouting that had immediately preceded it. It momentarily stunned the deputies.

Filbin turned to look at his sixteen-year-old partner. The kid looked shocked. "I'm hit!" he told Rich.

Bob was knocked completely off the porch by the force of the bullet. Lying against a car in the driveway, he had been hit in the thigh; blood was pumping out through the hole in his pants.

"Goddamnit!" shouted Filbin.

Bang. Another shot, a half-second later, twisted

Deputy Bear around and also threw him off the little porch. Bang.

He flew into the air "like a wild horse had just taken off with a rope attached to my wrist." He hit against the wall to his right, then smashed against the ground. He wanted to drag himself farther away from the door, but he couldn't move. Filbin's legs were paralyzed.

Just then, the house door slammed shut.

Crumpled against the car in the driveway, Bob felt "like my whole leg had been torn off." He was watching when Deputy Filbin got taken down.

"I was holding my leg to slow the blood down," Bob remembers, "trying to decide if I should just fall down and forget about the whole thing."

Watching Richard go down got Bob moving again. Somehow he managed to drag himself over to the patrol car, parked about thirty feet away. He struggled to get the door open, but it took time, because his hands were slippery with blood. When he finally managed it, he fell across the front seat and almost lost consciousness.

Bang. Another shot brought him back. He grabbed the radio.

"Car 55B requesting code-three assistance . . . car 55B requesting code-three assistance!" Code three demands immediate response from all available units, with sirens and lights.

"Code 999! Code 999!" he shouted into the radio. The signal means that officers have been hit in a shootout. It's the highest priority call, the police equivalent to a "Mayday!"

Barbara, the night dispatcher, was on the desk. Trying to keep cool, she had forced her voice to be calm when she answered. "Car 55B, this is dispatcher. Assistance is on the way."

Bang. The sound of the next shot carried over the radio to the station house, adding another compelling reason for the converging fleet of patrol cars to hurry.

Bang. Bang. Two more shots, four in all, fired within the last ten seconds.

But the shots were now aimed at the house.

Seeing light coming from the front door of the house, Filbin, lying paralyzed in a pool of his own blood, had watched it slowly opening up. During the fighting, one of the officers' saps had fallen across the door stoop, keeping it from being tightly closed. Now, as it swung outward, Deputy Filbin thought it was the people inside coming to finish him off. In desperation he had freed his revolver and blindly fired the four shots into the door to keep them away.

As Filbin fired, Deputy Bear was also reaching for his gun. But he'd been hit in the hand and because of that injury he didn't realize at first that his gun was gone. Despite Bob's efforts, somebody had managed to grab Bear's gun during the fighting at the door.

Bob had no idea where those last four shots had come from, so he assumed that the occupants in the house had opened fire again. He groped for the shotgun, and only with great difficulty managed to pry it from its rack under the front seat. Then the sixteen-year-old Explorer started squirming out of the car, his exit made easier than his entrance by the blood now covering the seat.

Holding the shotgun, he stood up uncertainly and staggered toward the house. He thought, at the time, that Filbin was already dead. His motive was vengeance.

"Hell," he thought, "I'm going to kill somebody."

There was still no sign of the car coming from Rosemead. Although it was supposed to have been there at the same time Richard and Bob arrived, it had gotten lost. The car was being driven that night by a relatively inexperienced deputy who had forgotten that Parlin was a dead-end street. During the shootout, he was trying to find a way around the factories.

Bob managed to reach the car parked in the house driveway. He propped his elbows against its hood and pointed the shotgun at the door. Filbin was still lying on the ground, and he wasn't moving. Bear was sitting under one of the house windows. He had taken Filbin's gun and fired a fifth round into the door to keep the people away.

Even that close to him, Bob thought Filbin had

been killed. Suddenly his partner moaned, "Please, dear God . . . somebody help me. . . ."

"Hang on, Rich. You'll be all right," Bob called out to him.

"Bob. Can you get Rich out of there?" asked Bear, who was on the other side of Filbin.

"I can't!" Bob shouted back. "I'm hit bad in the leg, and I don't know how long I'll last!"

"Cover the door," Bear replied. "I'll try it!"

Deputy Bear ran hunched over, so he wouldn't be seen from the windows. As he ran, he held his bleeding hand against his chest. He reached Filbin, grabbed him under the arms, and despite the pain in his hand, started dragging him toward the street.

"If the door opens . . . blow it!" Bear shouted to Bob.

"I will!" the sixteen-year-old replied loudly enough so the people inside could hear him. He was standing now in a pool of his own blood.

Somebody pulled the curtains aside in the living-room window.

"Stay away from that window or I'll blow your fucking head off!" Bob shouted as he aimed the shot-gun. He could still hear Filbin moaning as Bear reached the street.

"How is he?" he called out to Bear.

"Don't worry about him . . . watch the door!"

"I'm bleeding bad. I won't be able to stand here much longer."

"Hang on, kid."

Just then the door started swinging again. This time somebody was behind it. Bob leveled the shotgun and almost pulled the trigger. He stopped himself at the last split-second when he saw a woman at the door. It was the one who'd been standing in the living room, and she was screaming. "You killed my brother!"

"Shut that door!" Bob commanded.

"You pig! You goddamn pig. You killed him!"

"Close that door or I'll blow your goddamn ass off!"

The door shut, and Bob maintained his vigil,

weakening every moment. Finally the car from Rose-mead arrived.

It skidded to a stop in front of the house, and two deputies jumped out:

"Get Filbin to a hospital!" ordered Deputy Bear.

With the driver of the car helping, they managed to get him into the front seat, and the car took off. The other deputy from that car stayed. Also armed with a shotgun, he took up a position next to Bob behind the car in the driveway.

"You all right?" the deputy asked the sixteen-year-old next to him.

"I'm hit. In the leg." The kid was obviously about to collapse.

"Go ahead. Try to get to the street. I'll cover the house."

As Bob worked his way toward the safety of the street, he could hear the sirens of at least a half-dozen patrol cars rapidly approaching.

Parlin Street was filled within minutes by patrol cars parked randomly all over the place. The solitary set of red flashing lights on top of Deputy Bear's car had been joined by dozens of others. The strobe lighting and cackling static from all the police two-way radios gave the street an eerie and surrealistic ambience. Shouting men, wearing bulletproof vests, were running toward the house with shotguns, and almost all the residents of Parlin Street were standing out on the lawns in front of their houses, watching.

Bob had collapsed in the gutter.

Deputy Bear grabbed the driver of another recently arrived patrol car.

"You got to get me and the kid out of here!" he told the deputy who was driving. The men inside jumped out, carried Bob to the car, and placed him as gently as they could in the back seat. Bear got in the front seat, his hand by this time looking like a bloody meatball. They sped off, heading for Garfield Hospital, about five miles away. It was where they had taken Filbin.

A pair of Monterey Park units met them at the off

ramp of the freeway and escorted them the rest of the
way to the hospital. Garfield had already been alerted
that they were on the way, so a stretcher team was
waiting outside.

"Can you get out?" an attendant asked Bob as he
opened up the back door.

"I think so," Bob said, as he struggled to get up.
But as he tried, he saw it was useless; he couldn't move.

"No. You'll have to pull me out."

Two attendants did, helped by the Monterey Park
deputies.

"My God!" one of the officers said when he could
see Bob more clearly. "It's an Explorer."

They strapped him onto a stretcher; then, with an
officer on either side as escorts, they carried him into
the hospital. The car had parked in front of the wrong
door, so they had to carry the sixteen-year-old in
through the main entrance of the hospital to the emergency room on the other side. Several people in the
lobby gasped as he was carried past them, and asked
the officers what had happened to the boy.

When they placed him on one of the tables in the
Emergency Room, Bob started calling out to his friend
Richard, but there was no response. Within a few minutes a doctor walked in and asked him how he was
doing.

"I'm bleeding pretty bad. . . . Can you stop it?"

The doctor examined him, told him exactly where
the wound was, and started cutting his pants off.

"No! Don't cut them. The detectives'll want to see
them," Bob advised. "Let's just take them off."

When the doctor took off Bob's left boot to get his
clothes off, blood dripped out.

A nurse came in and asked Bob whom he'd like
them to contact. Bob asked them to get in touch with
his mother, then changed his mind and asked if he
could call her. That wasn't permitted, so Bob gave the
nurse his brother's phone number. He didn't want his
mom finding out from a stranger.

While he was waiting to be operated on, another

nurse, older and obviously part of the hospital administration, came over to him. She was carrying a metal clipboard and looked very businesslike.

"Robert? I have to ask you some questions."

"Yes?"

She asked the correct spelling of his name, address, service number, and then finally his age.

"Sixteen."

"Please, Robert. I have no time for games. How old are you?"

"I'm sixteen," Bob answered again. This was the most fun he'd had all day long.

After several more minutes of this the nurse was finally convinced. She left the room shaking her head in disbelief. Minutes later the word was around the hospital that they were caring for a sixteen-year-old hero.

Several reporters came in from the local newspapers, but by that time Captain Robert Trask of the sheriff's office had arrived. He was serving as the press liaison, and immediately asked them all to wait until the family had been notified.

Bob's twenty-nine-year-old brother, Andy, was the first one there.

"Hi, bro!" Bob greeted him with studied nonchalance.

Andy shook his head. "You know, I go off to Vietnam for a year and a half and I don't get a scratch. . . . You! You're just starting out, and you go and get shot!"

"I'm okay."

"Sure you are."

His sister Anita, brother Danny, and his mother all arrived together. His mother ran over to him and embraced him, crying and asking if he was all right. Bob told them that he was fine, but as he spoke, they could see blood seeping through the sheet the nurses had thrown over him. He asked everybody who came into his room about Richard, and everybody told him that his partner was doing fine.

A couple of hours after he had arrived at the hospital, Bob was wheeled into surgery. It had taken that

long because the operating room was being used for
Deputy Filbin. He was being brought out as Bob was
brought in.

The last thing Bob remembered before being
knocked out for the operation was a doctor telling him
not to worry. "You'll both be home in a couple of
days."

For his actions, Bob was awarded the Honor
Medal with crossed palms. It's the highest award the
Boy Scouts of America of which the Explorers are a
part, can present. He also received a law-enforcement
award from the federal government, and the
distinguished-service award of the Sheriff's Department.

In a special ceremony, attended by several high-
ranking Los Angeles County officials, Sheriff Peter Pit-
chess said, "During these times, when the demands on
law enforcement are ever-increasing, Robert's actions re-
flect great credit upon today's youth, and it gives me
great pleasure to extend our appreciation by honoring
this outstanding young man."

The main building of DeWitt Clinton High School is a huge, turreted, gothic-type structure that looks like it could have been used as the setting for the horror film *Rosemary's Baby*. The school is seventy-five years old, and much more steeped in tradition than most of New York's newer but somehow more temporary public buildings. There are 4,400 students at the all-boys facility, making Clinton one of the nation's larger high schools. It's a big, tough, high-energy place, heavily but workably integrated, which makes it exceptional.

In keeping with a custom dating back to the turn of the century, all the students are called "Clinton men" by their instructors. Of course, that is more the school administration's hopeful aspiration than it is a statement of fact.

While some of its students have won honors and brought honor to the high school with their academic achievements, traditionally Clinton has been known for the success and strength of its athletic teams. The long, dark corridors of the old main building are lined with dusty trophy cases filled with three-quarters of a century's worth of awards won on the playing fields by the men of Clinton.

Located down at the end of the main corridor, hanging alone on the wall next to the principal's office, is a plaque that was not awarded for athletic prowess. This one was presented posthumously, by the local chapter of the Jewish War Veterans, to a Clinton student named Henry Schwartz.

Henry was not the type of Clinton man who traditionally brought honor and glory to this institution. While in school, he was a quiet kid, the kind who is

109

passively ostracized by the club-oriented swingers who dominate teams and organizations with their swagger and easy ability. Henry was a loner who spent most of his time just trying to get by in his classwork. After his death, the newspapers reported that he was so bright that his fellow students called him "the professor." In fact, he had no nickname around school that anyone could remember, and he was only an average student who had mortal difficulties trying to earn passing grades and who spent most of his spare time working at a part-time job after school.

Henry's plaque hangs on the wall in the high school essentially because of the noble and frighteningly violent way he died.

Clinton is located in the Kingsbridge section of the Bronx. It's one of the few neighborhoods in the borough still maintaining a substantial white middle-class population. It's one of the shrinking fringe neighborhoods whose inhabitants exist behind double-locked doors and gated windows, always on the lookout, with a mixture of justified fear and exaggerated paranoia, watching as the massive slum center of the Bronx continues its inexorably cancerous outward growth.

The death of Henry Schwartz, and the way he died, was the grim realization of the residents' worst fears. A neighborhood boy, a good boy, had been brutally murdered by savage and barbarous raiders from that encroaching ghetto. If one young boy could have his promisingly admirable, peaceful, and law-abiding life ended with such tragic abruptness, then nobody in the neighborhood was safe.

At Clinton, Civil Liberties is an elective course, and since the students don't have to take it, these days most of them don't. It hadn't always been that way. In the late 1960's, for instance, when student involvement in various social causes was brand-new and heady stuff, the course had been oversubscribed. Since that time, however, there had been a gradual de-escalation of that passion for involvement. Students were becoming more concerned with the harsh realities of the outside world that their parents were always telling them about. Like having to get a job when they graduated. Idealism was giving way to pragmatism, and if a student had to take an elective course, it would most likely be one of the more career-oriented selections, like business law or speed reading.

In recognition of this contrary trend, the instructor of the Civil Liberties course, Mr. Purcigliotti, tried always to make the class discussions as relevant and as down-to-earth as possible. Vague principles were discussed only as they related to real-life situations.

One of the most successful applications of this approach was the classroom discussion of the issue of "getting involved" if a student saw another person in danger. This controversial subject had been red-hot in New York, at least since a young woman named Kitty Genovese had been repeatedly stabbed and finally murdered in the borough of Queens in the 1960's. A whole gallery of neighborhood residents had watched that bloody ten-minute-long spectacle, but no one had tried either to intervene or even vigorously to seek out other help for the young woman.

Mr. Purcigliotti, called "Mr. P" by his students, to avoid using up valuable classroom time in repeated pronunciation of his five-syllable name, thought frequently during these discussions that people living outside New York would be surprised at the classroom consensus on the issue of involvement. Most of his students felt, in the case of Miss Genovese, that the bystanders were right not to get involved. Living in the city was enough of a hassle without unnecessarily adding the risks of injury, death, liability in a lawsuit, or, at the very least, having to take off valuable time from work to give unpaid testimony in criminal court against one stranger in behalf of another stranger. It just wasn't practical, and at an all-boys school like Clinton, discussion on this issue could go on unfettered by any need to grandstand for the benefit of the ladies in the audience. Freed of the demand for macho bravado, the fellows would try even to top each other with stories of how they would energetically or ingeniously avoid trouble if they saw it. Of course, there were exceptions.

Henry Schwartz sat right up in the front row of the room. He didn't participate in the class dialogue in any of his other courses, but this one was different to Henry. Whenever the discussion turned to involvement, he would vigorously advocate doing as much as possible, regardless of the personal consequences. Mr. P. would soberly caution restraint. During one spring-day class, Henry had raised his hand and stood when Mr. P. called on him.

"I can't see how we can watch somebody being killed or beaten up and not do something to help." Henry spoke with sincerity and conviction.

"It's just not that cut-and-dried, Mr. . . . " Mr. P directed classroom discussions standing in front of his big teacher's desk. After Henry had spoken, Mr. P walked behind the desk and looked down at the class seating chart, searching until he found Henry's name.

" . . . Mr. Schwartz."

Walking back around to the front of his desk, Mr. P sat on top of it and continued. "There are a lot of things you have to think about—like getting killed, for instance." Mr. P smiled easily and looked around at the rest of the class, holding out his arms in an exaggerated shrug as he said that. Predictably, the other students nodded, whistled, laughed, or just called out their unequivocal agreement that nothing was worth going that far for.

But Henry persisted. "Sometimes you have to take chances . . . to help someone else."

"But, Henry," answered Mr. P, for the moment remembering Henry's name from the seating chart, "why can't you just call a cop? They get paid to take chances."

"What if there's no time to get a cop? Can't we make a citizen's arrest?"

"Whenever you do something like that, you take a chance that you're going to get hurt, or sued," cautioned Mr. P. "It just doesn't pay."

"Well . . ." Henry could be stubbornly steadfast when he believed strongly in something. "I think every citizen has to look out for his fellow citizens. No matter what." With that, Henry sat down, his statement followed by low-energy hooting and derisive catcalls from the skeptical, jaded members of the student "in" crowd, wondering what Henry was "trying to prove." Courage had become a very uncool concept.

Months later, in his emotion-charged speech at the Mosholu Jewish Center, Henry's high-school principal explained to the packed audience how Henry had died a hero. Telling the crowd about Henry's statements during his Civil Liberties course, Mr. Weissberg concluded by saying that "he had a strong commitment to justice, and he died coming to the aid of others, because he knew no other way."

The audience attending the memorial service was obviously touched by his remarks. They listened, at first, in respectful silence. As soon as the speech was over, however, they shouted—frustrated, frightened, and angry, directing their emotions at the high-ranking police officials sitting on the dais. Most of them had not known Henry personally, but they took the assault on him as an assault on the entire community. They had come to the center to pay Henry and his family their respect, but they were also there to demand that their neighborhood immediately get increased police protection.

The emotions generated in the Kingsbridge and adjacent Norwood sections of the Bronx by Henry's death were reflected throughout many other areas of the city. The crime, which happened on a Monday around noon, dominated the early newscasts that evening. And the next morning the story of the impending impeachment of President Nixon was temporarily pushed out of the local headlines and replaced by the story of Henry's murder.

"TWO YOUNG BIKE THIEVES KILL YOUTH WHO CHASED THEM," said *The New York Times*.

"SLAY BIKE RESCUER," said the *Daily News*.

Because both of the suspects in the murder were thought to be of Puerto Rican origin, the racial aspects of the crime helped fan the flames of anger and hysteria. To many people, Henry's death was just the latest phase in the continuing battle of us (the law-abiding, mind-our-own-business, white middle class) against them (the ever-increasing, high-crime, only semicivilized black and Puerto Rican ghetto dwellers). It was just the latest atrocity in a grand design to force whites to flee from their last remaining enclaves in the Bronx.

Because of that community reaction, and because of the heinousness of the crime, police officials in the Bronx assigned their best men to the job of catching Henry's murderers. Within twelve hours, Tony Santana, age sixteen, was apprehended, and every television station and newspaper in the city prominently displayed the pictures of his being taken into the station house, arms handcuffed behind him. Public sentiments were such that, at another place and time, Santana would have been lynched by an outraged citizenry.

The reaction of the Puerto Rican community was slightly more complicated. They, too, were shocked and disgusted by the murder, but they were also embarrassed by it. As soon as the Santana boy was arrested, and his address was printed by the newspapers, his family began receiving hate mail, most of it from fellow Puerto Ricans, condemning the Santanas for having brought Tony into the world, and their struggling community into still further disrepute.

The irony was that Henry, the victim, and Tony, one of the alleged perpetrators, were more similar than dissimilar. Both were sixteen years old, both were hardworking industrious teenagers who had never been in trouble before, and both were being respectably brought up by concerned and dedicated mothers who happened to have been divorced. Tony's involvement in Henry's murder was one of those awful coincidences, a tragic accident, a classic example of being in the wrong place at the wrong time.

George San Inocencio was entirely a different matter. He was the actual killer. Tony had just been with him when the terrible crime was committed, and murder was almost a logical and inevitable progression for George to follow. At nineteen years old, he was a neighborhood bully, a bad egg who had already been arrested six times for such diverse crimes as child molestation and the attempted murder of a police officer. Most of those cases and several others were still pending against George at the time of Henry's murder.

He was precisely the kind of person Mrs. Santana would have forbidden Tony to hang around with. Aware of all the complicated problems and unsavory temptations confronting a kid growing up in a bad neighborhood, she took great pains to screen Tony's acquaintances. Since her divorce, especially, she had exercised so much control over her sixteen-year-old son's social life that many of her friends warned her about raising a "pansy." But despite her hawk-eyed vigilance, Mrs. Santana could not screen all her son's friends, so Tony had met George a few weeks before, their loose relationship based solely on a mutual interest in automotive mechanics.

George and Tony lived next door to each other in the rundown Tremont section of the Bronx. It's another world, but geographically it is located just about a mile and a half south of Norwood, Henry's neighborhood. Jerome Avenue, one of the main drags in the Tremont area, is perpetually in shade around there. The avenue's rusting, hulking elevated train tracks keep out the sun and permit just two times of day—darkness and twilight.

Once he hopped off the train, Tony walked slowly down the long, gloomy, urine-stinking steps, from the dilapidated Burnside subway stop, down to Jerome Avenue. Nobody else got off at that stop, so Tony's step echoed on the wooden platform. When he pushed out of the squeaky exit gate, he walked across the street and turned left onto Burnside Avenue. Blinking a couple of times to get accustomed to the brightness out from under the El, Tony headed up the block.

He was coming home from a morning of summer-school classes, and he didn't have to be at work until four that afternoon. He had a job at the local McDonald's hamburger place, which was just across the intersection of Jerome and Burnside.

With nothing better to do, Tony had decided to

check out the action at the bodega. It was part small-time grocery store, part greasy candy store that also served as an informal neighborhood gathering place.

It was already getting warm and sticky, even though it was still before noon, and four or five kids from the neighborhood had already drooped themselves on the steps and sidewalk in front of the hangout. George was there, and, as always, he was much more animated than the rest. Drinking a can of beer that was only minimally disguised in a little brown paper bag, he was strutting back and forth, loudly and obnoxiously puckering his lips at every woman who walked or even drove past him.

George was the epitome of the swaggeringly bellig-erent, defiant, incorrigible ghetto punk.

"Hey, faggot . . . where ya been?" he called out when he saw Tony approaching. "I been waitin' for ya."

"Watch that 'faggot' shit," Tony warned halfheart-edly. "I've been at school," he added, as he was walking past George and into the seedy little store to get a soda. After putting his money down on the dirty counter top, Tony walked out, sat on the step next to some of the guys, and took a long pull on his cool drink.

"What's the matter? No work today?" George had an irritating way of asking questions. He always made them sound like grating insults or challenges.

Tony ignored him for a second, then took another swig of his Coke before answering calmly, "I dunno yet . . . I gotta check with the boss around four o'clock."

"Well. I gotta car we can look at in the mean-time."

"What car?" Tony responded, careful not to com-mitt himself to doing anything with George.

"A VW. A red one. It's a seventy-two, and I'm thinkin' of buyin' it."

"Where's it at?" asked Tony. He loved cars, and his curiosity was overcoming the instinctive suspicion he held for his brash new semifriend.

Sensing that Tony was on the verge of agreeing to go with him, George pressed his argument. "Not too far . . . . C'mon, man I'll ride you on the bars of my bike."

"How far?" Tony was still searching for a way out.

"Fifteen minutes." George answered. After a few seconds, taking Tony's silence for assent, he picked his bike off the curb and motioned to the handlebars, for Tony to hop on.

Henry Schwartz was getting ready to leave his apartment at about the same time George and Tony, the reluctant sidekick, began pedaling north toward the Norwood section for their fateful rendezvous. Henry was on his way to the Capital Ice Cream Parlor, a family-owned sweet shop and restaurant, where he had been working for the last two and a half years. In his mother's words, "Henry was a very enterprising kid" who had been working at various jobs, part-time and during the summers, since he was twelve years old.

Since then, as a matter of principle, Henry had never taken an allowance, managing to save what he made to buy the things he really wanted. He had gotten a stereo set that way, and now, like Tony Santana and ten thousand other kids their age, Henry was saving to buy a car.

He worked the counter at Capital. It was a popular spot in the neighborhood, a homey little restaurant, painted off-white, the basic motif, except for the brightly colored signs hanging on the walls and big front window facing the street. Made of cardboard, the signs advertised some of the Capital specialties, like the well-known "Dynamite Freeze Pop."

The owners of the place, Mr. and Mrs. Albert Saliban, were nice, friendly people of Eastern European descent. Like two little windmills constantly in motion, they were industrious and eager to please, especially their regular customers. At first they had been reluctant to hire Henry, because they felt they needed somebody older, but he had been so persistent, and persistently mature in his requests for work, that they finally took him on. Now they loved him. He was like part of the Saliban family, casually but expertly tending the counter, scooping ice cream, making the customers feel right at home with his easy, charming manner.

Henry had to be at the restaurant by noon in the summer. He had already been out of the house that morning, but by eleven o'clock he went back upstairs to get dressed for work and straighten his room. The four-room Schwartz apartment was crowded but comfortable, on the top floor of an old but well-maintained three-story apartment complex. Henry lived there with his mother, Phyllis; stepfather, Danny Gallo; and his kid brother, thirteen-year-old Eric. There were only two bedrooms, so the boys shared one, Henry sleeping on the top half of a bunk bed; Eric, who was not nearly as agile as his big brother, got the bottom. The walls of the room were amply decorated with the pictures and signatures of famous people. Henry was an avid autograph collector and the proud possessor of short scribbled messages from such celebrities as Agnes Moorehead, Marlo Thomas, Debbie Reynolds, and Larry Blyden.

He went downtown to the theater district frequently. When he didn't have enough money to see a show, he'd just hang around the stage doors, getting the stars of the Great White Way to write something on scraps of paper that eventually made it to the walls of the boys' bedroom. Actually, he aspired to a career in show business himself. Henry wanted to become a singer, and according to his mom, "Oh, boy, could he sing." He'd been taking lessons for the last year several years, and to be as great a singer as his idol, Johnny Mathis, was "Henry's biggest dream."

After their mother and father were divorced, when Henry was eight years old, the boys and their mother became much closer-knit. They would frequently spend their evenings at home, the three of them gathered around the big piano in the living room, one of the few luxuries in the modest apartment. Henry would sing, Phyllis played the piano, and Eric provided the background vocals.

"He was more even than a son to me," says his mother with bitter resignation. "We were friends." In her late thirties, with reddish hair, she under normal circumstances has the energetic vivaciousness and displays the maternal excesses commonly and good-naturedly associated with "Jewish mothers."

"The three of us would sit around that piano and sing until the neighbors complained. Then we would move over to this sofa"—she almost smiles when she remembers—"and we would just gab, sometimes all night long." Wistfully emphasizing something that was irrevocably lost, she repeated, "We were friends. The three of us were friends."

On one of their last all-night gab sessions, Henry told his mother that he had a problem. Since the sixteen-year-old had just started dating a month or so before, Phyllis had a fairly strong feeling that he was going to ask her something about girls. "There was no subject on earth that Henry and I couldn't talk about," she says proudly. "If something was wrong, or if he had some kind of problem, he just came to me, and we tried to work it out together."

"Hey, Ma . . ." he started awkwardly, looking with slight shyness at his hands. They were sitting on the sofa; Eric was reading in the bedroom.

"What, Hen? . . . Talk to me."

"Well, you see, it's like this. . . . How do you ask a girl out that you really like, like a lot, but you're sure she's going to turn you down?"

"And what makes you so sure?" Phyllis wasn't going to let him become an easy prisoner of adolescent insecurity.

"Well . . . she's really popular."

"Popular, shmopular, you'll never know if you don't ask."

"Henry was like a father to me." Eric fitted easily into the inseparable trio. He has a thoughtful, introspective personality, not generally associated with kids who've just reached their thirteenth birthday. "After my parents got divorced, it was a little rough at first. But my mother, and me, and Henry always stuck together."

Happily, when Phyllis married Danny Gallo in 1971, this closeness continued. He's a friendly, easygoing man who never tried to push himself on the boys.

The net result was that they took to him naturally. Even the singing sessions continued.

"Henry wanted to study music," his mother says. Whenever she talks about her son now, her voice is quiet and edged in melancholy. "He sang beautifully." Henry had even had several chances to sing semiprofessionally. When the boys were growing up, Phyllis used to take them, by bus, to one of the dozens of inexpensive summer resorts located not far from the city in the Catskill Mountain area. There, on rainy afternoons during the general recreation hours, Henry would sing for the pleasure of hard-pressed mothers and their restlessly squirming offspring.

"Henry had perfect pitch, and you know what else . . . ?" Like most mothers, Phyllis loves to brag about her boys. "Henry would have made it big in show business. He had the personality."

It was on one of these annual treks to the Catskills that Henry had first demonstrated his uncommon spirit and courage. When he was only ten years old, he saw a small child fall, unnoticed, into the deep end of the resort pool. Without hesitation, Henry, at the time a weak swimmer, jumped in and with great difficulty and even personal peril managed to save her life.

"Ever since he was a boy—I guess he was still a boy—but anyway, ever since he was little, he couldn't just walk by if he saw someone was having a problem," says his mother. "You want to know what kind of kid he was? If he saw an old person falling over in the street, he'd run in front of a bus to pick him up." Crying now, she continues, "This is how he was—he couldn't think to do anything else."

On the morning he was to die, Henry left the apartment and walked downstairs after making his half of the bunk bed. It was about 11:15. The store was only fifteen minutes away, but Henry liked to be there early. When he got outside, he shaded his eyes from the sun and looked up at the sky. He smiled because it was a cloudless day, perfect swimming-pool weather for his mom and Eric. They had left the apartment a couple of hours before, having wisely decided to spend what was surely going to be another oppressively hot July afternoon in the water of the pool at Van Cortlandt Park.

For a city boy, Henry had a great love of the outdoors. If he had left the house with his mother and brother that morning, he would probably have greeted this glimpse of the clear summer sky with one of his traditionally exuberant cries of, "Hey, Ma. Look at that sun!" followed by a playful, teasing poke at either Phyllis or Eric, and the beginning of an impromptu game of tag along 211th Street.

As the mother of one of his friends said in a letter to Mrs. Gallo after Henry's death, "He was joyful, teasing, and light-hearted, but it was always in a kind, not ever in a cruel way." For all his teasing, Henry had impressive dignity for a sixteen-year-old. He was tall, more than six feet, towering over most of the kids in the neighborhood, and he used his height to good advantage. Acting as a sort of roving neighborhood diplomat, Henry would frequently intervene in disputes, particularly if they became fights, and even more particularly if they were uneven.

Like all good big brothers, he had also spread his protective wings over his own kid brother. Eric is a small boy. Slightly on the chubby side, his round face is dominated by a relatively huge pair of tortoiseshell eyeglasses. Eric is bright and precocious, but he has a couple of physical problems. He suffers from diabetes. Of more immediate concern, however, in Public School 34, where Eric was a fifth-grade student at the time, was his size; he was small enough to be easy prey for any bully with a mind to terrorize him. Which is exactly what one young fellow in particular took casual delight in doing regularly. It got so regular, in fact, that Henry was forced to take one afternoon off to see the fellow and convincingly demonstrate that Eric had a friend who would not tolerate the terrorizing of his younger brother.

"He was always sticking up for me," Eric says. "I'm too small, and I can't fight that well, and sometimes, around here, you have to. Henry always protected me."

His mother adds, "It wasn't in Henry's nature to refuse to help someone who needed help."

Around his own neighborhood, Henry was much more accepted than he was in the highly organized, clubby atmosphere of his high school. In Norwood, he had proved often enough that his quiet reserve should not be interpreted as weakness.

Walking down Henry's block, 211th Street, is almost like being on a dead end. With the cemetery on one side, and trees on both, it has a near-suburban feeling to it. But as soon as you turn onto one of the neighboring streets, the one- and two-family homes and the smaller buildings begin giving way to larger apartment houses and generally bigger buildings. At that point, a pedestrian is instantly reminded that he is in the Bronx.

Henry walked with a long, loping stride. Whenever he and Eric went walking, as they often did, Eric would pantingly and constantly remind his brother to slow down. Even on days like today, when Henry had no special need to hurry, he glided easily and rapidly along.

Gun Hill Road is the main street in that section, and when Henry reached it, he turned right, heading for the ice-cream parlor, about a mile away. But that was as close to Capital as he got.

"Henry!"

One of the younger boys Henry recognized from around the neighborhood was yelling to him from across the street, obviously distressed. Henry checked out the traffic, then hurried across the wide, busy four-lane thoroughfare. He put his hands on the kid's shoulders. "Take it easy a second and tell me what's going on."

"Two kids are stealing my friend's bike!"

"Where?"

"Right down the block! At the oval!"

"Two kids?"

"Yeah. Maybe they're Puerto Rican!" added the agitated and obviously frightened twelve-year-old, wanting to be exact. Up to this point, Henry didn't know whether a crime was really being committed. Temporarily snatching a bicycle and taking it for a joy ride was a common form of teasing, and usually, after a half-hour or so, the bike was returned and no harm was done. Still, this kid was really upset, and Henry knew what a bummer it was actually to have your bike stolen. His had been grabbed just a few weeks before. And it sounded like the two alleged bike thieves came from outside the neighborhood, which made the jest theory unlikely.

After a momentary hesitation, Henry made up his mind. "Okay, you wait right here . . . I'm going to call a cop." He had compromised responsibly. Having to get to work, but still wanting to ensure that justice was done, Henry had decided to flag down a patrol car and report the incident to the police.

He didn't have to look far. A police car had just pulled over a block away. Henry half-walked, half-ran over to it.

"I think something is going on over at the oval," he said hurriedly to the officer inside. The policeman was just in the process of reporting in to the station house when Henry spoke to him. Still holding the two-way radio microphone in his hand, he looked up at the tall sixteen-year-old.

"What is it?" the officer asked, evidently preoccupied with the importance of his imminent call to the precinct.

"I think some kids are trying to steal another kid's bike," Henry answered anxiously, waiting for the policeman to burst instantly into action.

"Where did you say this was happening?" the officer asked politely, relieved that it wasn't something more serious or pressing.

"Over on Reservoir Oval."

"Well, what did you see?"

"I haven't really seen anything yet," Henry answered, slightly embarrassed at his lack of firsthand information. "That kid over there told me about it," he added almost defensively, pointing to the boy waiting fidgetingly across the street.

"I've got to make this call in to the precinct," responded the officer, looking back at Henry. "As soon as I do, I'll take a ride over there. . . . Where did you say this was happening?"

"At Reservoir Oval," Henry said, more subdued, the aroused gusto gone from his voice.

"At the oval," the officer repeated, again politely. "Okay, see you there . . . in about five minutes." He was turning away from the window even before he finished that sentence, his mind already switched on to his more pressing duties. "Car 12 to base, car 12 to base . . ."

Feeling a bit silly, and convinced that nothing menacing was going on, Henry impatiently decided that, still, he should check the situation out. He walked back across the street to where his informant was waiting anxiously, and said, in an almost tired voice, "Come on. Let's take a look."

"But what about the cop?" the worried youngster inquired, looking back over his shoulder at the parked patrol car.

Without looking back, Henry answered, "He'll be there in five minutes," as he headed off in the direction of the oval, eating up the distance with that long stride of his. With renewed confidence, the twelve-year-old went right along, trotting to keep up.

With Tony on the handlebars, George pedaled with some difficulty uptown on the Grand Concourse, the almost European-style boulevard that runs north and south, dividing the Bronx in half. As recently as five years ago its name was neither so pretentious nor so inaccurate as it now seemed. There really was grandness to the avenue, the broadest and one of the longest in all New York City. But as Tony and George were riding past the still-elegant-looking old buildings that line the Concourse, it had fallen into the advanced stages of decay. The ugly, ever-spreading slums, master already of the bordering side streets, had reached the avenue, and on every other block there was at least one abandoned building smeared with insoluble graffiti and littered with long-neglected trash.

As you head north on the Concourse, the neighborhood becomes more stable, and more like it was. It doesn't happen instantly. Gradually, there are fewer boarded-up buildings, and more people outside their apartments, sitting on benches, or going shopping, or doing other things that are uncommon and considered foolhardy in the fringe neighborhoods of this city.

When he got to the northern end of the concourse, George continued to work his way up through the side streets until he got to 212th Street, in the Norwood section. It was unfamiliar territory for Tony, and it made him slightly uneasy. He was relieved when George pointed to the red Volkswagen parked on the corner. There was a "for Sale" sign taped on one of the rear side windows. At least George had been telling the truth about the car.

Tony hopped off as George rolled the bike to a stop. "This is it," George said, walking around the car, trying the locked doors, as if he already owned it. "Whattaya think?"

"I dunno. But if you're goin' be foolin' around wid it, ya better call the man." Tony wanted to see the owner of the car before he looked too closely.

"Yeah. I'll call the man," George replied, distracted by a kid riding around the block for the second time on a good-looking ten-speed bike.

Tony was peering in through one of the closed windows of the car, holding his face pressed against the glass, trying to shade out the glare of the sun. Suddenly he heard a scream. He looked up in time to see that George had taken his own bike and thrown it in the path of the youngster who had been riding by on the ten-speed. The kid shrieked at the unexpected assault, and ran off down the block, abandoning his bicycle and screaming for help.

"Hey, George!" Tony called out when he realized what was happening. "Leave that kid alone . . . he didn't do nothin' to you!"

"Shut up!" was George's only reply.

Still standing next to the red VW, Tony watched as George jumped on the commandeered bicycle and started pedaling away toward Gun Hill Road.

Momentarily left alone by George's sudden flight, Tony got scared. He ran to where George had left his own bike, hopped on it, and rode furiously after his fleeing companion. "Hey, George . . . wait up!"

Disregarding the traffic, both George and Tony sped across Gun Hill Road, but halfway up the block George suddenly jumped off the stolen bike and carelessly dumped it between two parked cars. Tony slid the bike he was riding to a stop right behind George.

"What's the matter?" he asked.

"Aw, this piece of shit ain't worth a shit . . . it's no damn good."

Tony started to complain. "I dunno what you're doin' stealin' that bike anyway. . . . You crazy, man? How come you did that?"

"Shut up. And get off my bike."

"What am I supposed to do?" Tony asked. "I ain't takin' that bike," he said, gesturing over to the dumped contraband. He was confused, and he was starting to get very nervous. He was no punk, but he was extremely uncomfortable about pulling stunts like this one, particularly in a strange neighborhood, particularly one in which Puerto Ricans are still aliens.

"Get back on the bars," George ordered contemptuously, making room for Tony on his handlebars. Tony hopped back on, without having time to think through his next move. But as George pedaled down toward the park, Tony decided to take leave of his unstable companion.

"Let me off. I'm goin' to get a train."

George looked back over his shoulder. Seeing that nobody was following, and that the coast was clear, he pulled the bicycle over to the curb and roughly deposited Tony there.

The park they were approaching is called the Reservoir Oval. It's a fairly large, pleasant area of grass, trees, a pool, and playground, surrounding a central reservoir that is part of the city's public water supply. Private homes and apartment buildings face the park, which is used, mostly, by playful children and elderly area residents, who play checkers or just sit and chat on one of the oval's many shaded benches.

Tony and George went on with their argument as they continued walking down Tryon Avenue, which runs into the street circling the oval. Thinking that the heat was off, they were moving casually now, turning right onto that encircling street, which is called West Reservoir Oval.

They were on the oval, approximately halfway between Tryon and Wayne, the next street that runs up to the park, when somebody called out to them to stop.

It was Henry.

He was still with his little friend, who proudly walked alongside him, confident that Henry was going to be the angel to avenge the terrible crime of bike stealing.

"Is this the bike?" Henry asked his friend, motioning to George's bicycle.

"No. It's a white one. A ten-speed," his little friend explained with dignity. So far, he was enjoying the scene immensely. He felt like the hero's sidekick in a Western movie.

"All right," Henry called out with great moral authority. "Where is that other kid's bike?"

"Hey, brother," George started to say. "C'mon. We ain't got the bike."

"Don't 'brother' me," Henry answered sternly. "We don't like people coming around here to rob other people's bikes."

"I didn't come here to steal no bike," Tony answered back defensively. "I just came here to look at a car that this man up the block is selling."

George didn't say a word. He just stared at Henry, his eyes quickly glazing over with malevolence and hatred. Tony continued to be conciliatory.

"Hey, man. We're sorry. My friend left that other bike down the block there," he explained, pointing back up Tryon Avenue in the direction they had just come from. "I didn't even know what was goin' on."

"Shut up!" George exploded at Tony. Then, turning to Henry, "And you better fuck off, Jew boy, before you get hurt."

"You better watch your language, mister." Henry was offended, but he was controlling his temper. "Now, where's that bicycle?"

"I told you, man. It's back up there." Tony said, still trying · to salvage a peaceful getaway. "C'mon, George . . . let's split out of here."

"I ain't goin' noplace until this four-eyed bastard shuts his face up." George was really heating up.

"You're damned right you're not going anyplace. The cops will be here in about two minutes," Henry shot back. George's taunts were getting to him. "And if you didn't do anything wrong," he said, turning back to Tony, "then you've got nothing to be afraid of."

"I ain't afraid of nothin'!" George shouted, throwing a wild roundhouse right that hit Henry on the side of the face. Henry stumbled backward, taken by surprise. His twelve-year-old companion was frightened and confused for the first time, and ran over to the curb to wait out whatever was going to happen.

Henry straightened his eyeglasses, which had been knocked awry by George's blow. It was another turning point for Henry. He could either engage the thieves or retreat and find what was keeping that cop.

He turned to face George, who wasted no time in coming at him. They started trading blows, and it was obvious right from the start that once his bluff was called, George was really no match for the taller, stronger Henry.

Suddenly George pulled out a knife.

"Hey, man. You crazy?" Tony called out desperately. The situation was deteriorating rapidly. "Let's split out of here."

"I ain't goin' noplace till I cut this motherfucker," George said as he struggled awkwardly to get his knife open. It was a K-55 gravity knife, the kind that is normally opened with a flick of the wrist. But George, the nickel-and-dime junior hood, was having problems with it. Henry had drawn back several paces and was watching in horrified amusement as George repeatedly cut his fingers trying to get his blade to stay open.

"Don't be stupid," Henry cautioned. "Put that thing away."

"I'll show you who's stupid," menacingly warned George. His fingers were bleeding, and the pain was driving him to greater excesses.

"I'm telling you to put that knife away," Henry repeated. But George finally managed to get the blade to stay open, and grinning, he began to circle, slowly stalking his adversary. For about thirty seconds Henry circled in time with him, always keeping George in front of him. "The cops are on their way . . . you're just making more trouble for yourself." Keeping his eyes on the shiny long blade, Henry continued to talk to George. "Put it away before somebody gets really hurt." George had managed to back Henry up against a parked car.

"Yeah!" George suddenly yelled out. "You!"

With that, he plunged the knife deep into Henry's chest, the blood gushing out. "It was horrible," Tony said later. "It came out like a fountain."

Mortally wounded, Henry was also surprised by the attack, and angry. He looked from the gaping wound in his chest, back up at his adversary, and went at him. Henry swung another punch at George, but it missed and only made the blood flow that much faster. George had just leaned back when he saw the slow-motion blow coming. The momentum of his own swinging arm drove the dying sixteen-year-old to his knees. On the ground, he was swaying sickeningly back and forth. His head slumped over, Henry was moaning now.

Around West Reservoir Oval, a crowd had started to gather. Several adults had watched the whole bloody episode from the sidewalk across the street, but as in the case of Kitty Genovese, nobody intervened. Like most of Henry's Civil Liberties class, these people had apparently decided that getting involved would be too reckless.

George didn't notice these people. Only Tony did, and they served to frighten him even further. He grabbed George's bike, and in a panic hopped on it and started riding off.

With that first blow, Henry's little companion had also fled. He ran back up Tryon Avenue toward Gun Hill Road. This just wasn't turning out the way the movies did.

A half-block away Tony stopped the bike and looked back, in time to see George kicking Henry repeatedly and viciously, punctuating each swing of his leg with, "I'm goin' to kill you, motherfucker! I'm goin' to kill you!" Finally George swung his knife again, plunging it deeply into Henry's back.

"He didn't have to do that," Phyllis says now, her hands pressed against her face, as if trying to keep out the image of that second malicious, unnecessary blow. "Henry was already dying. He was hurt so bad . . . he didn't have to hit him again."

As soon as George struck that second blow, he looked up in the direction Tony had pedaled away on his bicycle. "Hey! Gimme that bike, you punk!" When Tony heard him, he threw down the bicycle. Frantically looking around for another escape route, he decided to jump over the stone fence down into the park. Once off the street, he looked back just long enough to see George run unhindered past the gallery of bystanders, pick up his bicycle, and ride furiously off.

Henry's body was lying in a pool of blood between two parked cars. For several minutes none of the spectators went any closer to him than they had been during the fight. The first person to approach him was his little friend, who'd come back. Bravely, the boy knelt alongside Henry's motionless body; for seconds he stared, hypnotized by the gushing blood. Then he screamed out for help.

Nobody moved.

Finally the twelve-year-old spotted a truck coming around the oval. Boldly, frantically waving his arms, he managed to flag it down. The driver jumped out took one look at Henry, and ordered the boy to help him get Henry into the truck. Once they had him inside, the driver sped off, heading for Montefiore Hospital, which is just a couple of blocks away.

As Tony ran blindly, panic-stricken, through the park, he could hear the police sirens building in intensity behind him. He felt sick to his stomach. He had to rest. Finally he sat down next to a group of old men playing checkers on one of the stone tables that dot the interior of the park. He was sweating and breathing heavily. The elderly players looked nervously at him, but said nothing, pretending instead to concentrate on their game. A group of children was playing nearby under the supervision of several counselors. One of them, a young lady, spotted Tony's obvious distress and walked over to him.

"What's the matter?" she asked. Tony could still hear the sirens, as police cruisers began combing the neighborhood.

"I just don't feel so good . . . that's all," he said unconvincingly. "I'm lookin' for the closest subway . . . I just want to go home."

The unknowing counselor kindly explained to Tony where he could find the nearest stop. As soon as she finished, Tony dashed off in the direction she had indicated, too exasperated even to thank her. He could still hear the sirens, but they were diminishing in intensity the farther he ran from that side of the park.

On the subway, the ride to the Tremont section took just five minutes.

Once out of the train, Tony ran the three blocks to his house, flying up the steps of his Creston Avenue tenement. The apartment was empty. Tony hurried into the bathroom to throw up.

At the swimming pool, Phyllis was chatting with some other ladies. Eric was swimming casually around, playing with a couple of friends.

"Mrs. Gallo . . . Mrs. Gallo! Please come to the office immediately. Mrs. Gallo, Mrs. Gallo, please come to the office immediately!" Phyllis had been paged before over the pool's public-address system, but the messages had never had such immediate urgency before. She looked apprehensively around at her friends, who quickly assured her that it was nothing serious. Nevertheless, Phyllis thought that she should take Eric with her to the pool office in the unlikely event it was something that would require her to leave the pool in a hurry.

"Eric! Come on out!" Eric had heard the P.A., and was already in the process of climbing out of the water when his mother called to him. He was also worried.

They hurried into the office, and were not reassured by the presence there of two somber-looking police officers.

"What is it . . . what's the matter?" Panic was starting to creep into Phyllis' voice. At first the officers said nothing. "Where's my son! Where's Henry?"

"Mrs. Gallo, you have to call Montefiore Hospital right now," one of the officers told her quietly, avoiding her eyes.

"What's the matter? Has there been an accident? Was Henry in a car crash?" Obviously in discomfort, the officer just asked her again to please call the hospital as soon as possible.

For a few seconds she fumbled around in her purse for a dime, until one of the veteran and usually inattentive pool attendants quickly offered her the use of one of the house phones. In a way, it was the worst possible indication of trouble.

On the phone, Phyllis was initially just as unable to get information about her son's accident from the doctor she was speaking with as she had been from the cops. Finally the doctor relented and explained that Henry had been stabbed, and that it was bad.

"How bad?" she asked. At this point, she was fast approaching hysteria.

"Very bad, Mrs. Gallo. You'd better get over here right away . . . the Emergency Room." Phyllis fought desperately for control. She closed her eyes to steady herself.

"Eric, we have to go to the hospital." A pool attendant offered to drive them to Montefiore.

Tony's nineteen-year-old sister, Brenda, came home at three in the afternoon. Tony was just walking out of the apartment at the time. She stopped him on the steps.

"Tony, what's the matter?" his sister asked when she got a close look at him. He looked sick.

"Nothing. I just don't feel so good."

"Well, why are you going out?"

"I'm just goin' over to McDonald's to see if there's work for me."

Once out of the building, he headed up Creston Avenue toward Burnside; 180th Street is a dead end there, and the kids from the neighborhood use the block as a stick-ball court. About half a dozen kids were there, but when Tony greeted them, they turned their backs on him. He was hurt and confused.

"Hey. What's the matter wid you guys?"

"*Pendejo*," was the only reply—Spanish for "coward."

"*Pendejo* for what?" he asked.

"George already told us he stuck whitey, and you was wid him, but you chickened out!" one of them grudgingly replied.

"George told you? That he stuck somebody?" Tony couldn't believe that George was stupid enough to come into the neighborhood bragging about having killed somebody. Because Tony had run away so quickly from the scene of the crime, he had been hoping that he'd made good his escape and that the grisly incident was behind him. George's conduct raised the dead specter that if these people knew about his involvement, then soon others surely would. Tony felt like throwing up again.

When Mrs. Gallo reached the entrance to the Emergency Room, an orderly was waiting for her. He escorted her and Eric quickly to an elevator that was being held for them.

"Is my son alive?" It was now the only question that mattered.

The orderly said nothing, which told her everything.

"I want to see my son!" she cried out. Not knowing what to say, the orderly forced himself to concentrate on the floor-number indicator, trying to will the elevator to go faster.

Once on the appropriate floor, Phyllis was led to a doctor's private office. Mr. Gallo and Mr. Schwartz, Phyllis' former husband, were already there. She remembers how "those faces told the story."

The doctor whose office they were in started gently to explain all of the emergency procedures that the hospital had taken when Henry was brought in. He told Mrs. Gallo about the massive tranfusions of blood, and of the heart-message techniques, and of how every surgeon in the hospital who was not involved in an emergency situation was called in to work in the frantic effort to save Henry's life. Finally the doctor said, "Mrs. Gallo, we did everything humanly possible. . . . We couldn't save him."

"You're a liar!" The careful dam she had struggled to build against this eventuality burst apart. Her son was dead. No, no, Henry couldn't be dead! He was too full of life. Too young to be dead. Phyllis started to bang her feet, as if she could stamp out that unbearable truth.

"How am I going to tell Eric?" she asked sobbingly, after her husband had managed somehow to calm her. "How am I going to tell Eric?" she demanded of nobody in particular.

There was no work for Tony at McDonald's that day. Business was slow, and he had already worked seven days straight, so Sam Monroe, the manager, told him to take the night off. Tony asked if he could hang around long enough to have a burger and a Coke; the manager assured him that he could. So Tony picked up a Big Mac and sat at a table already occupied by several co-workers on their afternoon break.

Like Brenda, Tony's sister, they noticed that he wasn't looking very well, and told him so. He assured them that he was all right and took a bite of his burger. It made him instantly sick, and he ran to the men's room and threw up again.

At home, later that evening, Mrs. Santana confronted her son.

"Tony. You have to tell me what's the matter with you." She worked for the city's municipal hospital system as a bookkeeper. In order to provide her children with every possible opportunity to escape the inevitability of Creston Avenue, she also worked part-time at another job. Her greatest fear was that her children would get into trouble somehow, and that she wouldn't be around to help them out. "Tell me the truth, Tony. Are you taking drugs?" In the heroin capital of the world, Tony's symptoms led her logically to that conclusion.

"Oh, Mami. You know I don't take no drugs."

"Then what?" she demanded.

"I just don't feel so good. That's all."

"Well, tomorrow you're going to see a doctor."

Tony agreed. With that settled, the family sat down to an evening of television, and were all in bed by midnight. The cops came at about two in the morning. At first Tony wouldn't let them in. More than one mugger had used the guise of being a police officer to gain access to one of the tenement apartments on Creston Avenue.

It was only when the detective in charge put his identification up to the peephole on the apartment door that Tony realized, finally, they had come for him.

His mother screamed when the officer mentioned murder. Tony started to lie, telling the cops that he had no involvement and no knowledge of what they were talking about. But his mother knew him, and knew he was lying. "Tony! For God's sake, tell the truth!" He did. The cops took him to the station house, handcuffed and bathed in the glare of television lights.

A nationwide alert was immediately put out for George San Inocencio. He was described, accurately, as armed and dangerous, and as the actual murderer of Henry Schwartz. He hid for a week with relatives in Brooklyn, then decided finally to surrender.

Henry Schwartz, in keeping with the traditions of his religion, had already been laid to rest. Two months

later, after school was back in session, a plaque was
hung on the wall in the corridor outside the principal's
office:

TO HENRY SCHWARTZ

. . . for his dedication to human rights and
deep feeling and understanding of the brother-
hood of man. Who gave his life for his be-
liefs . . .

September 26, 1974

It wasn't the kind of award that traditionally hung
in those hallowed corridors; but then again, Henry was
not the type of Clinton man who traditionally brought
honor and glory to this institution.

There's an old one-room red-brick schoolhouse about eight miles outside of Thompsonville, Illinois, that's been restored and is used now for square dances and other community events. Like a brightly colored navigational aid placed to guide lost sailors home, it rises above a small cleared patch in the middle of a boundless brown sea of soybeans. The long, cultivated bean rows around it run all the way up to the crests of the rolling hills on the horizon, darker lines drawn on the dark, fertile dirt of Franklin County.

When the big midsummer sun sets in fire behind those hills, it leaves the soybean fields in shadow but lingers awhile longer on the schoolhouse spire. For maybe five minutes the line of red light floats slowly up to the wind vane on the peak, until finally that, too, is dark.

At sunset on Saturdays, the 4-H Clubbers turn on the long strings of outdoor lights they've put up behind the schoolhouse in the middle of those dark fields, creating an oasis of brightness and happy sounds for their weekly square dance. And by 8:30, the dusty road leading in is lined with dozens of cars carrying families from the surrounding farms. These are true-grit, hard-working families coming in ready for a party after six long days of cultivating their soybean fields.

Angus Mack Gaither and his family had been coming to these square dances since they were started several years back. By this time the skinny, fair-haired, inexhaustible twelve-year-old could spin his partner with the best of them. Wearing his best pair of overalls and a brightly patterned plaid shirt, Mack looked like a real-life version of one of the boys in *Seven Brides for Seven Brothers*.

Typically, he would dance from the minute they all got there until his dad told him it was time to leave, around midnight. His only occasional breaks came whenever the two old gents who served as fiddlers and their colleague on the banjo decided it was time to grab a breather and a beer.

Under the lights, which were soon surrounded by a million mad bugs, everybody ate homemade potato salad, fresh corn on the cob, and sizzling hamburgers from the open grills, and drank beer and soda chilled in tall tin garbage cans filled with ice.

While the kids danced, ate, flirted, played tag, and danced some more, the grown-up men smoked pipes and talked thoughtfully of farm prices and weather. This is rural southern Illinois, and farming is not merely the principal industry; it is everything.

In one large circle Mack's father was leading a discussion on the lateness and paucity of the rain. He was something of a phenomenon in the country. At seventy-five, he still put in a full twelve- to fourteen-hour day on his four-hundred-acre soybean farm located just a mile and a half from the small town of Thompsonville. He was sixty-two when Mack was born, still looked at least fifteen years younger than he really was, and had never been seriously ill.

He was a short man with a mane of white hair. He had a great sense of humor, and his anecdotes, told while trading hogs or at the feed mill on the barber shop, were legendary in the country. He was the community's elder statesman, a walking, talking farmer's almanac, whose advice was sought after and to whom attention was paid.

Standing next to Mr. Gaither was his older son, J.C. At twenty-six, J.C. was deservingly accepted into this informal farmers' council as his father's protégé and partner. While young Mack was already tending more toward school and scholarly pursuits, J.C., whose real name is Jewell Charles, was the epitome of the modern young farmer.

Cleta, Mack's mother, had spent the early part of the evening helping the other ladies to heat up and dish out the food everybody had contributed to the dance. She was a bundle of friendly energy, expertly urging the shy ones to take another portion, while playfully shooing away the more determinedly gluttonous.

Now, as the party was winding down, Cleta was knitting and chatting near the bonfire with the women's group. It was almost midnight when she looked over to her husband, caught his eye, and nodded. It was the subtle, silent kind of communication people have when they've been together for several decades, and in this instance it meant that it was getting on time to go home.

Mr. Gaither, whose name was also Angus Mack, said good night to his friends and sent J.C. over to retrieve little Mack from the whirling circle of square dancers.

After the boys had helped their mother hose off the empty pots she'd brought loaded with home-cooked food, they all got into their old four-door Chevy and joined the procession of headlights heading home from the schoolhouse.

The four-hundred-acre Gaither farm is small when compared with the huge factory-farms that dominate the agricultural industry, but it's fairly large by the standards of Franklin County. Soybeans are the basic cash crop, but some corn, milo, and wheat, are grown to feed either the family or their livestock.

Working a farm this size usually requires two men putting in six days a week—most of the year, at least twelve hours a day. On Sundays there's traditionally no work done in the fields, but there are still the animals to be tended. The Gaithers kept thirty head of milk cows and about a hundred hogs, raised mostly for slaughter.

In a good year, if the planting, cultivating, and harvesting went exactly according to schedule, and if the weather held up and the price of soybeans remained stable, the family could anticipate an income of about eight thousand dollars. And much of that money had to be set aside for fertilizer and equipment replacements for the following year's planting season.

Mr. Gaither got up between five and five-thirty every morning, and Sundays were no exception. He was already out in the big old barn feeding the livestock when his boys joined him at about six.

They greeted their father and started to work on their chores. As Mack was milking one of the cows, he looked over and saw his father gingerly rubbing his stomach. In that dim light, the twelve-year-old couldn't tell for sure, so he walked over and saw that his father looked different than he'd ever seen him before. Mr. Gaither, the man who continually amazed his neighbors with his indefatigable vitality, was in pain.

J. C. came over also and asked his dad what was bothering him.

"Maybe that sun got to me yesterday," Mr. Gaither answered, "or maybe it was something I ate at the dance last night."

Mack looked at his older brother but didn't say anything. It was true that his dad had worked long and hard cultivating the beans on Saturday, and it was true that the day had been suffocatingly hot and humid. But so were many other days, and the heat never seemed to get to the seventy-five-year-old farmer's farmer before now.

Mack ran to get his mother, who was already up fixing breakfast. After a struggle, she persuaded her husband to knock off for the rest of the day, although she was unsuccessful in urging him to go and see doctor. He had simply never been really sick before, and he refused to admit to being that sick now.

At two-thirty the next morning, Cleta was wrenched awake by her husband's agonized delirium. He was in a terrible fever, but he was also shaking unconsciously, as if being tortured simultaneously by fire and ice. His cries had been so loud that they woke J.C. and Mack, who shared a room on the opposite side of the farmhouse.

"Call the ambulance!" Cleta frantically ordered J.C., as she held tightly to her husband to keep him from shaking off the bed. At twelve years old, all Mack could do was bring his mother the wet towels she was putting on his father's burning forehead.

With a total population of fewer than two thousand people, the town of Thompsonville is just a dusty crossroads, punctuated by a handful of relatively prominent buildings, mainly the public school, some agricultural supply stores, and the firehouse. There is neither a hospital nor an ambulance. The closest ambulance is operated by the Poulson and Freeman Funeral Home, in Benton, about ten miles away.

"The ambulance is on the way!" J.C. ran into the room as soon as he'd completed the call. "Should I call Dr. Swinney?"

"No. He's on vacation," Cleta answered despairingly. "There's got to be a doctor in Benton."

Two weeks later, Angus Mack Gaither, Senior, died at the age of seventy-five because of complications brought on by an intern's failure to quickly diagnose a ruptured appendix.

He was buried in the little cemetery behind the Pleasant Hill Church, about a mile and a half down a gravel road from his farm. It's a small white building with a steeple and a bell that the Gaithers can hear from their fields.

On the day they buried Mr. Gaither, the church building was filled to overflowing with scores of people from all over the county who'd come to pay their last respects.

After the service, about twenty-five neighbors spontaneously came over to the farmhouse to give Cleta their condolences and give J.C. their best wishes. The burden of running the farm had now passed to him. But his father had taught him well, and with Mack and the help of their intrepid mother, the farm seemed in good hands.

Mack had done odd jobs on the farm, helping with the chores almost from the time he was old enough to walk. Most of the heavy work, though, had been shared by his father and J.C. With his father's death, that changed. Despite the fact that he was only in the sixth grade, Mack graduated into the ranks of adult farmers.

His basic responsibility was still to school, but early each morning, before he left, and as soon as he got home in the afternoon, Mack would be out in the fields, plowing and cultivating alongside his brother.

It went that way for three years and three modestly successful harvests. Like most small farmers, the Gaithers never prospered, but they did always manage to pay the bills.

J.C. married a pretty girl named Janice, and the two of them moved into the other farmhouse on the property. Located just down the road from the slightly larger main house, it dated back to the days when the four hundred acres had been divided into two different farms; until J.C.'s marriage, the house had been closed up.

One Saturday morning in the middle of the fourth planting season after the death of their father, Mack walked over to J.C.'s house. Now fifteen years old, Mack was going to help his brother bring home a bull that J.C. had bought for breeding purposes. It was about seven-thirty when Mack got there. J.C. still hadn't come outside, so Mack went ahead and started getting his brother's pickup truck ready for the ride.

When J.C. finally came out his front door, he wasn't saying much, and he looked awful.

"What's the matter, J.C.?" Mack was concerned. His older brother, like his father, never complained about any kind of pain or illness.

"I'm not feeling so good." J.C. was pale and perspiring. "Do me a favor and call up Earl Gunter and ask him to go with you to get the bull."

"Sure, J.C."

"I'm goin' inside to lie down on the couch."

By the time Mack and neighbor Gunter got back to the house with the new bull, J.C. was unconscious. His wife and Cleta were there, desperately trying to get him to respond by putting cold towels on his face and talking to him. But there was no response.

The same ambulance from Benton that had carried his father three years before now took J.C. to the hospital. Janice and Mack rode with him. There wasn't enough room for Cleta, so she followed closely behind in the family car.

They kept J.C. in the local hospital for only about thirty minutes. It didn't take the staff there long to realize that his affliction was beyond their limited capabilities to handle, so the ambulance left immediately for St. Luke's Hospital, the closest facility with experts in neurosurgery, located in St. Louis, 180 miles away.

At the height of the planting season, J.C., the stalwart, steadfast rock of a young man, had suffered a stroke. He was thirty years old.

Mack and Janice again rode in the ambulance with J.C. His mother had to arrange for the neighbors to come over to the farm and take care of the animals. As soon as she'd done that, Cleta was also going to head for St. Louis in her car.

J.C.'s young wife cried most of the way. Mack did his best to comfort her, but he needed comforting himself. He was in shock. That morning his world had been orderly. Now it was chaos. He was only a freshman in high school. His mother was fifty-six years old. With J.C. sick, the two of them were charged with the almost impossible task of holding onto and working a four-hundred-acre farm bequeathed under the most unhappy and untenable circumstances.

It was a beautiful sunny morning, and as Mack fought back his own tears, he could look out at the rolling hills and the just-plowed fields full of workers getting ready for the annual planting.

Whenever there was a lull in the conversation, either Janice or Mack would suddenly blurt out, "He's going to be all right!" only to lapse again into silence, stunned by the lack of conviction in their own voices. Mack's father's death was still too fresh a memory for the fifteen-year-old to discount that awful possibility.

The ride was endless and dreary, despite the sunshine. There's no good highway betweeen Thompsonville and St. Louis, so the ambulance had to make the best possible time on one of those two-lane rural roads that have a traffic adventure waiting around each turn. Despite what seemed a reckless pace, it took them almost four hours to cover the 180 miles.

The ambulance entered the city limits with its red lights still flashing and its siren engaged whenever necessary to clear away the cars in front of it.

It was the first time Mack had ever been in the big city, and the awesomeness of that experience conspired with his brother's condition to push the kid to the edge of collapse. For the first time in his life, he felt faint. Six hours before, he had walked over to his older brother's house to help him with a new bull. Now he was, in effect, the older brother. The burden of the farm had passed again.

"My father had always told us both no matter what happened, hold onto the farm. He told us no matter how rough things might get, never to give it up."

When Mack remembers that time, and specifically that ride, he gets uncharacteristically misty.

"So when I was fifteen years old, I inherited the tradition and the spirit and the feeling that a family farm is a lot more than just a piece of ground. It was our heritage and our way of life, and I didn't know how I was going to keep it together."

For the next two hours Janice and Mack sat on a metal bench outside the Emergency Room, watching, without comprehending, all the hustle and bustle of that frightening place, still not getting any word on J.C.'s condition.

Finally Cleta arrived. She had driven to St. Louis with her brother, Clyde Summers. She clutched at Mack's arms as soon as she spotted him, and asked if he knew anything about J.C.'s condition. After the fifteen-year-old confessed that there was no news, she asked for the attending physician.

When they found the doctor, the bewildered family was told that J.C. had suffered a stroke of some kind, that the extent of the damage was unknown, and that it would be at least two weeks before they could get a realistic prognosis.

They were given no reason for optimism, except that J.C. was apparently not dying. He was still in a coma, but his condition had stabilized.

After that hurried conference with the doctor outside the Emergency Room, Mr. Summers suggested that they go downstairs for coffee. By this time it was midafternoon, and nobody had eaten anything all day.

In the little coffee shop on the ground floor of the hospital, Cleta decided that she would stay near J.C.

"Are you goin' to stay in a hotel?" asked Clyde.

"No, I'm goin' to stay right here in this hospital," said the determined little lady. "I want to be there when J.C. wakes up."

"But, Ma . . . you can't stay in the hospital!" protested Mack. "There's no place to sleep."

"I'll sleep on those benches in the Emergency Room."

When Mack continued to protest, Mrs. Gaither closed off all argument. Her mind was made up. She had stayed by her husband's side during his final illness, and now she refused to leave her elder son.

"Mack," she said, looking straight and hard at her fifteen-year-old, "you're the man of the family now. You got to get home and take care of the farm."

"But, Ma!"

"Don't worry about me, Mack," she said, holding up her hands as if to stop traffic. "You just get on home and take care of things until J.C. and me get back."

Mack made the long, quiet drive back to Thompsonville with his Uncle Clyde. Janice had also decided to stay in St. Louis, at least for the night.

When Clyde pulled the Chevy up into the big dirt driveway in front of the barn, he and Mack saw eight or ten pickups already parked there. They belonged to the neighbors.

Mack jumped out of the car and hurried into the large red barn where he had spent so many happy afternoons as a kid playing in the hayloft. Now his neighbors were there, tending to the livestock and straightening the place out.

When they saw Mack, the group came quickly over and eagerly began asking questions about J.C.'s condition.

"He's about the same as he was when we left here," was all Mack could tell them. He was near tears, despite his efforts to be manly and in charge of himself. His neighbors saw that, but didn't say anything. They only spoke to offer their time and services, helping him with the farm in any way they could. Their offers were totally unconditional.

"I'll help," said one.

"We'll be here," said another. "Call us whenever you need anything."

For the next two weeks Mack worked getting the fields ready. Despite J.C.'s illness, the soybeans still had to be planted. Everything depended on the new crop, and the neighbors, all farmers themselves, realized that and turned out to help.

Men who had spent long, hot days in their own fields spent their evenings and weekends working on the Gaither farm. They used their own tractors and even insisted on paying for their own gasoline.

The women also helped. After they had cooked and cleaned their own homes, they would walk over in the afternoons and take care of the Gaither house. Mack was touched and grateful for all the help, but he wasn't surprised.

"You know, it just comes natural to farmers. When a neighbor is in trouble and needs help, people lend a hand. We sure needed them, and they turned out."

About three weeks later, Mack went back to St. Louis to help his mom bring J.C. home. His brother had regained consciousness, seemed to be in good health, but was as weak as a baby.

When they got him back to Thompsonville, J.C. sat convalescing on the porch in front of his house. For a few days he watched Mack, at times helped by neighbors, at work in the fields. By the end of J.C.'s first week at home, he was already getting restless. Mack was doing a good job, but there was so much to be done.

By the end of J.C.'s second week at home, he was up and doing light work around the house and in the barn. In three weeks, the big six-footer was back in the fields, despite the protests of his mom and his wife.

He seemed to thrive on work. Suffering no apparent after-effects of the stroke or whatever it had been, he was soon putting in full thirteen- or fourteen-hour days.

Mack and he worked side-by-side. The fifteen-year-old would occasionally ask his brother to take it easy, but J.C. would just let out his tender laugh. He was amused and touched by his "little" brother's concern, but he was feeling good and saw no reason to slow down. J.C. was a plainspoken man and "a farmer through and through, according to Mack.

Because of the fifteen-year difference in their ages, the two of them had a relationship closer to that of uncle and favorite nephew than brother to brother. But they got along very well together. J.C. took pains to teach Mack everything he knew about farming, but he realized that Mack's ambitions, unlike his own, probably lay outside the farm.

Even though he was only a high-school freshman, Mack was already talking about going away to college and maybe even becoming a lawyer or a politician.

There was hard work all that summer, but things seemed to be going all right for the family. By harvest time J.C. was back to full stride, and Mack was doing very well in school.

The harvest was good, but J.C. decided after it was all in and work around the farm had slowed that he was going to earn a little extra money. He started working in the oilfields, the tall steel forest of rigs and derricks that dominate the fields starting about ten miles south of town.

He'd been at it for a month when Janice called Cleta in the middle of the night. J.C. had suffered another stroke. This time it was a massive, crippling cerebral hemorrhage.

They rushed him to Franklin Hospital in Benton. He was there for a week. This time, J.C. did not com-

pletely recover. When they brought him home, he was
conscious but paralyzed. The handsome young farmer
with dark hair and blue eyes could no longer even feed
himself.

One night after Dr. Swinney left, telling the family
that there would be no change in J.C.'s condition for
the foreseeable future, Janice told Cleta and Mack that
she was leaving J.C. She moved out. This time had been
much too much.

Mack, at twelve, had understood the significance
of his father's words about holding onto the farm, no
matter what; but the real responsibility for carrying
them out had been his big brother's. Now, when he was
sixteen, the burden had shifted—this time for good—to
Mack.

J.C. was moved back into the main house. His
home was closed, and is still sealed shut.

With the help of his amazing mother, Mack put
out the crop. He hired another high-school student to
help him. Bruce Higginson's family were laborers in the
oilfields, so the seventeen-year-old was free to take the
job working with Mack.

Mack also got help from his neighbors. Two who
turned out, Ernie and Percy Payne, even insisted on
bringing their own sandwiches with them. They didn't
take a real lunch break. They would just grab a few
minutes late in the day and eat out in the fields, standing alongside their tractors. The two brothers didn't
want to go into the house for a proper lunch, because
they were afraid it would be too much of an imposition
on Cleta.

The cynical pragmatism that causes so many city
people to avoid getting involved in the lives of their
neighbors is not the prevailing mood in Franklin
County.

But the greatest share of the work, and all the responsibilities, were still Mack's. He had become head of
both family and farm at an age when most kids are
struggling with decisions like whether or not to try out
for the freshman football team.

"Most people would have run away from it," says

Joe Williams, one of Mack's closest friends. "Mack was just in the ninth grade, but he still made it work."

Kim Blades, another of Mack's friends and former classmates, agrees. "When things really got bad, Mack had to depend on a lot of other people for support, but when it gets right down to it, he relied only on himself."

Alan Patton, his high-school principal, added that Mack was much more than just independent. "He's outgoing and intelligent. He's had to make adult decisions and do a man's work, even though he was only an adolescent. But he's always come through, and that's made him mature far beyond his years."

His school, Thompsonville High, is small, about one hundred students. Thirty-one were in Mack's class, "one of the largest classes we've had in years," according to Mr. Patton.

In the school, like the town, everybody knew almost everything about everybody else. The teachers and the school adminstrators were fully aware of what was happening to the Gaither family, but while they were all very sympathetic, Mack didn't receive any preferential treatment.

"That's not the kind of help he would have accepted," says Mr. Patton. "Mack always insists on being treated the same as everyone else."

In the four years he was in high school, Mack never missed a day of classes. He was rarely late, and only occasionally left early, and that was during planting or harvesting, or when there was a flare-up of some problem at home. He never asked for an extension on a pending term paper, the rescheduling of an exam, or any other special consideration. While running the farm virtually on his own, Mack still managed an A average. Unsurprisingly, his classmates fondly rechristened him "Superman."

Not satisfied with a burden that was just herculean, Mack refused merely to get by in school. At Thompsonville, for instance, the average course load is four or five subjects. Mack always signed up for seven or eight, and they were always the most demanding. All of the traditional high-school nemeses, calculus, trigonometry, and chemistry, were part of his curriculum. During his entire high-school career, Mack never had a single free study period.

His perseverance and achievements are relentlessly extraordinary. In addition to the farm, family, and schoolwork, he made time to participate in many extracurricular activities.

He loved drama and played the principal role in several productions of Thompsonville's Theater club. The casting in one play was inspired. He played the title role in *Young Abe Lincoln*.

"You know something?" says friend Joe Williams. "He was great at it. . . . Damn! He even looks like Abraham Lincoln."

A historical footnote of perhaps more than passing coincidence: Lincoln was also a self-made man and the product of a tough, early-years apprenticeship spent in the farmlands of rural southern Illinois. Comparison is almost unavoidable. Mr. Patton, the school principal, says of the Lincoln analogy, "They're two of a kind."

In his freshman year, Mack developed an even greater interest in the world of politics. To learn more about the process, on a practical level, he joined the school's debating team. One of their most memorable outings was to a statewide mock United Nations debate, held at nearby McKendree College.

Dozens of teams were there, representing much larger high schools from throughout Illinois. Thompsonville, led by Mack, portrayed the delegation from the USSR in the competition.

In the tense, packed auditorium, Mack, with all the outward assurance of an experienced diplomat, delivered a passionate but reasoned defense of "his" nation's position in the debate. With a performance that Kim Blades later called "brilliant, absolutely brilliant," Mack carried the day for Thompsonville. The school was declared the Illinois state champions, and Mack was offered a special scholarship to McKendree College.

Success often breeds smug self-satisfaction, but that wasn't the way it worked with him. According to

Kim, it had exactly the opposite effect. "He was never the kind of person to hold his own success over anybody else's head. He was just a normal friendly guy. He was never condescending, and he never acted like a big shot."

Another classmate, Susan Johnson, emphasized his sincerity. "There was this one new kid in our class who was really unpopular. You know, the kind of guy who just doesn't fit in anywhere. In the beginning, nobody would talk to him or invite him to any parties. Well, that really upset Mack, and he used to go out of his way to include this guy, and get the rest of the kids to go easy on him. Mack wasn't a 'goody-goody' or anything like that. He just didn't think it was right to treat anybody that way."

Alan Patton was more than just Thompsonville's principal. Doubling as the school's guidance counselor, he forged close relationships with many of his students, and with Mack, especially, he became almost a surrogate father. Recognizing both the boy's need and obvious abilities, Patton spent hours advising, suggesting, and teaching his star pupil.

"Maybe city people wouldn't be able to understand what kept Mack going," he reflects. "In wide-open country like this, a man does feel closer to the Almighty. Maybe it's not very sophisticated, but it's true. Mack always had an unswerving belief and faith that if he kept doing everything he was able to, then somehow things would work out."

Typically, Mack would get up at about a quarter past five, and for the next hour he would study, completing the schoolwork left unfinished the night before.

By half past six he was out in the barnyard checking on the livestock. He fed and watered them and checked for anything unusual.

Disease spreads fast in farm animals, and farmers have to be constantly aware of even the slightest abnormality. If they aren't, an infectious disease can wipe out their animals in a matter of days.

From the yard, Mack would walk out into the fields to check on the crop.

At that hour, the sun hasn't had the chance to dry out the soybeans, so they sparkle with early-morning dew. Mack would walk down the long rows, his clothes getting wet as they absorbed the chill and dampness of both the beans and the misty air. The mist would clear by seven-thirty or eight o'clock, when the sun had the chance to burn it off.

It was Mack's favorite time of day, and the only time he could be leisurely enough to feel pride in what he owned and what he was doing.

Except for planting or harvest time, maintaining the crop didn't call for continuous hard labor. But aside from irrigation and fertilization, "there were always a hundred little chores and odd jobs to be done." Every day there was something to be fixed or built or repaired. The grass had to be cut, the fence painted, or a field replowed.

Whatever the season, the hours before breakfast were busy ones, and when he had done what he had time to do, Mack would walk back to the house.

Once inside, he would pick J.C. up out of bed and start getting him ready for the day. He would carefully bathe and shave his older brother, get him dressed, into the wheelchair, and down to the breakfast table.

After a quick breakfast made by his mom, Mack would be off. During his first two years of high school he'd wait at the crossroads for the bus. When he was old enough, he drove their slightly battered 1967 pickup truck to school.

The schoolday was filled, but the bell ending his final class was just a signal that he was free to go back to work in the fields. Except for those rare occasions when he stayed to rehearse a play or some other extracurricular activity. Mack went straight home. Cleta would have a late lunch ready, and as soon as he finished that, he'd pick up where he had left off in the fields that morning. To lengthen his working hours, Mack had night lights installed on both the combine and his tractor. That way, he could work the fields until nine-thirty or ten o'clock in the evening.

After he washed the day's dirt off, there would be

the evening meal. Fighting the accumulated exhaustion, Mack would always tell his mom and brother about whatever exciting events had highlighted his day. They were confined to the house, and he always tried to make them feel part of his life outside the farm.

When J.C. had been put to bed, Mack was finally free to do his schoolwork. Because he was such a conscientious student, that often meant studying until one or two in the morning. Four or five hours later, it would all start over again, unrelenting.

"Most grown men could never have carried that load," says Mr. Patton. It is the kind of understatement the quiet people of Franklin County are known for.

But assuming that the biblical myth is true, and that good does triumph over evil, and virtue over adversity, it certainly doesn't always work in the short run.

Mack's problems continued to get worse.

On a Sunday morning in April 1974 he got up at about four-thirty. It was earlier than usual, because he had more to do than he usually did. Forgoing his customary study hour, Mack was in the yard by five o'clock. Still below the horizon, the morning sun was just starting to color in the shadows.

Mack began his day, as he customarily did, tending to the animals. He started there, because he could find his way around the barn and the pens in the dark.

From the barn, he moved into the fields, and he was out there when the sun finally broke on the horizon. He worked, cultivating the long bean rows, expecting after some time passed that his mother would be calling him in for breakfast. As was their Sunday custom, they were going to the eight-o'clock church services. That meant he had to be in the house by seven-thirty if he was going to have time to eat and change his clothes.

Mack wasn't wearing a watch, but like most farmers, he carried a clock around in his head. At one point, it just seemed later than seven-thirty.

Mack started walking toward the house, but as his apprehension grew, he started running. Frantically he stumbled right through the wet soybeans, soaking his clothes in his headlong rush toward the house. Once inside, he called out for his mother. There was no answer. He ran to her bedroom. She was there, in bed, unconscious and breathing heavily.

Mack tried, but he couldn't wake her. Cleta had also suffered a stroke during the night.

"Oh, no! Not again!" he cried out, standing over his mother's bed, but she couldn't hear him.

He called the ambulance in Benton, for the fourth time in four years. As soon as that was done, he called a neighbor to come over and look after J.C. Then, in the few minutes left before the ambulance arrived, Mack got his brother up and dressed, did the same for his mom, and carried her over near the door, so there wouldn't be any delay once the ambulance got there.

Cleta was taken to Franklin Hospital. For the first week, she was only semiconscious. She couldn't recognize anyone or feed herself.

Mack visited her every day on his way to and from school. Worried because the local hospital was understaffed, he made the four-thirty wake-up his permanent regimen. That way he was able to do the chores, get J.C. ready for the day, and still have time enough to drive the ten miles out to the hospital before going to school.

He'd feed his mother breakfast, then get on to school by nine o'clock. Mack would leave school at eleven, feed his mother her lunch, then be back in school by twelve-thirty.

"I knew that if it was me in the hospital," he explained, "then she would have always been right there."

For the three weeks Cleta was in the hospital, Mack also had to find time to study for his rapidly approaching senior finals.

While she hadn't been as totally ravaged by the stroke as J.C. had been, Mrs. Gaither still needed constant attention after she finally came home from the hospital. So to Mack's already impossible burden of a large farm, an invalid brother, and a demanding academic schedule was added the need to care for his elderly, heartbroken, and crippled mother.

Earlier in the year Mack had made a final decision

to go on to college after he graduated from Thompsonville High. Farming was part of his blood, but he
wanted to expand his horizons, thinking always that he
could come back home after he had earned his degree.
Because of his impressive record, he had been offered
scholarships to a dozen colleges and universities, among
them the Air Force Academy, West Point, and Harvard.

Harvard was his first choice, and when word came
that he'd won a scholarship there, it was one of the high
points of his life. He talked it over with Mr. Patton, his
mom, J.C., and Joe Williams. All of them enthusiastically agreed. Mack would accept the offer; he would be
going to Harvard.

It was the first time anyone could remember a resident of Franklin County going all the way to Boston to
go to college. Most of the kids went to schools in the
area. Joe, for example, had decided on Rend Lake Junior College, about twenty miles from Thompsonville.

"Most of the people around here never even heard
of Harvard," Mack points out with amusement, not dis-
dain.

Before Mrs. Gaither had suffered the stroke, they
had even planned the financial arrangements. In obedi-
ence to his father's wish that they never lose the farm,
the family had decided that they would rent it out until
Mack came home. The way they had it figured, the rent
paid by a tenant farmer would have been just enough
for Cleta and J.C. to get by. Only the fields were to be
rented; Mrs. Gaither and her elder son would be staying
on in the farmhouse. She would manage the house and
the care of J.C.; Mack planned to come down from
Boston as often as he could to help his mom and make
sure everything was running smoothly.

The plan was shattered when Cleta suffered the
stroke. Now she was unable to care even for herself.
Mack wrote to Harvard explaining the situation and requesting more time to think about his future plans. The
college, which had offered a $5,250 scholarship, was
sympathetic, but needed an answer by the end of May.

Mack desperately wanted to go, but with the further collapse of his family situation, it seemed impossible.

Doctors at the hospital estimated that it would cost $1,300 a month to care for Cleta and J.C. Even with the generous scholarship offer, Mack would have had to work while attending school in order to cover just his own expenses. With the added financial burden of his mother's medical care and the housekeeper that would now be needed, there seemed to be only one logical but painful way out. Mack would have to sell the farm his family had owned for half a century.

"It was the hardest, biggest decision I've ever made, and maybe will ever have to make." For weeks he considered his limited alternatives. "At first I figured I'd ask the state for help. But then I was sure that they would want me to sell the farm. I knew I'd probably have to do that eventually, but I just couldn't make that decision until I had thought out all the other possibilities."

While he wrestled with this apparently insurmountable problem, there was no respite from his daily routine. Actually, things got tougher for him. It was the beginning of the planting season, an unavoidable responsibility. He was also right in the middle of his final exams.

When Mack had finished disking the fields and plowing one evening, he came into the house for dinner. Several of his neighbors had come over and prepared a meal for him and the family. As Mack ate, everyone silently watched him. He looked up from his plate, conscious that something was going on.

"What's up?"

His mother, whose speech had not been impaired by her illness, answered. She gently explained how both she and J.C. were determined that Mack go to Harvard. They would manage, somehow, if he went. But if he didn't go because of them, it would break their hearts.

It was Alan Patton, the school principal, who came up with the answer several days later. Ever since Cleta had been stricken, he had been agonizing over the plight of his friend and protégé.

"Somewhere, somehow," he told a group of Mack's classmates, "we've got to find somebody to help that family and get them some financial aid."

The school newspaper published his remarks, and several students offered to contribute either time or money to help the Gaithers. Mr. Patton formalized these efforts by setting up the Angus Mack Gaither Trust Fund. Barb Leebens, a reporter for *The Southern Illinoisan* newspaper, heard about the effort and ran a story about Mack's situation. It was later picked up by *Time* magazine and became national news. The response was overwhelming.

From virtually every state in the union, donations and letters of encouragement came pouring into Thompsonville. Paul Hellmuth, of Boston, gave Mack a thousand-dollar-a-year grant to help pay the medical expenses of Cleta and J.C. A nineteen-year-old senior from a high school in Liberty, Texas, sent five dollars. Mrs. Thomas Leach, of Tulsa, Oklahoma, contributed one hundred dollars a month for a year. Another woman, from Waukegan, wrote asking for Mack's measurements so she could make him some clothes for school, and there were scores of other gifts. Perhaps the most touching came from an eighty-year-old widow in Albuquerque, New Mexico. She sent Mack a little note. "I know how difficult it is to make some decisions. I know how it is to be alone. I would send you everything I have, as your story deeply touched me." Enclosed in the note was a money order for one dollar, made out to the trust fund.

On the last Sunday in May, the deadline set by Harvard, Mack wired that he would be gratefully accepting the scholarship offer. In all, he had received more than six thousand dollars in contributions, enough, at least, for the family to make it through his first year.

"It made me very proud to be an American," he said in his totally sincere, unpretentious way. "Generous people from all across this great country made one of my dreams come true . . . and I'm very thankful."

Mack graduated from high school in June. The exercises were held in the school gymnasium, and he delivered the valedictory address: "We observe today a beginning, as well as an end . . . a sense of anticipation for the future, a fulfillment in the accomplishments of the past. . . ."

Mack went off to Harvard and scored impressively in his first year there. Both his mother and brother also made great strides in their recoveries. Cleta is up and around again, and J.C. can sit up in his wheelchair and clothe and feed himself.

Despite going off to that fancy college back East, Mack plans to return to the county to live.

"People always come back. They may go away for a while, even a long while, but they always come back. There's something about farming and Franklin County that gets in your blood. It's the tradition, the family thing, and the sense of community. You can never forget it, no matter how far away you go. You always come back."

As soon as she saw the swelling below his right knee, Teresa asked Teddy how long it had been like that. It was Tuesday afternoon, and he was in bed. Since the weekend, he had been kept home from school with a fever and a cold. Teresa wondered, as she looked at it more closely, if this unusual swelling had anything to do with the way her young charge was feeling.

"I think I got it playing ball a couple of weeks ago," Teddy told her. He was sitting up in bed. The TV set was on, and the bed was littered with magazines and comic books, all there for the purpose of diverting Teddy from restlessness. He is the kind of kid who is totally unaccustomed to enforced inactivity. "But I don't really remember getting it," he added, more out of curiosity than concern, as they both continued the examination of the hard reddish lump, about half the size of his kneecap, located three or four inches below it.

Like most of the Kennedys, Teddy was a highly competitive, very active sportsman, energetically playing two-hand touch with his cousins on the lawn or racing his dad in the swimming pool outside his family's sprawling ranch-style house in McLean, Virginia.

The house sits on a hill overlooking the Potomac River and, except for the young patient and Theresa, was empty that Tuesday. Ted's dad was at the Senate; his mother, traveling in Europe. His sister, Kara, and younger brother, Patrick, were in school. As the children's governess for many years, Theresa had by now become almost a member of the family. She often served as surrogate head of the household when the Senator and Mrs. Kennedy were away.

"Well, my boy. How bad does it feel?" she inquired with a brogue that is as Irish as her name, Fitz-patrick. "Not great," said Teddy, already Kennedy-trained to minimize personal discomfort. Theresa knew this and reminded herself to bring the swelling to the Senator's attention as soon as he arrived home. And as the Senator drove his 1971 Pontiac Le Mans into the circular driveway about six o'clock, she was waiting in the hallway to tell him.

The Senator went directly to Teddy's room, where Kara and Patrick had joined their brother after school, and greeting all three, he examined with a gentle touch the swollen area on his son's leg. The swelling puzzled the Senator, and Theresa recognized the concern in his eyes.

"I'm going to call Phil Caper, son," he said. Dr. Dr. Philip Caper is one of the bright young men on the staff of the Senator's Subcommittee on Health.

The Senator telephoned his subcommittee office in the Dirksen Office Building on Capitol Hill and was told that Dr. Caper had left for the day. He was attending a formal affair that evening and had gone home to change. The Senator reached him there.

"Phil. It's Ted Kennedy. I'm sorry to bother you like this at home, but Teddy's got a little problem."

"No bother at all, Senator. What is it?"

The Senator described the swelling.

"I'll be dressed in a few minutes, and then I'll come right out."

"Thanks, Phil. I'll be waiting."

The drive from Dr. Caper's Georgetown apartment to the Kennedy home took less than a half-hour. The Senator met him at the door.

"Don't you look elegant!" Ted said as the doctor approached in his formal wear.

"I always dress this way for house calls," Phil quipped. "Now where's the patient?" He was led down the long photograph-lined hallway to Teddy's room. Teddy was alone in his room, and homework had replaced the magazines and comics.

"Teddy. You know Phil, don't you?"

"Hi, Dr. Caper." The twelve-year-old waved. He

was dressed in a fresh pair of pajamas which Theresa had insisted he put on as soon as she heard that a doctor was being called.

"Hello, Teddy," Phil replied, and moving to the bed, he added, "Now, let's take a look at that leg." He rolled up the pajama leg and probed the swollen area. "How long has this bump been here, Teddy?"

"I don't remember, exactly. About a few weeks, I'd say."

"Does it hurt?"

"Sometimes a little," Teddy admitted reluctantly.

"When?" the doctor countered, with a side glance and a wink at Teddy's father. "Doesn't it hurt all the time?"

"Well, it hurts when I walk or run on it."

"I thought at the time," Dr. Caper said later, "that it was probably just a bruise Teddy picked up somewhere. Whenever you see an injury like that, however, you have to be concerned about the possibility of something like a bone tumor—very concerned. But despite the fear, the chances of that are remote."

After giving Teddy the rest of a routine examination, Dr. Caper stood and walked to where the Senator was standing.

"I don't think it's anything serious, but I'd like to keep a close watch on that swelling." He was speaking in the conspiratorial tone doctors use in front of children. Teddy pretended politely not to notice what the grown-ups across the room were talking about.

"Let's give it a while," Dr. Caper continued. "If it doesn't go down in two or three days, then have Theresa call me."

The Senator agreed, reminded Teddy to thank the doctor for his inconvenience, then walked with Phil to the door. Like the doctor, the father was contemplating the remote but still terrifying possibility of something awful.

"Thanks for driving out tonight," he said. "I really appreciate it." Then he added, deeply preoccupied, "Oh, I almost forgot—have a good time tonight."

Two days later, the Senator was in Boston for an important speech. Mrs. Kennedy, a lifelong devotee of music, was attending an Austrian music festival and wasn't due home from Europe until the following week. So, Theresa, keeping to the letter of the doctor's careful instructions, was constantly and zealously inspecting Teddy's leg, much to his dramatically overstated but somehow unconvincing displeasure.

"I'm going to call your father, and then, young man, I'm calling the doctor."

"What for?" Teddy protested mildly. He was still propped up in bed.

"Because, if you must know, I don't like what I'm seeing," Theresa replied.

"Oh, it's nothing."

"I will be the judge of that," she said imperiously as she turned and strode with great dignity out of his room. Teddy was smiling as he picked up something he'd already started reading from the pile of stuff on his bed, and instantly forgot about the leg.

There is a phone in Teddy's room, but Theresa didn't want to talk in front of him. She was very much concerned about the leg's lack of progress, and she was sure the Senator would want to hear about it.

She reached him in Boston.

"Yes, Theresa. How are you and the children?" The Senator was concerned. He knew from experience that it must be important or Theresa would not have called.

"It's Teddy, Senator. I don't like the looks of his leg at all."

The Senator listened to the rest of her explanation, told her to call Dr. Caper immediately, then added that he'd be back first thing the next morning.

He planned a weekend trip. Not due back in Washington until the following Monday, he was going first to visit his mother, Mrs. Rose Kennedy, at her home in Palm Beach, Florida. The call obviously altered his plans.

Checking in, as he had the day before, Dr. Caper saved Theresa the need to call. When she explained how the leg was still swollen, he told the governess to drive Teddy to Georgetown Hospital for tests.

She was to ask for Dr. George Hyatt, who was the

head of the Department of Orthopedics at the prestigious facility.

Dr. Caper met her and Teddy in the lobby of the orthopedics floor of the hospital later that afternoon. Teddy was quickly taken in for X-rays of his leg.

Within thirty minutes, Drs. Hyatt and Caper could have a preliminary look at the pictures. Both agreed that the "bruise" was ominously suspicious. "We knew that something was definitely going on," says Dr. Caper.

Theresa and Teddy, who was visibly limping but still bravely unconcerned, left the hospital. Phil had told Theresa that he'd probably be calling in the morning. He and Dr. Hyatt agreed to talk again that evening, as soon as Dr. Hyatt had had a chance to review the X-rays more carefully.

He called Phil at home when that review was completed.

"I think it's a serious problem," Dr. Hyatt opened the conversation, his voice heavy with regret. He went on to say what both men already suspected: that Teddy has a cancerous bone tumor. Dr. Caper was trying to be scrupulously thorough and professional as they spoke, but he also felt the grievous sorrow of a family friend. Cancer isn't always an unbeatable enemy, but it is relentless, and the fight against it is profoundly frightening and difficult.

"The Senator will be back in the morning," Dr. Caper concluded the conversation. "I'll tell him then."

Waiting at the arrival gate at National Airport, the young man was in agony. It's harder sometimes to be the bearer of bad news than to be the recipient. How, exactly, do you tell your friend, a father who has already suffered incalculable grief, that his son probably has cancer?

He spotted the Senator easily, a head taller than most of the rest of the line of arriving Boston passengers. When Ted was finally into the terminal proper, they shook hands in the heavy way people do when something momentous is going on, and walked quickly past a fast-gathering pack of admirers. The Senator wanted desperately to avoid having to engage in polite chitchat with the well-meaning autograph seekers.

Phil didn't say too much until they were safely inside his car.

"I'm afraid it's serious."

"How serious?" asked the Senator. He already suspected the worst.

Dr. Caper told him about the X-rays, and about what Dr. Hyatt and he had diagnosed as the problem. Talking as they drove down the pretty, tree-lined interstate and crossed the Potomac into the District of Columbia, Phil continually stressed the tentative and preliminary aspects of their findings.

In twenty minutes they had arrived at Georgetown Hospital. Phil escorted the Senator up to Dr. Hyatt's office. The men spent only the barest minimum of time on introductions, then sat down to talk about Teddy's problem. Dr. Caper deferred to Dr. Hyatt.

"Senator, to be frank, we think that Teddy has a bone tumor on his right tibia. That's the inner of the two bones in the lower leg."

"That's the bruise?" asked the Senator. His composure was intact, yet his inner urge was to dash home and take his son in his arms, or cry out against the unfairness of this new tragedy.

"Yes, we think so," Dr. Hyatt responded. "But I'd like to make several more tests, and call in additional consultants."

Bewildered but patient, Teddy was returned to the hospital that same day, and through Friday and Saturday, teams of experts from the Du Pont Clinic of Wilmington, Delaware, and the Mayo Clinic of Rochester, Minnesota, probed and poked in their examinations.

The end result was agreement with Dr. Hyatt's initial diagnosis. A complete examination was decided on, with X-rays of the entire body to determine if the cancer had spread.

Saturday morning the Senator and his son had a long and frank conversation in Teddy's hospital room.

"What's the matter with my leg, Dad?" the twelve-year-old asked. Although young, he sensed his father's deep concern. Something serious was upsetting his dad.

The Senator had anticipated the question. He had discussed this with Dr. Caper at the airport the day before, and had been groping for a response.

"Well, son," he began, avoiding the boy's eyes, "you have a 'rough spot' on your leg which Dr. Caper and the other doctors have to examine more closely."

"Will it be all right?"

"I hope so, son."

Teddy smiled, still full of spunk and mischief, despite all the discomfort of the last few days. "Well, then, can I go to the party tonight?"

One of his friends was having a birthday party, and missing it had been Teddy's major preoccupation all morning.

"I don't know, son," replied his father—also smiling now, admiringly. "Let me ask Dr. Hyatt." The Senator, in the face of that optimism, had decided to put off telling his son until he himself was absolutely certain.

The doctor agreed that Teddy could go to the party after all.

Early that Saturday afternoon, the Senator spoke with his wife from a phone in the hospital. Joan booked immediate passage home. She was there by Monday.

Teddy was allowed, at his own insistence, to go back to school on Monday. He was a seventh-grader at St. Albans School in Washington, and after a week away he was anxious to get back to his classes and his friends, even briefly. Since the doctors had told his father it would be best, the twelve-year-old was allowed to go in, still troubled slightly by his leg and by a lingering cold.

The biopsy to determine if the tumor was indeed malignant was scheduled for Tuesday, the next day. It was to be Teddy's first operation, but he took the preparations in stride. The only real change in him in the hours leading up to surgery was a slowly escalating impatience to know exactly what was going on.

There were, by this time, a half-dozen specialists on the team caring for Teddy, but Dr. Caper continued to fill the role of "Teddy's doctor." Sitting in on all the consultations and diagnostic tests, he was also the liaison, constantly updating and reassuring the Senator and Mrs. Kennedy that everything that could be done for their son was being done. Phil had frequent talks with young Teddy, trying as honestly and as completely as possible to answer his questions. Two words that still didn't enter into these conversations, however, were "cancer" and "amputation."

Aside from his conversation with Dr. Caper, someone else arrived at the hospital to look after and cheer Teddy in the hours before that first operation. It was Louella Hennessey Donovan, now almost seventy years old and the semiofficial nurse for the entire family for most of the last forty years. Louella had been just out of nursing school when she was originally hired by Mrs. Rose Kennedy to care for her daughter, thirteen-year-old Patricia (Pat Lawford). Pat had been admitted to a Boston hospital for an emergency appendectomy. It was the summer of 1937; at the time, Teddy's father was just five years old.

In the decades since then, Louella had seen the big family through all its ailments and injuries. Among her more pleasant responsibilities have been assisting at the births, and being in charge of the care, of all twenty-eight of the grandchildren of Joseph P. and Rose Kennedy, including young Teddy.

Called by the Senator at her home in Boston the night before, Louella had arrived in Washington on the first plane Tuesday morning. Teddy was in his hospital bed when she walked in, pleasantly surprising him. Louella is more than a nurse to the Kennedy children; she's a trusted friend and, like Theresa, almost a member of the family.

"Lulu!" he said happily, as he sat up to hug her. "It's great that you're here"—almost as if he were glad to have his old friend involved in this latest adventure. Louella held Teddy extra tightly, and ended her embrace reluctantly. She spoke only after she was sure of her own composure.

"I guess you've got a sore leg there," she managed.

"Oh, they say so," admitted Teddy, quickly quali-fying the doctor's appraisal, "but the pain's not that bad."

"Well, as long as you're in the hospital," Louella said matter-of-factly, "then I might as well stay here with you for a few days." She also had a great deal of experience dealing with Kennedy understatements.

When the time for the biopsy arrived, Teddy kissed his father and his mother, who had arrived from Europe the day before, and was wheeled into the operating room.

Dr. Hyatt, assisted by three other physicians, and with Dr. Caper observing, gave Teddy a general anes-thetic, then made a small incision and removed a piece of the suspected tumor. The tissue was examined by Dr. Lent Johnson of the Armed Forces Institute of Pathol-ogy, an expert pathologist. Looking up from his micro-scope, Dr. Johnson said, to the surprise of no one, "It's malignant, but it looks like a chondro." The other doc-tors in turn examined the tiny sliver of frozen flesh and bone and confirmed the finding.

It was devastating news, but it was not as tragic as they had originally feared. Teddy's disease was chon-drosarcoma, a fast-growing cancer of the cartilage. It is one of the rarest of childhood bone cancers, and also, relatively, one of the most controllable. Nearly seventy percent of its victims have survived for at least ten years after being treated. If Teddy had developed osteosar-coma, which is primary bone cancer, his chances for survival would have been far less. Only twenty-three percent of the victims of osteosarcoma survive even for five years. In one respect, however, the two are the same. Survival in both cases is wholly dependent on early amputation.

Still anesthetized, Teddy was wheeled back to his room. His parents stood by waiting for him to recover consciousness. They were unaware of the firm diagno-sis, yet Joan was already in tears at the sight of her pale, lethargic son.

She leaned over him, gently calling his name as she wiped the tiny sweat beads from his brow. The Senator stood beside her, his arm around her shoulder. Teddy would open his eyes briefly, smile reassuringly at his parents, then slip back into slumber.

They were in the room for forty-five minutes before Dr. Caper gently knocked on the door, interrupting the bedside vigil. The Senator asked him for the results of the biopsy, but instead of going into details there, Phil told them that the rest of the medical team was waiting in the hospital conference room.

The six doctors, waiting uneasily around the big conference table, almost jumped to attention when Teddy's parents walked into the room. The Senator quickly asked them all to remain seated. Joan was still softly crying, almost childlike, as Ted helped her into one of the two empty chairs. Dr. Hyatt, sitting at the head of the long table, had assumed the role of chairman. He quickly confirmed that the sample was malignant, but just as quickly qualified his statement by explaining the critical distinction between bone cancer and Teddy's cancer of the cartilage.

While Ted and Joan had been with their son, the doctors had been meeting in Dr. Hyatt's office. They were discussing the various courses of therapy open to them and had unanimously agreed that Teddy's leg must come off immediately. The only remaining discussion was whether it would be amputated below or above the knee. Because there was some concern about the possibility that the cancer had already spread into the knee joint, the decision was quickly made, again unanimously, to take it off above the knee.

Their findings and their decisions shattered the parents, who sat numbed and voiceless opposite the medical experts. Joan leaned over and put her head against her husband's chest. For the moment, they were alone in the room with their misery, oblivious of the six embarrassed men uncomfortably watching their private suffering. But Senator and Mrs. Kennedy recovered their composure quickly. The discussion then turned to an emphasis on the positive.

Joan, particularly, kept pressing the doctors as to what Teddy would still be able to do. They repeatedly assured her and her husband that at his age and with his temperament, Teddy would be able to do many of the things he had always done. He would still be able to swim, sail, and even ski if he wanted to.

Toward the end of the forty-five-minute meeting, Ted asked the doctors when the operation would be performed. "As soon as possible" was the response, and Joan's relative calm again began dissolving.

There was a complication, however, to an immediate operation: Teddy's cold, which, as the doctors had accurately predicted, was exacerbated by the anesthesia administered during the biopsy. So the operation was scheduled for early Friday morning, three days away.

Teddy remained in the hospital for the entire time between the biopsy and the final operation. After recovering from the initial surgery, he again became a model of calm unconcern. Watched over carefully by his parents and Louella, Teddy was allowed visits from some of his cousins and from Kara and Patrick. He also had a radio and television set in his room—which led to the next crisis.

Teddy had been in and out of the hospital at this point for almost a week—long enough for the ever-vigilant Washington press corps to find out about it. Particularly in the capital, it is extremely difficult for any of the Kennedy family to do anything extraordinary without its being reported in the newspapers and on radio and television. Because Teddy still didn't know exactly what was happening, his parents were afraid he might find out he had cancer by hearing it on the evening news. The Senator wanted to tell his son what was coming, but the doctors strongly advised him not to do that until twenty-four hours before the operation. The doctors also told the Senator that it would be absolutely disastrous if Teddy found out about the pending amputation from anybody other than his parents. So the problem was keeping the news from him until Thursday.

On Wednesday, a tense Ted Kennedy had an urgent meeting with Richard Drayne, his press secretary. It was decided to tell the reporters who were flooding the Senator's office with inquiries approximately what was happening, but then ask them to hold off on the story until the day of the operation. To the credit of the profession, they agreed, but Ted and Joan still agonized over the threat that somebody in the highly competitive business would be tempted to break the news embargo.

Thursday morning was the day before the scheduled operation and the time the Senator had set for telling Teddy what was going to happen. But in the morning, when Ted and Joan went into Teddy's room to talk with him, they discovered that he had awakened still suffering from his cold. The operation would have to be postponed again, at least until Saturday.

The pressure from the media was becoming undeniable. Newsmen were calling from as far away as Europe and Asia to get the story on this latest tragic chapter in the saga of the star-crossed family.

The anxiety and distress the family was suffering because of the imminent operation were hugely aggravated by their fear of premature disclosure.

As Teddy napped later that Thursday afternoon, the Senator ordered the TV set and radio surreptitiously removed from his son's room. The Senator personally supervised the process, but his son woke up when he heard the noise.

"Where are they going with the TV, Dad?" he asked sleepily.

"Ummm . . . well, son, I thought we might give some of the other children on the floor a chance to watch it," answered his father, extremely relieved that he had been able to come up with a satisfactory answer that he would also be able to follow through on.

Teddy thought about it for a second. "Then, "You mean kids that can't afford a TV, Dad?"

"Yes, son. That's just what I mean. Is it all right with you?" he asked, now confident of the answer.

"Sure," Teddy responded charitably but matter-of-factly, as if there were really nothing more to discuss. "But can I have one on Sunday, so I can watch the Redskins?"

"Yes, son. I promise," answered his father, again having to restrain an almost overpowering impulse to crush Teddy in an embrace and let his pent-up sorrow dissolve.

Teddy wouldn't have had much time for television anyway. Throughout the day the huge Kennedy clan trooped in for visits. Steve and Jean Smith, the Senator's sister and brother-in-law; Eunice Shriver and Pat Lawford, Ted's other sisters; and his sister-in-law Ethel Kennedy were among the visitors. At day's end, almost all of Teddy's uncles and aunts had stopped by to say hello.

In midafternoon there was an important telephone call. His father picked up the phone, listened for a moment, and said, "Hello, Mr. President." The two men spoke for a few minutes; then Ted handed the receiver to his son. President Nixon spoke to Teddy briefly, wishing him a speedy recovery. The twelve-year-old thanked him politely, then gave the phone back to his father, who again thanked Mr. Nixon and hung up, deeply touched by the president's thoughtfulness.

Later that day, a newspaper in Sydney, Australia, broke the story that Teddy was in the hospital for tests, and that cancer was suspected. United Press International's New York office called the Senator's press secretary and explained that because the story had been broken, UPI had an obligation to carry it over the wires. Dick Drayne protested and finally persuaded the service to run the story in brackets, reporting the facts as they were known, but asking the editors to hold the story until the morning of the operation.

Every newspaper in the nation complied with the family's wishes. No one released the story until Saturday morning. By then, Teddy already had been told.

On Friday morning, Ted and Joan had a bedside breakfast with their son. When they had finished, and an orderly had removed the trays and a nurse had given Teddy his medicine, the three were finally alone.

"Son, we know what's wrong with your leg now."

"What, Dad?" Teddy asked, looking from his father to his mother, who was tightly holding his hand. She was sitting on the edge of the bed, and her husband stood beside it.

"It's very sick," the Senator said; "very sick."

"How sick, Dad?" Teddy pressed. He wanted to know when it would be better.

"I'm afraid your leg has a kind of cancer inside it."

Joan desperately tightened her grip on her son's hand.

"Cancer, Dad. Does that mean I'm going to die?" Like most twelve-year-olds, Teddy had heard of cancer only vaguely, and usually in the context of death.

"Oh, no, Teddy!" his parents exploded simultaneously. Both of them then spent the next few minutes assuring their son that his affliction was certainly not terminal.

"What, Dad?" If he wasn't going to die, then what else was happening?

"The doctors have to stop the cancer from spreading into the rest of your body, son."

"How?"

"Son, they're going to have to take your leg off," the Senator finally said, wishing that there were some way he could substitute his own leg for his son's.

"My leg, Dad?"

"Yes, Teddy. It's the only way."

"But, Teddy, they'll give you another leg!" His mother, taking courage from her son's calm example, but sensing his growing bewilderment and the beginnings of despair, hastened to reassure him that he would still be able to do all the things he liked to do. She wisely concentrated on this positive aspect. The impending loss of the leg was described as another challenge to be confronted and surmounted, another adventure to be mastered.

Dr. Caper, who had been standing outside the room, was summoned to add his professional assurance of Teddy's rapid recovery. Later, Dr. Hyatt also came by to reinforce the promise.

The twelve-year-old responded bravely, asking the adults when the operation would begin and telling his mother not to cry anymore. He assumed the role of the comforter, crying now chiefly because his folks looked so unhappy.

In the early evening, Teddy was placed under sedation. The operation was scheduled for eight o'clock the next morning.

In an ironic twist of timing, Kathleen Kennedy, the twenty-two-year-old eldest child of Ethel and the late Senator Robert F. Kennedy, was getting married on Saturday. Her uncle Ted was to give the bride away. The ceremony was at Georgetown's Holy Trinity Church, three blocks from the hospital, and scheduled for eleven o'clock.

Ted and Joan spent Friday night at the hospital. They knew that several hundred people were coming to Kathleen's wedding, and were aware of the extensive planning and the couple's expectations, so they urged Ethel to proceed with the ceremony as planned. Ted explained that he would make every effort to attend, if his son's operation went off without complications.

Surgery began at about eight-thirty Saturday morning. Dr. George Hyatt led the medical team that first cut through the skin, muscle, and other tissue, then through the bone above the knee. By ten o'clock it was over.

As the doctors walked out from the operating room, they assured the anxious parents that Teddy had "tolerated the operation well." The Senator asked if there had been any unexpected problems. When informed that his son was responding "uneventfully," Ted quickly left the hospital and headed for the church. Joan remained behind, in case Teddy came out of the anesthesia and asked for his parents.

Senator Kennedy got to the church just a few minutes before the ceremony was scheduled to begin. The family members there were relieved both that the operation was apparently successful and that Ted had managed to make Kathleen's day complete. Promptly at eleven o'clock, she was escorted by her Uncle Ted down the aisle, where the bridegroom, David Lee Townsend, waited.

The wedding service lasted fifty-five minutes. It ended with the guests all singing "When Irish Eyes Are Smiling." The echoes of that rousing and happy song were still bounding from the walls of Holy Trinity Church when the Senator kissed the new bride, congratulated her and David, and hurried back to the hospital.

By the time Teddy woke up the next morning, he had already been fitted with a temporary aluminum leg. The doctors had wanted to replace the void with something, so they had fitted the prosthesis immediately. The twelve-year-old was still groggy, and even uncharacteristically irritable, but at his father's urging he began pulling himself out of bed. The Senator, with the assistance of a doctor who specialized in physical therapy, helped Teddy stand upright.

"Come on, son," his father encouraged him. "You can do it."

It was difficult for him, and painful to put any weight on the artificial leg. Still, the doctors felt he should make some effort at walking, so with one arm around his father and the other supported by the therapist, he took his first faltering steps.

"It hurts me, Dad."

"I know, Teddy. Just a few more steps."

"It was like a big, bad dream for the Senator and his wife," Louella Hennessey said later. "They were the most concerned parents I've ever seen. The Senator's heart was so heavy that first day, I thought it would break."

Teddy's parents were with him almost around the clock. Louella tried to remain in the background, leaving them alone with their son whenever her nursing duties permitted. When the Senator wasn't urging Teddy to try to walk, father and son would be reminiscing about some of the good times they'd had and would be having the following summer. The Senator kept talking as cheerfully as he could manage, trying to keep Teddy's mind off his loss.

Whenever Ted and Joan took a brief respite from their nearly unbroken vigil, Louella would come into the room. That night, she was sitting in a chair near the foot of Teddy's bed when he woke up.

"Hi, Teddy," she said softly, reassuring him that he wasn't alone.

"I guess I'm kind of sleepy," he replied. Still under heavy sedation, he was very groggy and floating in a kind of twilight world.

"I'll just sit down right here and keep you company for a while," Louella said, sitting on the edge of Teddy's bed. He complained to her about some pain in his missing leg. "Phantom" pain in an already amputated limb is a common medical phenomenon, particularly in the period immediately following surgery. As Teddy told Louella about it, the regular hospital nurse came into the room on her rounds.

"What's bothering our young friend?" she asked Louella.

"He has a bit of pain in his leg," Louella answered. Both women understood the nature of Teddy's discomfort. "Roll over, Teddy," Louella said, turning back to the twelve-year-old. "I'll rub your back."

"Well, *I* can help you, Teddy," said the second nurse. She was assigned to Teddy and was determined to do her part in caring for him. "Let me do it."

Teddy hesitated. He certainly didn't want to hurt the hospital nurse's feelings, but he would be so much more comfortable with an old friend than with a stranger.

"Teddy has such a sweet disposition," Louella said later. "I could see how apprehensive he was of hurting the nurse's feelings; that's why he started to explain to her right then and there how long I've known him and his family."

"Could Lulu do it?" Teddy finally asked the staff nurse in a small, sincere voice. "You see, she was there when I was born, and I trust her so much."

"Of course she can, Teddy. I understand."

"It was the greatest compliment I've ever received in my forty years of nursing," Louella remembers with tears of pride.

Over the next few days, Teddy gained confidence in his ability to walk. By midweek his father, who had initially urged Teddy to take his first, faltering steps, was urging his son to slow down. "He aggressively assaulted the learning process." As his mother had accurately predicted, Teddy's boundless enthusiasm reduced the loss of his leg to the status of merely another problem to be solved and mastered.

By the end of his first week in the hospital, he was walking the distance from his room all the way down the hall to the elevator and down to the physical-therapy area by himself. Thirteen-year-old Kara and six-year-old Patrick were invaluable in helping their brother through this new challenge. As he walked through the hospital corridors, they would walk alongside him, playfully making bets that he wouldn't make it to the end without resting. Teddy almost always won. His progress was remarkable. As the wound from the surgery healed, he spent more and more time out of bed.

With the news that another Kennedy had met misfortune, public response was compassionate and overwhelming. More than fifty thousand letters and get-well cards were sent to Teddy in care of the Senator's Washington office. Local florists were asked, after delivering hundreds of arrangements to Georgetown Hospital, to donate them to other children's hospitals and orphanages in the Washington area.

The Thursday following his operation was Thanksgiving, and normally the Senator's office would have been closed. Yet volunteers poured in to help the staff handle the mail from all over the world. Gifts arrived too, from children Teddy's age or younger, and the Senator's staff wanted Teddy to see some of them to help bolster his spirits.

Teddy was most impressed by the drawings and petitions bearing the signatures and best wishes of entire classes, and even entire schools. When he asked his mother how he could answer all the letters, she suggested a handwritten note which was later duplicated and mailed to everyone who had written.

On Friday, November 30, thirteen days after his leg had been removed, Teddy walked from Georgetown Hospital through a large crowd of newsmen, unassisted except for a pair of crutches. An artificial limb had been fitted a few days earlier. Gripped between his elbow and his crutch was a football that the Washington Redskins' coach, George Allen, had delivered when he learned that Teddy was an avid Redskins fan.

For the next several days Teddy was home in McLean, slowly making up three weeks of back homework. He also devoted a substantial part of each day to therapeutic exercises and learning to walk on his artificial leg. The house returned to its usual uproar as Teddy, aided by his brother, sister, and assorted cousins, "tackled the learning process with extraordinary vigor." To ensure the ultimate return to law and order, Theresa Fitzpatrick occasionally voiced mild disapproval of the unrestrained enthusiasm, but even the children could see that she loved every minute of it.

The Senator and Joan rearranged their schedules so that they could spend more time with Teddy. They remained in constant touch with his doctors, and Phil Caper visited Teddy twice each day to observe his progress.

The X-rays of the rest of the twelve-year-old's body proved negative, and the doctors were reasonably confident that the cancer had been arrested.

Still, Teddy's prognosis was uncertain, and despite his apparently excellent recovery, the doctors could not be sure that they had done everything possible to lessen the odds that the cancer would recur. In the following weeks, conferences were held to discuss further preventive treatment.

Teddy did his best to remain unconcerned with the stream of specialists visiting his parents. His attention was diverted by the mail and the gifts which continued to arrive. About a week before Christmas, he and his dad visited the Senate office. It was a weekend, and the two were alone to inspect the hundreds of gifts piled high against a wall. Teddy spend a happy hour opening boxes and trying to select the gifts he would most like to take home. When he had made his selections, he walked into his father's private office, where the Senator was going through some papers. "All set?" his father asked, looking up as Teddy came in holding a big bundle of toys and other gifts.

SQUARE NUMBER 1:

DR. HYATT EXPLAINING TEDDY KENNEDY"S X-RAY TO TEDDY.

SQUARE NUMBER 2:

TEDDY KENNEDY JUMPING OUT OF CHAIR AND EXCLAIMING "WHAT"!!!!!!!!!

SQUARE NUMBER 3:

DR. HYATT CALMING TEDDY DOWN, SAYING: "NOW TEDDY, JUST TAKE IT EASY".

SQUARE NUMBER 4:

TEDDY KENNEDY SOCKING DR. HYATT IN THE NOSE.

SQUARE NUMBER 5:

DR. HYATT, ON THE X-RAY TABLE AT GEORGETOWN UNIVERSITY HOSPITAL.
　　　　　　　　　　　　　　DIAGNOSIS - AMPUTATION OF NOSE.

SQUARE NUMBER 6:

DR. HYATT IN SURGERY AT SAME HOSPITAL MENTIONED ABOVE.

SQUARE NUMBER 7:

XXXXXXXXXXXXXXXXXXXXXXXXXXXXXXXXXXXXXXXXXXXXXXX

DR. HYATT ALL BURIED UP!!!!!!!!!

"There sure is a lot of stuff," Teddy replied happily.

"There sure is." The Senator grinned as he rose to leave. "What are you going to do with it all?"

"I don't know," answered Teddy, experiencing the warm glow of somebody whose options are all happy ones.

As he and his dad drove through the empty streets of the District, heading home, Teddy made a decision.

"Dad, I want to give the rest of the toys and stuff to kids in the hospital."

When they reached home, the Senator phoned Phil Caper, told him of Teddy's decision, and asked him if he would make the necessary arrangements. Phil called Children's Hospital in Washington. With Christmas barely a week away, the hospital officials were delighted, and on the following day, Sunday, father and son went bearing gifts.

Hospital personnel met them at the car, which was overflowing with colorfully wrapped packages.

Teddy personally distributed the gifts to the young hospital patients.

Christmas was spent at his grandmother's home in Palm Beach, Florida. One of Teddy's most prized gifts was from the Miami Dolphins football team. Not to be outdone by their archrivals in Washington, the world-champion Dolphins had also given Teddy an official autographed football.

But once the pleasant distractions of the holiday season were past, Teddy's father, tortured by the desire to do everything he could for his son, began a kind of pilgrimage around the country. Visiting such noted cancer-care centers as the Memorial Sloan-Kettering Hospital in New York City, he talked with and listened to the experts. Finally the Senator called a medical summit meeting at his home in Virginia.

The Kennedy children warmly dressed in their winter clothes, stood outside and watched the steady procession of cars pulling up the long circular driveway. Phil Caper, who had coordinated Teddy's care from the beginning, was there, as were Drs. Hyatt and Johnson, who had participated in the youngster's initial operation. They were joined by a gallery of medical giants, all pioneers in the fields of cancer research and pediatric immunology.

There were eight of them in all, and joined by the Senator and Mrs. Kennedy, they sat around the big dinner table.

Dr. Caper opened the informal meeting. "We know that there is a finite chance that the cancer can recur. We don't know what that chance is, but we think it is very small. The question today is whether we do something to reduce it even further."

For the next four hours an energetic discussion went on about which, if any, of the several therapeutic disciplines represented around the table would be adopted for Teddy. Several were rejected because they were still in the "very experimental" stages of development. Others were scrapped because they were appropriate only if the patient had active cancer, which Teddy did not. Finally, it was decided that he would be started on a two-year course of treatment involving the powerful anticancer drug methotrexate.

Unlike the decision to amputate Teddy's leg, this decision was by no means an easy one. "We didn't know for sure if we were doing the right thing," Dr. Caper told Stuart Auerbach, the medical reporter for *The Washington Post*. "We may have been better off to do nothing. But decisions in medicine are made that way. We tried to balance the benefits to Teddy against the risk."

If Teddy's amputation had been an ordeal, at least it was a short ordeal. The chemotherapy was three days of unequivocal unpleasantness, relentlessly scheduled every three weeks. Beginning in February 1974, Teddy and his father would fly up to Boston on Friday afternoon as soon as the twelve-year-old got out of school. There, he would check into the Boston Children's Hospital, where work with the methotrexate had been developed. Then, for the next six hours, he would be given massive, painful injections of the drug, two thousand times the normal dosage. It is a toxic substance that kills both cancerous and healthy cells. To avoid killing the patient as well, Teddy was then also given massive doses of an antidote a few hours later, and then periodically for the next three days.

In addition to the discomfort of having to spend the whole weekend in the hospital, there was the added fact that the medicine made Teddy very sick. He was impatient to be done with it, but only occasionally did it make him irritable.

To reduce the amount of time Teddy had to spend in the hospital, the Senator learned to give the injections of the antidote. That way, his son could be home in Virginia by Sunday night, in time for school the next day. Of course, the Senator's amateur skills were the subject of continual lighthearted abuse from Teddy and the other kids around the house. "Oh-oh, here comes the mad scientist!" was the warning echoed throughout the house.

In March, less than five months after his amputation, Teddy showed the Kennedy toughness by joining the family on a skiing trip to Vail, Colorado. An expert skier, he had to learn all over again, and "he aggressively assaulted the learning process."

A special ski was fitted to his prosthesis, and he started on beginner's slopes—skiing, sliding, and falling down the hillside. Nobody babied him. He had been able to ski before, and his father's enforced nonchalant attitude was that he could learn to ski again. But Teddy couldn't see how his parents suffered every time he lost his balance. When an embarrassed reporter finally asked him how his leg was doing, Teddy replied casually, looking back up at the slope he had finally managed to conquer, "I just don't think about it much."

By the bottom of the third inning, the baseball game had been turned into a rout. In the Hoboken, New Jersey, Little League contest, the home team, called the Young Democrats, was on the short end of a nine-to-one score against the team sponsored by local businessman C. C. Casalino. The old wooden bleachers of Stevens Park, though, were still packed, despite the lopsided score. As a matter of fact, thought Carmen Ronga, the coach of the trailing Young Democrats, it was one of the largest and most vocal crowds he could remember, and he didn't want to disappoint them.

"C'mon, c'mon, let's go, fellas. . . . We can still pull this one out of the fire." Clapping his hands as he walked up and down in front of his bench, the coach certainly didn't seem like a man whose team was eight runs behind. After the Young Democrats failed to score in the third inning, Mr. Ronga did some shuffling.

"Okay, listen up. We're making some changes," he said, as he pulled his lineup sheet out of his back pocket.

Crossing out some, and putting checks next to other names on his list, he benched many of his starters and brought in the reserves. The Little League has a salutary rule that every kid on the team must play at least three innings of each game, and get to bat at least once.

Ronga then made his big move, bringing his left fielder in to pitch. The coach was a bit apprehensive. He knew the new pitcher could throw hard, but he was afraid that the big crowd had made her nervous.

"Okay, honey. This is it. Go out there and blast it past them."

As she walked out to the pitcher's mound, slamming the ball in an out of her glove, it was a historic moment for Little League baseball. For the first time, the organization, which oversees leagues for 2¼ million young boys around the world, was to have a girl playing—and pitching, no less—in one of its games.

Twelve-year-old Maria Pepe took about a half-dozen warm-up pitches, then signaled to the catcher to throw the ball around the infield. She was ready. The umpire, a Hoboken taxi driver by profession, called, "Batter up!" and while the crowd shouted its support of Maria, around came her arm, the pitch, "Ball one!"

"Ohhh!" the crowd sighed. Maria took off her baseball cap, wiped her forehead with the back of her glove arm, and flipped her ponytail back over her shoulder. In a few seconds, she was ready, and threw again. "Ball two!"

"Come on, Maria! You can do it! Blow it past him!" She smiled, recognizing her dad's voice roaring out from the bleachers. She kicked at the dirt around the pitcher's mound, taking her time. Getting the signal from her catcher, she let loose with her fast ball.

"Strike one!" The batter had taken a mighty cut at the third pitch, but Maria had indeed blown it past him. "Yeah!" The crowd was on its feet. The excitement in the slightly faded green-plywood confines of Stevens Park was like pennant fever; it was as if a World Series were at stake. She threw again.

"Strike two!"

A called strike. The batter had been so confident that Maria's first pitch into the strike zone had been a fluke, he watched her next pitch all the way, anticipating a ball. But she had fooled him, and the count was even at two balls, two strikes.

"Two, four, six, eight. Pitcher's got a bellyache!"

The members of the C. C. Casalino team had taken off the kid gloves. They were all up, standing near their bench. If Maria was going to play as an equal in the Little League, then she had to take the razzing, just like the rest of the boys.

"No batter. No batter. Come on, Maria, strike him out!"

The Young Democrats responded in kind, giving moral support to their pitcher, the source of their huge popularity with the crowd.

"Strike three!"

The batter had gone down swinging, and from the stands the crowd enthusiastically roared its approval. Maria had struck him out. Both sides went scoreless after that, the game ending in an anticlimactic nine-to-one victory for the C. C. Casalino team.

"But wasn't Maria great?" Coach Ronga smiled. "I'm going to make her the starting pitcher in next week's game against the Hoboken Elks."

Maria pitched in that game against the Elks, and played right field in the game after that. Unfortunately, she couldn't lead her team to victory in either contest, the Young Democrats losing both games by lopsided scores. But Maria had won another victory—the respect of her teammates and coaches.

"Her fast ball is as good as or better than any of the boys'. And she's not a bad batter, either," said her coach.

Then the bombshell hit. Responding to all the publicity generated by Maria's entrance into the formerly all-boys league, the national office of Little League, Inc., of Williamsport, Pennsylvania, issued a statement. With it, they revoked the charter, and canceled the league insurance, not only for Maria's team, but for the whole Hoboken league. Ten teams, with two hundred ballplayers, were affected by the draconian reaction. A representative of the national office broke the news of the charter forfeit to Hoboken's recreational superintendent, Joseph Pullano.

Mr. Pullano was devastated. Like most of the city's officials, he had expected some reaction from the national group, but nothing so humorless or severe as this. It was his unhappy task to pass the news on to James Farina, the sponsor of Maria's Young Democrats. Mr. Farina, confronted with the choice of losing Maria or the whole league, reluctantly agreed to drop his twelve-year-old star righthander from the lineup. He asked Coach Ronga to assume the unenviable responsibility of telling Maria and her parents about the decision.

"They had me over a barrel," Mr. Farina said later. "I didn't want to drop her from the team. Especially after she showed us all how well she could do, once she had the chance. But the national office didn't just kick our team out of the league. They knocked the whole Hoboken city league out! And we didn't want to jeopardize the two hundred other kids who play Little League baseball in this town." Mr. Farina also pledged that he was not going to take the action meekly. He promised to go over the rule book carefully, to find if there were any legal grounds "to fight this thing."

When a reporter for the Hoboken *Evening News* asked the national representative if the Hoboken league would get their charter back now that Maria had been dropped, the spokesman was evasive. "This is always a possibility." But he added, "They would have to reapply." It was as if the national office wanted to go beyond just getting Maria out; they wanted to punish the entire city for the absolute effrontery of allowing a girl on the field.

Maria Pepe, the twelve-year-old at the center of the great Little League controversy, grew up in Hoboken. The city of 50,000 is actually a working-class neighborhood of older apartment buildings and single-family brownstones, all crowded together in long gray rows. The town is exactly a square mile in size, and is a blue-collar community squeezed into the middle of the dense industrial section of New Jersey. Best known as Frank Sinatra's home town and the setting for Marlon Brando's *On the Waterfront*, it lies between the piers of the west bank of the Hudson River and the smoky factories and refineries of Bayonne, in the shadow of the state's largest cities, Newark and Jersey City.

The dimpled and pretty Maria had been playing sand-lot baseball in the city with the boys long before her foray into the Little League. Her family lives in the ten-story Church Towers, one of Hoboken's largest buildings. From their seventh-floor-apartment windows, Maria's mother, Angie, could watch her playing baseball in the vacant lot across the street, near Our Lady of Grace Church.

"The boys in the building were so nice to my Maria." Angie loves to talk, especially about her daughter.

"She was almost always the only girl in the games, but they always let her play. They even used to watch out for her crossing the street and all. They loved her, and she loved the game."

Maria started playing baseball at about the age of five, when she would shyly ask the boys in her building if they would let her play with them. She had to ask quite a few times, but by sheer perseverance she was finally given a chance to get into a ballgame. After that, the boys never objected. Maria was a good ballplayer, and on the roughly drawn baseball diamonds of the vacant lots of the city, whether or not you were a good ballplayer was all that really counted.

Although Maria loved sports, she was never considered a tomboy. Once off the field and out of her playing clothes, the slender twelve-year-old was as feminine as any other girl her age.

"I just like playing baseball, and I'm pretty good at it," Maria was telling a small group of her girlfriends who had come over for dinner during the height of the crisis. As Angie cooked, they were sitting on the floor in the living room of the Pepes' apartment, reading the newspaper clippings of her ouster. At one point Maria frustratedly asked a rhetorical question: "What's the big deal?" She already knew the answer from the painful experience of the last few weeks.

Felicia Gilletti, a non-ballplayer who was one of Maria's best friends, was perplexed and concerned about what was happening. She tried to explain her feelings to Mrs. Pepe, who was walking in and out of the kitchen acting as sympathetic mediator and audience for the troubled kids.

"Your daughter's just an all-round kid," Felicia was telling Angie, who already knew. "She's lots of fun to be with, and when she's with us girls, she acts the same as we do." Felicia turned away from Mrs. Pepe and addressed the room at large. "Those Little League people shouldn't have made such a big fuss about her playing baseball. They made it sound like she was some kind of freak."

"Yeah!" "That's right!" everyone animatedly agreed.

"Let's eat," said the constant Angie. "The lasagna is ready."

It had been in the spring of 1972 that Maria came home with some papers for her parents to sign. It was Saturday, the only day Patsy, her father, had off, and he and Mrs. Pepe were sitting around the Formica table in the apartment kitchen. The atmosphere was weekend-casual. Her bathrobed folks were reading the *Jersey Journal* and sipping coffee.

The papers Maria handed them were her Little League application forms. She told them that she wanted to try out for a team in the Hoboken league, called the Young Democrats. Patsy was astounded. He took his glasses off and put the newspaper down. A longshoreman who had been working the piers for the last twenty-nine years, he was something of a tradition-alist. "But, honey"—Mr. Pepe smiled gently as he rested one of his big burly arms on his daughter's shoul-der—"the Little League is for boys. They ain't never going to let a girl play." Maria was an obedient child, and though she was disappointed, she was ready to ac-cept any reasonable decision. But she was also curious.

"But, Daddy, what if I can play better than the boys can?"

"That don't count, sugar. It's for boys, not for girls."

"Why?"

Mr. Pepe furrowed his brow and thought for a while. Unable to come up with a logical answer quickly enough, he turned to Mrs. Pepe. "You tell her."

Maria's mother dutifully and gamely charged into the breach. "It's just always been that way." But that answer was also unsatisfactory to Maria. It didn't even sound right to her parents. Sensing an opening, Maria seized the opportunity to explain that the coach of the team, Carmen Ronga, had told her she could go to the tryouts. If she was good enough, the coach had added, he'd let her play. All she really needed now was her parents' permission.

Totally on the defensive, and under the unswerving gaze of his daughter, Mr. Pepe equivocally told Maria that they would give it some thought. "Uh . . . I don't know. Let your mother and me think about it." As twelve-year-olds almost always do, Maria happily accepted the vague "maybe" as a definite "yes."

"Thank you Daddy!" she squealed, as she kissed both of them on the cheek and ran out of the apartment on her way down to the lot across the street. She had ostentatiously left the papers on the kitchen table in front of them.

"You know something? . . . She's right." It was Mr. Pepe who spoke first. He was smiling again and shaking his head back and forth. He picked up the application forms and leafed through them.

"I dunno, Patsy," said Mrs. Pepe as she walked over to the stove to pour another cup of coffee. "What if she gets hurt?" She was worried about the roughneck boys Maria would be playing against

"Aw, c'mon . . . she's been playing ball with the same kids since she was this high," said Patsy, holding his hand at about the level of the tabletop. "The only difference now is that she'll have a uniform."

On the verge of giving their consent, Maria's parents thought it prudent to wait a few days. During that time, Patsy had the chance to speak with Coach Ronga.

"What's the story, Carmen? You gonna let her play?"

"Yeah, sure we're going to take her. Hell, she's better than half the boys in the league."

With that assurance, and not wanting to disappoint Maria, Mr. and Mrs. Pepe gave their consent. "It meant everything in the world to her. How could we say no?" said Mrs. Pepe. "And besides, I'd rather have her playing baseball with the boys than have her hanging out on the streetcorners like too many of the kids in this town are doing!"

So Maria was there on the first day of the league tryouts, and, as expected, she easily made the team. From the beginning of the season, however, her spot in the Young Democrats' lineup generated tremendous controversy. Although most of the initial reaction was favorable, some was not. There were parents of children on the opposing teams who were genuinely angry at the situation. It was as if her playing somehow detracted from their own sons' accomplishments. Several times grownups walked over to Maria and asked her questions like, "Shouldn't you be home playing with your dolls?" or, "Little girl, you should be ashamed, acting like such a tomboy. Do your parents know you're here?"

Most often, the taunts would not upset her. Occasionally they generated angry responses from her. "Yes, they do know I'm here! And I can play baseball as good as anybody."

The controversy also fostered a great deal of local interest in Little League games. With each successive game played by the Young Democrats, there were more spectators in the stands, and more reporters and photographers on the field. Finally the word got to the national office, and that was the beginning of the end of Maria's career in organized baseball.

Perhaps the result would have been different if Little League, Inc., hadn't been such a highly centralized and strictly administered institution. Started in Williamsport as a modest program for that Pennsylvania city's eight-to-twelve-year-old boys, it was a good idea that gradually spread to other Northeastern states after World War II. During the baby boom of the 1950's and 1960's, it blossomed throughout the country, until virtually every suburban community in the United States could boast a team, or if it was large enough, an entire league playing under the auspices of the Little League.

Run by a board of directors still operating out of the international headquarters in Williamsport, the Little League had not been without controversy, even before "The Great Sex Discrimination Case of 1972."

Conceived as a summertime diversion for boys, it has never had any problem attracting millions of applicants for its more than 100,000 teams in the United States and thirty-one foreign countries. After all, where else can a kid get to play baseball in a uniform and in a ballpark that with a little imagination can be seen as just one step removed from the major leagues? The criticism began when the adults involved started letting their own imaginations run amok. When the sponsoring businessmen who bought the uniforms or the coaches of the teams started imagining themselves another Charlie Finley or Casey Stengel, the nine- or ten-year-olds playing under them started suffering. Overly enthusiastic parents compounded the problem. Winning was definitely not supposed to be the name of the game, but according to the legion of Little League critics, it too often became exactly that. Maybe that was why they reacted so strongly to the threat perceived in Maria's place in the lineup of one of New Jersey's two thousand teams. The imaginations of the grown-ups involved just weren't broad enough to envision a tense seventh game of a World Series being played, say, between the Yankees and the Dodgers, but complete with a ponytailed girl stepping into the batter's box.

By the time Maria played her third game as a Young Democrat, even her parents were being subjected to abuse and scorn by a vocal minority of Little League fans. Mrs. Pepe, who attended all of Maria's games, was frequently asked why her daughter "wasn't home learning to sew or cook" or why Angie "was letting her nice little girl play baseball with all those filthy boys." The attacks were by no means limited to strangers. One afternoon Angie was bringing a basket of laundry down to the machines in the basement. She got into the same elevator with two women she'd known for years, also heading down to do the wash.

"It's not right, Angie," immediately said one of them.

"What isn't?"

"Maria's playing in the Little League. What's she trying to do, wreck it for all the other kids?"

"Girls should stick to girl things, and boys to boy things. All the neighbors are talking about it," joined in the other women.

"Well, I'm surprised at you two!" responded Angie angrily, after recovering from her momentary shock. "This whole excitement is ridiculous. Imagine two grown-up women getting so worked up because one little girl wants to play baseball." The elevator door opened onto the basement. Mrs. Pepe added one footnote before storming over to an empty washing machine. "She's got just as much right to play as any other child!"

The taunts directed toward the hulking Mr. Pepe were understandably more subtle. Occasionally one of the fellows would make some smart remark, like, "Hey, Patsy . . . in a couple of years she'll have to get custom-made uniforms!"

"Ha-ha." A good line always got a few laughs from the guys on the pier.

"That's wasn't funny, Joey." Patsy abruptly terminated any attempt at merriment that was at Maria's expense.

Of the people most displeased at Maria's Little League career, surprisingly, the majority were women. Whatever their private feelings, most of the men publicly supported Maria's precedent-setting activities. Her father's longshoremen's local, for instance, took a poll when the debate was really raging. They unanimously decided that they were behind her all the way.

"Let her play if she's good enough to make the team" was the prevailing sentiment.

That summer, when she wasn't playing ball at Stevens Park, Maria spent her spare time playing informally on the field across the street from her home. Of all places in her world, Maria was most comfortable there among her friends. At the critical time, they were the most supportive. Michael McInerney, who was always there on the field, was "sort of" Maria's boyfriend at the time. When anyone who walked onto the lot wanted to argue the issue of girls playing in the Little League, he would take up the challenge. "Maria's just about the best friend I could ever have, and all this really makes me mad!"

At fourteen years old, Michael was more sophisticated in the area of women's rights than many of the adults involving themselves in the heated issue of Maria's aborted attempt to play baseball.

"I think if a girl is good enough to play, she should be allowed to play. Maria is good, she has a lot of guts, and she would have been good for the team."

Maria's abbreviated career was marked by escalating unpleasantness, but it got really ugly only after the edict from Williamsport. From that point on, she was more than just a trend-setting girl in a formerly all-boys world. Maria was publicly made the cause for the disenfranchisement of the city's entire league.

The calculatedly severe action taken by the corporation's board of directors had exactly the desired effect. The pressure on Maria and her parents for her to quit the team built enormously. Where once she could count her coaches and teammates on the Young Democrats as ardent supporters of her right to play, most now began to waiver, and finally became polite opponents of that right. But it was the grown-ups who really let her have it. When she was outdoors, she would be stopped by adults she scarcely knew or didn't know at all.

"Little girl, because of you, my son Johnny can't play baseball anymore. Now, how does that make you feel?"

"Maria, do you think it's right for you to spoil the summer for two hundred other children?"

"Maria, just because of your pride, all the other kids are going to have a rotten time."

Walking down the streets near her home, she was like Alice in Wonderland, reeling in dismay from verbal blasts coming first from one side, then the other.

At first she would face the attackers with her hands on her hips and her chin proudly raised. "I should be allowed to play. I can play as good as anyone!"

"But you're a girl . . . a girl . . . a girl." Like a curse, it echoed in Maria's head. It was as if she had committed some terrible crime, or suffered from some disease or deformity that automatically should have excluded her from the league.

The cumulative effect of the personal attacks made her quiet and thoughtfully introverted. She was a spunky kid, and would, under ordinary circumstances, never run away from a fair fight. Maria's playing ability on the field had silenced the challenge of the skeptics, but there was no real answer for people who criticized just the fact that she was a girl, and one who had cost the entire league its right to play.

Slowly walking home down Willow Avenue the day after her third game, she reached a decision. As she walked past the school and across the street toward her building, Maria decided to throw in the towel. "It was just that I didn't want to hurt all the other kids' chances to play ball," she explained later. "And I already figured that I'd caused people enough trouble. . . . I just didn't think it was fair anymore."

With that decision made, she walked into the apartment. She was surprised to see Mr. Ronga, her coach, there talking to her parents. There was an awkward pause in their conversation when the adults saw her coming in. Maria, still standing by the door, quickly realized that they had been talking about her. "I'm going to quit," she said before they could say anything to her.

"I think it would be the best thing to do, dear," her mother consoled her.

Mr. Ronga had come over to the Pepe home to explain to Maria and her folks the reluctant decision that he, and Mr. Farina, the team sponsor, had made to drop her from the team. The decision she had reached by herself spared them that embarrassment.

After announcing what she was going to do, Maria walked quickly through the living room and into the bedroom she shared with her sister, Michele. Shutting the door quietly behind her, Maria stood there for a second before throwing herself on her bed in tears.

The little room, Maria's sanctuary in her unhappiness, was symbolic of her problem. It was all pink and ladylike, with two bamboo-canopied beds on opposite sides of the room. Displayed on the walls on Michele's side were posters of such 1972 heart-throbs as David Cassidy and Mick Jagger. In Maria's corner, hanging on the walls and pasted on the mirror over her dresser, were pictures of her favorite ballplayers and pennants emblazoned with the names of her favorite major-league teams.

After her resignation, Hoboken officials began criticizing the Little League for having forced her out. As the negative publicity mounted, the national office issued its first formal statement on Maria's situation. Robert Stirrat, one of the public-relations men for the organization, told skeptical reporters that the rule that makes girls ineligible "was backed up by a wealth of evidence, physiological and medical." He claimed further that girls shouldn't be allowed to play because baseball was a contact sport, and little girls were more prone to injury than boys the same age.

It was an old argument that had always been successfully invoked whenever any young lady sought to challenge the league's "boys-only" rule. But times were changing, and in Maria's case there were plenty of people to assist in the process of change. Later in the same week that Maria had been dropped, the Essex County chapter of the National Organization for Women interceded in her behalf. The organization filed a suit against the National Little League, charging the organization with discriminatory practices. NOW alleged that the league, which uses public land to play its games, had discriminated against Maria because she was a girl.

The Pepe family found out about the lawsuit when Patsy got a call at home from a reporter for the Hoboken *Evening News,* asking him for a comment. Everyone had been sitting in the living room watching television when the call came. Angie had answered the phone, then called Patsy over to talk with the reporter. As he began speaking, Mrs. Pepe told Maria what it was all about.

"It's a reporter. . . . Women's lib has started a case about you getting thrown out of the Little League."

"Really?" was the only response that Maria could manage, fixing her eyes on her dad as he continued speaking to the newsman.

"Well . . . I approve of the action. Not only for my own girl . . . not only for Maria, but for all of the other girls who might want to play." He paused just long enough to wink at Maria. She started squeaking in delight, then smothered her own laughter with the back of her hands. Patsy put his hands over the receiver. "Maria! Shush!" Mrs. Pepe whacked her playfully on the back of her head. Then, after the mini-disturbance had quieted, Patsy continued with his interview. "Maria and Mrs. Pepe and me don't want to jeopardize the other kids' chances of playing ball—no way. But if the ladies bringing the case feel it's right, then I say go ahead—hell, they even have women jockeys nowadays, don't they?"

After he hung up the phone, Maria ran over and hugged him. "Thank you, Daddy." But after a couple of minutes had passed, she became quiet again. "Mommy, does this mean that all those people are going to be angry again?"

"No, dear. I think they'll understand."

"That's the trouble with the world today."

"What do you mean, Maria?"

"All those people getting so worked up about me wanting to play baseball. It just doesn't seem right." Her mom agreed with her.

The national office reacted calmly, even disdainfully to the news of the legal action. Mr. Stirrat announced that a court fight would prove useless. He pointed out that a federal court in Boston had just thrown out a lawsuit filed by a team in suburban Newton, Massachusetts, which had also sought to challenge the "boys-only" rule.

During the following week, Frank Yacenda, a field representative for the State Division of Civil Rights, announced that medical opinions were being sought to determine if girls between the ages of eight and twelve were really physically inferior to boys in that same age group. But Maria's attention had been diverted elsewhere by another telephone call her dad had received. It came from Jackie Farrell, the public-relations director for the New York Yankees.

"Hello, Mr. Pepe? My name is Jackie Farrell. . . . I work with the New York Yankees. Listen, on behalf of Mike Burke, the president of the club, and Ralph Houk, the skipper, and all the fellows on the team, I'd like to invite Maria to spend a day with the Yanks. Yes, that's right, we'd like her to be a 'Yankee' for a day . . . come to the stadium, meet some of the guys, have lunch with the team, and then, of course, watch the game. It's against the Tigers. . . . No, no, I'm not kidding."

When Patsy explained the details of the invitation to his daughter, Maria was happier than she had ever been.

"You mean it, dad? You really mean it? I'm going to meet the Yankees?"

The following Saturday, on Patsy's day off, Jackie Farrell drove out to the Pepes' apartment in Hoboken. Maria had been dressed and waiting for hours before his scheduled arrival. With her, and just as pleased with the prospect of visiting the stadium, were her younger brother, eight-year-old Mark, and her older, non-sports-oriented sister, fourteen-year-old Michele. The three kids and Mr. and Mrs. Pepe piled into the car, and they were off to see the "House That Ruth Built."

During the ride, Maria was bubbling with anticipation. "Mr. Farrell, can I really get to meet Mel Stottlemyre? How about Bobby Murcer? I can! !" Each time she received an affirmative answer, she would squeeze, shake, or pound her brother or sister. "Did you hear that, Mark? Did you hear that, Michele?" Michele was trying to be more composed, as befits an older woman, but in the end she also succumbed to the contagious excitement, helping to fill the car with happy chattering.

The hour ride from Hoboken across the Hudson to the Bronx was endless, but when they finally arrived at Yankee Stadium, it was strictly red carpet. Mr. Farrell whisked Maria and her family right into the club offices. Mike Burke greeted them there, smiling as Maria stared, astonished, at all the old photographs and other memorabilia of the legendary Yankee teams from the past. They were all there, and Maria acted as expert and guide for her family. "Look! That's Mickey Mantle. And that's Yogi Berra. Whitey Ford! I wish I was a lefty. There's Joltin' Joe DiMaggio. . . . The Babe! And that's Lou Gehrig."

"Would you like to meet a few of our more recent ballplayers, Miss Pepe?" asked Mr. Burke.

"Oh, would I!"

Burke took Maria's hand, and the whole Pepe clan followed as he led the way through the labyrinth of corridors leading through the huge old stadium, out onto the playing field.

"Maria, this is Ralph Houk, our manager."

"Hello, Mr. Houk. You're doing great so far this season. Do you think the Yanks are going to win the pennant?"

"I don't know, Maria, but we're sure going to give it a try." Even before the manager had finished his answer, Maria was distracted by some of the ballplayers at batting practice. She nearly swooned when she saw Ron Blomberg smashing easily thrown warm-up pitches deep into the outfield. As she looked at everything with wide-eyed amazement, it was the scale of the place that stunned Maria into silence. From the grass in front of the Yankee dugout, the stadium seemed to stretch forever in all directions. It was the biggest place she'd ever seen.

"Maria." It was her mom who broke the trance. "Come over here for a minute; they want to take some pictures."

The rest of the day was a montage of thrilling experiences for Maria. She got her picture taken with all her heroes; she received an autographed baseball, a batting helmet, a tour of the Yankee dugout, and an armload of books about the team.

For the game, Maria and her family were seated in a private box right behind the Yankee dugout. She cheered wildly, greeting players by name whenever they took the field or went up to bat. The only disappointing aspect of the entire beautiful day was the score. Detroit beat the Yanks two to one.

As they were leaving the stadium for the ride home with Mr. Farrell, one of the photographers asked Mrs. Pepe how all the publicity and attention were affecting Maria. "I don't know. Patsy and I worry about it. We don't want to see Maria hurt. She's such a good girl. At first she was very upset by the decision . . . we all thought it was unfair, but, you know, you can't fight City Hall." Watching Maria excitedly reviewing the day with her brother and sister, Mrs. Pepe's anxiety seemed to vanish. "She seems to understand now."

When one of the newsmen asked Maria how she felt about what was happening to her, she answered with, "Aw, I just want to play ball."

In a few weeks, after the excitement of having been a "Yankee for a day" faded, Maria had to content herself again with sand-lot baseball. The closest she got to the Little League after her ouster was rooting for her old teammates from the sidelines.

The Hoboken league managed to start up again after a brief hiatus, but it was without support, franchise, or insurance coverage from the national headquarters. The city was still being punished for having allowed Maria to play, but instead of folding the league, civic leaders announced that organized baseball would continue. The city government assumed the responsibility for any game-related injuries. But despite the fact that Hoboken was going it alone, Maria was still barred from playing, in the hope that the national organization would reinstate the league's chapter.

While order—and baseball—resumed in Hoboken, the legal action started on Maria's behalf was causing chaos among the fifteen men on the national board of the league. A three-day hearing held before the State Division on Civil Rights was producing some very unexpected results. The weight of the evidence given by expert psychologists and doctors supported the conclusion that girls between the ages of eight and twelve could play baseball with no greater risk of injury than boys in the same age group. The major legal prop in the Little

League's policy of excluding girls from play was being called out on strikes.

Sylvia B. Pressler, the division hearing officer, finally ruled that the league had been unlawfully discriminating against Maria, specifically, and against all other New Jersey girls who wanted to play Little League ball.

"The Little League," concluded Mrs. Pressler, "is as American as hot dogs and apple pie." She added that there was absolutely no reason, physical or psychological, "why that piece of Americana should be withheld from Maria or any other girl."

Hoping to send the legal fight into extra innings, the Little League appealed to the Appellate Division of the State Superior Court. Beaten on the argument that little girls were more fragile than little boys, the national office changed its game plan. Relative safety no longer the issue, the league maintained that it was a private and not a public accommodation. As such, the league contended that it was exempt from New Jersey's law against sex discrimination.

It was an old principle, basically the same argument that certain Southern school districts had used to prevent racial integration. It had been unsuccessful then, during the civil-rights movement, and it failed again to impress the judges in what was becoming a critical battleground in the women's-rights movement.

The court case propelled Maria reluctantly back into the headlines that she had shared in New Jersey, off and on, for two years with such issues as Watergate and the energy crisis. Team sponsor James Farina called the Pepes to relay another invitation to Maria. In the wake of the renewed attention, she was being invited to appear on the television program *To Tell the Truth.*

The aim of the game-show panel, naturally, was to determine which of three contestants was "the first girl to play in the Little League." Before the program, Maria confessed to some stage fright. "Being on TV makes me a lot more nervous than playing baseball ever did." On the set, she was seated by host Gary Moore alongside two girls who had never played baseball before. For the three days before the show Maria had been tutoring her partners all about her ballplaying experiences in the hope that they could fool the panel.

All the hard work almost paid off with the five-hundred-dollar grand prize, which is awarded only if a contestant can fool all four panelists. When Gary Moore asked, "Will the real Maria Pepe please stand up," panelists Bill Cullen, Peggy Cass, and Alan Alda had all guessed wrong. Only perceptive veteran Kitty Carlisle managed to select the "real" Maria.

"She was the only one who really showed how much her feelings had been hurt by getting dropped from the team," said Miss Carlisle, as she picked out Maria.

Maria and her partners received only the fifty-dollar consolation prize, but shortly after the program she won a more significant victory. The court finally ruled in the court case, and it ruled in Maria's favor. Said Mr. Stirrat from the league's national headquarters on hearing the news of her victory, "I wasn't totally surprised. Nothing has been going our way lately."

The court had ruled that Little League was indeed a "public accommodation, because the invitation to play baseball is open to children in the community at large, with no restriction whatever." The court added that the league is "public in the added sense that, characteristically, local governmental bodies make the playing fields available to the local leagues without charge."

The day before the court's decision, there had been a huge demonstration in Trenton, the capital. Eight hundred mothers and their children had marched on the State House, asking to see their legislators. Worried over the reverses suffered in court and how an adverse ruling would affect the future of the Little League, the crowds angrily cried for legislative action. Armed with more than fifty thousand signatures on hundreds of petitions of support, they were demanding a state law that would protect the Little League against an influx of girls.

The attempt at political muscle, however, proved as ineffective as the league's rapidly diminishing legal prospects. A new law that would have exempted the organization from the old law against sex discrimination was defeated by three votes after an emotional debate on the floor of the State Assembly.

School was back in session by the time the issue was being resolved. When Maria walked into the apartment after school on that afternoon, Angie handed her a newspaper account of the disturbances in Trenton.

"Aw, Mom, don't make me read it. I already heard about the whole thing from all the kids at school. . . . And I feel so bad about starting all this trouble."

"But, Maria, I still think you were right."

"I think I was right, too," said Maria as she sat down heavily on the couch. "But I can't help feeling bad about upsetting all those people." She let out a sigh. "So I don't want to read about it in the newspapers."

In court, while the demonstration was raging in Trenton, the league was down to its last legal resort. It was a specious argument that sought to appeal to the judges' puritanical instincts. There are no rest-room facilities in or near many of the ballfields used by Little League teams. Therefore, the league argued, the "bodily privacy" of a girl playing baseball could not be guaranteed.

"Why, I've seen some of the boys doing it right on the field!" league attorney Michael Loprete had passionately exclaimed during his unsuccessful argument. The court wasted no time in disposing of the "privacy" argument.

Although Maria had been reluctant to listen to news of demonstrations, she eagerly listened as her mother read the reports of her legal victory. "Hurray!" she shouted, parading around the apartment living room.

Michele and brother Mark had listened with her to the good news. As Angie read, the trio formed a kind of conga line. Maria was in front, with her arms upraised in twin victory signs. Mark was behind her, with his hands on her waist, and Michele was behind him.

"We won! We won!" they were all yelling as they

marched around and over the living-room furniture and through the rest of the house.

By the time Patsy had come home from work, about an hour later, the excitement had died down. When Mrs. Pepe told her husband the news of the victory, he knocked on the girls' bedroom door and went in to congratulate Maria.

"Not bad. Not bad. How do you feel about the whole thing now? Do you think it was worth it?" he asked her.

"Of course she does, Daddy," answered Mark, an enthusiastic and very proud younger brother. The kids were all sitting on Maria's bed, bubbling happily, as they read and reread the newspaper accounts of the court's decision.

"Well, what do you think, Maria?" Patsy asked again.

"I'm happy, Daddy," she said softly. "I'm mostly happy for all the other girls who'll get the chance to play."

"But what about you, sugar—aren't you happy for yourself?" asked Patsy with uncharacteristic softness.

"I guess so, Daddy, but . . ."

"But what, Maria?"

"I'm too old to play now."

The victory had come too late for Maria Pepe. At thirteen she was already over the Little League hill, and no longer eligible to play.

The next spring, the first under the new ruling, 50 girls joined the 175 boys who turned out to register for the Hoboken Little League. "I never expected that many," said Joseph Pullano, the town's recreational superintendent, with a wide grin. "And you know something else?" he added as he walked among the crowds of young hopefuls who were throwing baseballs around and practicing slides into second base. "Just from talking with them, I figure that at least twenty of them know something about what they're doing."

In June 1974, defeated in New Jersey, and facing dozens of legal challenges in other states, officials of Little League, Inc., announced from Williamsport that they would "defer to the changing social climate" and permit girls to play on their teams. The statement went on to say that the board of directors felt it would be "imprudent for an organization as large and as universally respected as the thirty-five-year-old Little League to allow itself to become embroiled in a public controversy"—rather like shutting the barn door after the livestock have fled.

The only roadblock to the official recognition of girls' right to play was the organization's federal charter. It referred only to "young boys," saying nothing about young girls. So the national office petitioned Congress for the necessary change.

On December 26, President Gerald Ford signed legislation that officially opened the Little League baseball program to participation by girls. According to an announcement by Ron Nessen, the presidential press secretary, the charter had been changed to refer to "young people" rather than just boys. In addition, the new law deleted reference to the promotion of manhood" among Little League players.

When it happened, and girls were formally admitted, the action rated only a small item in the back pages of the newspapers. Nobody even called Maria for a comment.

In Saigon in the spring of 1975, there was panic and terrible confusion. All around the almost tropical city once known principally for its broad boulevards and French colonial motif, the forces of the Saigon government were retreating in disorder as the Viet Cong advanced. Many high-ranking South Vietnamese leaders had already fled the country, some reportedly taking part of its gold reserves with them. President Ford, through his ambassador, Ellsworth Bunker, had ordered the immediate evacuation of all American civilians and all but the most essential military and diplomatic personnel. The long war was almost over, but it was ending in an orgy of violence.

Wendy Grant had just arrived in the besieged and battered capital of the rapidly diminishing Republic of Vietnam. A dedicated woman from Boulder, Colorado, Mrs. Grant and her husband, Duane, had spent most of their adult lives caring for homeless children and all the last decade trying to alleviate the specific suffering of the orphans of the brutal wars in Southeast Asia.

She had come to Saigon from Phnom Penh, the once serene capital of the former military government of Cambodia, escorting forty-one orphans out of that city just days before it fell to the Khmer Rouge. Already the adoptive parent of three American and four Vietnamese children, Wendy had adopted two more baby girls in Phnom Penh, two-month-old twins, because that was the only way to get them out of Cambodia quickly enough.

She had sought a temporary haven in Saigon for all the children she was escorting. They were already in the process of being adopted by American and Canadian families, but the torturously drawn-out interna-

tional procedure was still uncompleted. Wendy, and the
organization she had co-founded, called Friends for All
Children, had counted on a respite of several weeks in
Saigon during which time the necessary documents
could be obtained and processed.

But the life of the regime in Saigon, now mortally
wounded, was measured in days, not weeks, and the
adoption process was complicated by numbers. The
Friends organization also ran four orphanages in the
Saigon area, caring for six hundred homeless Vietnamese children. Most of them were abandoned babies, and
again, all were in the process of being adopted by
American, Canadian, Australian, or British families.

Because intense fighting was expected in the
streets of the city at any time, the decision had been
made to get the kids out as soon as possible.

Under the pressure of American public opinion,
the Ford administration persuaded its State Department
and what was left of Saigon's to waive most of the time-
consuming procedures. Wendy had obtained a laissez-
passer, a diplomatic pass covering all the children. All
the other formalities could be taken care of once they
were safely out of the war zone.

The first group of forty-one Cambodian children,
including Wendy's two little girls, was flown safely to
the United States and Canada aboard commercial airliners. Many of the rest were to be airlifted out on military planes President Ford had generously offered as
part of a "vast humanitarian effort." In all, two thousand orphans in facilities run by several American-
based organizations were to be flown out by the United
States government.

"This is the least we can do," the president had
said, "and we will do much, much more."

The first U.S. military plane made available for
what would become popularly known as the "baby lift"
was a gigantic Air Force Galaxy C-5A. It had just arrived at the Tan Son Nhut air base with a cargo of ammunition for whatever was left of the broken army of
South Vietnam. The Galaxy would carry a much more
precious cargo on its outward flight, 228 small children

from the Friends orphanages. It was bound for Travis Air Force Base in California, where many of the children were to be met by their adoptive parents.

Wendy, incidentally, hated the expression "baby lift." She felt it somehow reduced the children to the status of commodities and overlooked the fact that most of the children the orphanages evacuated from Vietnam were already in the process of being adopted.

A second plane was leaving Tan Son Nhut for Australia the same day that the Galaxy was heading for California. Its passengers were the tiny babies thought too young or too sick for the grinding, arduous twenty-hour flight to the United States.

Wendy was anxious to leave Vietnam. She had already been away from home for several weeks on this trip, and wanted desperately to be reunited with her two new little girls and the rest of her family, waiting nervously for her at their home in Colorado. But the Friends for All Children office in Saigon could not spare her. Even with the laissez-passer, there was still an enormous amount of administrative work that had to be done before the six hundred babies could be moved halfway across the world.

When it became apparent that she would not be able to make the Galaxy flight, Wendy asked Margaret Moses to take her place on board. An experienced person was needed to coordinate the Friends personnel and the other women who had volunteered to care for the children during the flight. Besides the staff people, these volunteer escorts were mostly secretaries working in the United States embassy and wives of members of the American defense attaché office.

"Damn you, Grant!" Margaret had playfully told Wendy before the flight left. "I knew you'd get me to America somehow!"

Margaret Moses was an Australian volunteer worker in her mid-thirties. With another Australian woman, Rosemary Taylor, she had been working in Saigon at the Friends orphanages for the past five years. Both women were very well known in Saigon's foreign community for their tireless heroic efforts in behalf of the thousands of war orphans.

Margaret's mother was also in Saigon at the time, assisting in the emergency evacuation. Up until the moment Wendy's trip back to the United States was postponed by the exigencies of the situation in Saigon, both Margaret and her mother had been scheduled to fly out on the Australian plane together.

The 350-ton Galaxy had been hurriedly converted into a passenger plane for the rescue mission. Seats had been bolted onto the upper deck of the cavernous cargo hold. Then, in order to carry out as many children as possible as quickly as possible, canvas slings were hung in the lower hold. Additional children were strapped into them, sitting nine or ten across.

Fully equipped with diapers, baby bottles, and blankets, the C-5A, the world's largest jet aircraft, had been made into an ark to ferry helpless infants away from danger. The Australian plane was scheduled to leave a half-hour later.

Wendy went back to the Friends office after the process of loading the lively infants had been completed.

"I remember feeling really sorry for myself that the plane was going and I had to stay behind." When she remembers, Wendy's voice breaks, and she chokes with emotion. "I'd been away so long, and I missed Duane and the children."

Commanded by Air Force veteran pilot Captain Dennis Traynor, the great airplane lumbered down the runway at Tan Son Nhut and under full power began its long climb to cruising altitude.

Trouble came at twenty-three thousand feet, when the huge cargo-loading entry doors at the rear of the double-decker airplane suddenly and apparently without warning blew out. At that altitude, the atmosphere is extremely rarefied, and the airplane is pressurized to keep the air inside normal for breathing. When the doors exploded, the airplane instantly depressurized.

Air Force Sergeant Jim Hadley was one of the medical technicians on board to help care for the children; he was on the upper deck when it happened. He was interviewed later by the Associated Press. "You could see the hole in the back of the plane. You could see sunlight streaming in. Things started flying around. Eyeglasses. Pens. Pieces of insulation tore off the ceiling. The pillows exploded. . . ."

The emergency oxygen masks appeared automatically when the pressure in the passenger area dropped so drastically, but with two or three infants in a single seat, there weren't enough to go around. Many of the masks couldn't be used at all. Their connecting hoses were designed for grown soldiers and were not long enough to reach the faces of the little children seated under them.

"We had to keep moving them from kid to kid," said the sergeant.

The situation on the lower deck was even more chaotic. Many of the hastily slung canvas hammocks came loose, roughly dumping the frightened children onto the deck. So many had neither oxygen nor a secure seat as the plane careened toward the crash landing.

With the explosion, apparently caused by an improperly sealed rear cargo door, Captain Traynor lost most of his steering controls. Pieces of the door or other loose wreckage had violently smashed into the airplane's towering tail section, putting those contols out of operation. Steering with just his engines and the controls on the wings, Captain Traynor struggled to turn back toward Saigon, by this time about forty miles away.

"I felt like I was waiting to die," said one flight nurse, describing the moments after the captain fought to get his crippled airplane turned around.

He was heading for an emergency landing at Tan Son Nhut, but when realized that the plane would never make it, Captain Traynor crash-landed the C-5A in a paddy field about five miles from the airport.

When the 700,000-pound jet smashed into the rice field, it skidded, then broke into four huge pieces and scattered debris over an area of at least a quarter of a mile. Most of the escorts and children on the upper deck were rescued from the flaming wreckage by the heroic actions of the surviving members of the airplane's crew. Most of the people on the lower deck were crushed almost instantly. Seventy-eight babies and about half that many adults, including all but one of the regular members of the Friends staff, were killed.

Wendy Grant was in the office when the tragic news came. Bereaved beyond adequate description, she went first to the Seventh-Day Adventist Hospital near the air base to determine who had survived. Then she made her way to the makeshift morgues nearby where Air America helicopters had carried the scores of bodies, wrapped in army ponchos. Among so many others, her friend Margaret Moses had also died.

Margaret's mother had watched in horror as the helicopters ferried the casualties back toward the airport. She was there shepherding her own contingent of infants aboard the Australian plane. The pilot of her plane mistakenly informed his passengers that there were only a handful of survivors of the crash. After a moment of indecision, Mrs. Moses resolved to remain on board. After all, there were children to be cared for.

The next day, two chartered jumbo jetliners and two C-141 military cargo planes flew Wendy, what was left of her staff, the survivors of the crash, and nine hundred infants from orphanages all over the city out of Saigon for the United States. About three hundred others left for homes in Canada, Australia, and Britain.

Two weeks later, the war ended.

It had been the longest and most unpopular war in the history of the United States, and its terrible cost was almost incalculably high: 56,713 Americans were killed, 303,654 others were seriously wounded.

For every American soldier who died, eight South Vietnamese soldiers were also killed. For every one of ours wounded, at least a dozen of theirs were also shredded by mines, mortars, bullets, or artillery shells. And these grim statistics don't include the unpublished casualty count from what used to be known as "the other side."

But to the Vietnamese, the price of war was more

dreadful than even the hundreds of thousands of military casualties. For the hapless people of a country that for twenty years seemed hopelessly divided, it was a war in which towns, villages, and cities became battlefields.

The objective of the huge and terrible armies that faced each other wasn't so much the control of territory as it was the control of the civilian population. People were the front lines, and they died in heaps of thousands.

Out of a population that numbered about fourteen million, at least 1.5 million civilian men, women, and children were killed or wounded in the South alone, just between the years 1961 and 1973. By the time the Saigon regime finally collapsed, the landscape had been littered with corpses, despoiled, and made destitute by the flames of the endless fighting.

The scars of the fighting were everywhere. They were etched on the faces of the children of South Vietnam who lost one or both parents during the war.

When the international news first broke in early April 1975 that a massive evacuation of some of these war orphans would be taking place, it was condemned by North Vietnam as a "criminal action." Premier Pham Van Dong charged that "The immediate aim of the airlift is to try to make the world believe that many Vietnamese are anti-Communists to provide a pretext for perpetuating the United States' action in our country."

But the private efforts of American citizens to care for and open their homes to children whose families were destroyed by the war was without doubt the most humane and nonpolitical aspect of our tragic involvement in Southeast Asia.

Tia Grant's story is representative of thousands of others'. She is one of the Vietnamese children adopted by Wendy and Duane.

The U Minh forest, where she came from, is 150 miles south of Saigon. It lies astride the vast delta formed by the great Mekong River as it quietly winds its way to the South China Sea. A dense, hot, impenetrable jungle, U Minh was one of the few areas of South

Vietnam totally controlled by the Viet Cong. For that reason, Ba Xuyen province, which is part of the forest, was subjected to almost continuous air raids flown by both the Saigon government and the U.S. forces.

In overgrown terrain like Ba Xuyen, high-speed bombing runs are extremely imprecise tools of war. The crowded orphanage near the province town of Soc Trang is bitter testimony to the lack of precision demonstrated by the jet fighters. While the town itself was an island of relative calm, its orphanage was filled with children from the surrounding area whose parents were killed by napalm or shattered by fragmentation bombs.

Tia, whose real name was Thu Van, was a resident in the orphanage. She was born in a tiny village located just outside of Soc Trang. Records were kept only haphazardly, but by the best estimates, she was born in either 1965 or 1966.

In peacetime, the economy of her village would have been based on the paddy fields surrounding it, and social problems like a child left lonely would have been solved by the village council. But in Tia's life there had been no peace, and war had flattened most of the village fields and destroyed its communal way of life.

One day when she was only three or four years old, Tia's father went off to war. She doesn't remember either his leaving or the side for which he fought. What Tia remembers is when, a year later, her mother told her he'd been killed. Her grandmother had also died, caught out in a field during one of the random air raids, so her family by then had been reduced to Tia, her mother, her grandfather, and an older sister. They tried to survive by growing and selling vegetables.

The memories of a child are often obscured by time and exaggerated by perspective, but Tia remembers her grandfather very clearly, "a kind and wise old man with a long, flowing beard."

He was the master gardener, directing the planting and harvesting of their tiny crop. It was grown in a garden behind the one-room thatched cottage they all lived in. It was one of the dozen or so cottages in their village huddled together on a small raised patch of dry ground between the rice fields and the forest.

When things worked for the family and were marginally bearable, Tia and her mother would take whatever vegetables were not necessary for their own table and bring them to what was left of the marketplace in town. It wasn't much of a harvest, barely filling the two hand-woven baskets Tia's mother would carefully balance on her shoulders at the ends of a long bamboo pole. Together they'd walk to town, carefully listening for airplanes and taking cover in the murky drainage ditch that followed alongside the dirt road if they heard the unmistakable roar of a bomber approaching.

It worked minimally for a while, but then, according to Tia, her mother got sick. The little girl remembers sitting at the edge of her mother's bed wiping the sweat from her forehead and pinching her body. The pinching is a delta custom, thought to relieve pain and suffering.

Day after day Tia and her older sister brought their mother bowls of boiled fruits and vegetables, fighting to keep her strength up, but she continued to deteriorate. As Tia first told the story, her mother at the end just fell asleep. Presumably in a coma, she slept for several days. When she woke, she was paralyzed.

Then Tia—who'd been born into war, lost her father to it, and watched as her mother became crippled and infirm—was herself ravaged by illness. When the shy and hauntingly beautiful child was only five or six, she was afflicted by polio, a disease that's become almost an anachronism in the civilized world.

In the twenty years since polio vaccines have become universally available in the United States, for instance, the number of cases of that crippling and often fatal disease has fallen from a peak of fifty-eight thousand in 1952 to just seven in 1974. Even in those areas of Vietnam where the Saigon government had haphazardly reigned, U.S. forces and the International Red Cross had managed a partial distribution of the preventive Salk vaccine.

In the so-called "free fire zones," however, the

vast areas held by the guerrillas, most of the limited medical supplies went first to the soldiers. Inoculation of the civilian population against disease was an unaffordable luxury reserved for the tranquility of peacetime, and limited even then by the absence of refrigeration to keep the vaccine. In the savagely contested rural countryside of Vietnam, controllable diseases like polio killed and crippled tens of thousands of children.

According to the little girl, it was her grandfather who made the difficult decision to bring her to the orphanage at Soc Trang. The family was impoverished, and her mother seriously ill. With virtually no resources, and no medical facilities in the village, the old man knew the crippled child would just wither and die if left untreated.

Contrary to the apparent thinking of some of the American General Staff, life is as precious to the Vietnamese as it is to anyone else, and the abandonment of a child is just as emotionally tearing. As an old, sad man once told Wendy Grant, "It is our culture to care for our children."

But twenty years of war had torn the ancient culture to pieces, and noble traditions had been replaced by fatalistic expediency. Children would be unwillingly abandoned whenever it became apparent that their chances of survival were greater in an orphanage or some other place outside the range of the fighting.

At the height of our involvement in the war, it was common for desperately frightened young mothers to get out of their beds in makeshift village maternity hospitals and abandon their babies in the middle of the night. They'd often leave without ever having been tortured by the sight of their own newborn.

During the final two years of the war, there were at least twenty-five thousand lost, abandoned, or homeless children living in understaffed, underfinanced orphanages scattered the length and breadth of Vietnam. About five percent of the children had been fathered by American G.I.'s. Three out of every five of them died before they were three months old, and of the two who were left, only one reached his third birthday. The effort to evacuate the children to the West must be judged with that historical perspective.

Many more than twenty-five thousand children were taken in or adopted by Vietnamese families who were living in the cities and were slightly better off. Unfortunately, not all these placements were motivated by compassion and generosity. Reportedly, many middle-class Vietnamese who brought orphaned children into their homes did so to acquire cheap domestic help. Like Cinderella, but without the fairy godmother, these children in effect became servants of their adoptive households.

The orphanage at Soc Trang was one of the best facilities operating in the country. Called Co Nhi Vien, which is simply the Vietnamese expression for an orphanage, it's run by a French order of nuns, the Sisters of Providence. The orphanage is like a walled city, a sprawling place consisting mostly of one- and two-story mud-brick buildings, at least twenty-five or thirty years old. Cracked and crumbling back to dust, they are a legacy from the time France ruled as the paramount colonial power in Indochina.

The Providence orphanage lies just outside the town. Although it was never directly attacked by either side, Tia and the other children could watch from the orphanage windows as bombs burst in the nearby rice fields and forests. Those explosions were as much a part of her childhood as the seasonal monsoons that bring continual rains to the delta for half of each year.

Tia is a precocious, brave little girl, and she soon became a special favorite of Sister Sylvie, the mother superior. But she was often the object of the other children's ridicule. Her limbs had become so twisted by the disease that she would have to drag herself across the floor in an unavoidable parody of a crab. One of her feet was bent back up against her leg.

To alleviate the ugliest symptoms of the polio, the sisters decided Tia should learn to walk on crutches. She did, but it was extremely painful for her. All the upper muscles in her legs had been severely affected by the disease, and the new pressures brought to bear by her reliance on the crutches caused even further contractions.

Shortly before she was finally adopted, she was not only unable to walk; Tia was unable to stretch out her body. It was bent at a right angle.

Despite the pain and the pitiless advances made by the disease, her memories of Co Nhi Vien are good ones. The staff was kind, and as Sister Sylvie's favorite, Tia was occasionally rewarded with an extra portion of lemonade or a few piasters to buy an ice cream whenever she tried especially hard to master her crutches.

Everything outside the orphanage grounds, including the school in Soc Trang, was inaccessible to her, but the sisters made an attempt to instruct her as best they could. Tia learned a surprising amount of Vietnamese folklore, and can still sing many of the delta songs. She even sings "Frère Jacques," the classic French children's song. She sings it in Vietnamese in a voice of heartrending softness.

In the long run, it wasn't the illness or the inability to go to school that most distressed her. When the war in the delta finally eased off after America's direct participation in the fighting ended, people would frequently come by and take children away with them. They were being adopted, but Tia thought nobody would ever come for her.

At seven or eight, she was already older than most of the children still at the orphanage, and she was terribly handicapped.

"I could not walk, only crawl."

One afternoon, the mother superior told Tia that she was going to be transferred to another orphanage, in Saigon. A woman would be there to meet Tia, Sister Sylvie explained. The woman was an American, coming to take Tia back with her to the United States.

"No," reasoned Tia. "She's only coming to visit."

"But, Tia," patiently explained the mother superior, "she wants you to be her child."

"She's only coming to visit!" insisted the little girl who'd been through too much. The awful fear that Sister Sylvie was somehow joking or mistaken was more than she could bear. But the mother superior had been right. The woman was Wendy Grant, and she was coming to Vietnam to adopt Tia and bring her back home to Colorado with her.

Even before the fighting began to tear and eat away at the fabric of Vietnamese society, Wendy and Duane Grant had been sheltering and giving love and comfort to homeless children. All their kids are adopted. Originally there were just the two boys, Loren and Walter, and a girl named Lisa, who was the youngest.

The Grants' specific interest in the children of Vietnam began in 1964, with the escalation of America's participation in that civil war. The Grants had already decided to adopt another little girl, so that Lisa, only five at the time, would have a playmate. Mr. Grant is a physicist with IBM, and their large, rambling house just outside of Boulder could easily hold another child or two.

After reading some of the horrific newspaper accounts of the war, they decided to try to adopt a Vietnamese child. But they found that it was an almost impossibly complicated process. In the early days of the fighting, American adoption agencies refused to handle the placement of Vietnamese children. Despite the elaborate military arrangments, there was almost no formal civilian contact between the people of South Vietnam and the United States.

Through the American embassy in Saigon, the Grants finally got the name of a Vietnamese attorney living in that city. They were told that he might be able to help.

The Grants wrote to him and explained their desire to provide a home for one of the thousands of children already orphaned by the escalating war. He wrote back and said it could be arranged. In his letter was the photograph of a lovely ten-month-old girl named Thi.

When the frustratingly complicated adoption procedure was finally completed, Thi came to America, arriving in the spring of 1965. They gave her the Vietnamese name of Diahan. It was a name the other children could easily pronounce, but one that would still give Thi a sense of past and of cultural heritage.

Because Wendy and Duane had discovered and managed to surmount the difficult adoption process, and because the need for qualified parents was so great, they decided to assist other American families trying to do the same thing. Together with several former army doctors who had served in Indochina, they established a group initially called the Friends of the Children of Vietnam. It became the Friends for All Children after the war spilled beyond the borders of South Vietnam.

Their little committee had two functions. The first was to provide food, clothing, and necessary medical supplies to existing orphanages in Vietnam. The second was to provide counseling to American families interested in adoption.

They met intensive resistance all along the way. It was fueled initially by Vietnamese national pride and Saigon's refusal to admit that it was incapable of caring for its own children. The rescue effort was also delayed by bureaucratic complications in the United States and the unspoken reluctance on the part of the Justice Department's immigration officials to admit non-whites into the United States, even if they were children. Lastly, it was enormously delayed by the exigencies of the fierce fighting that relegated to the lowest levels of priority all administrative work not directly related to the war effort.

Eventually the group managed to overcome the difficulties. In their first year they were able to locate and place only a half-dozen children with American families. In 1973, two years before the final collapse, more than three hundred homeless children found new homes in the United States as a result of their efforts. The group ultimately matured from a little room in a corner of the Grants' home in Boulder. With tongue firmly in cheek, Duane refers to the room as his "ex-study."

In 1967, when the Grants were still informally helping others through the adoption process, the Australian Rosemary Taylor went to Vietnam for the first time. She'd also heard the horror stories of the agony being endured by the people there and wanted somehow to help in alleviating it. With her, the children had top priority.

There were thousands of orphans everywhere. The older ones—and in Vietnam that meant over four— lined the streets of Saigon, begging for food and hustling odd jobs. It was common to see an infant in the exclusive care of another child four or five years old. And there would be additional hundreds of homeless children whenever the countryside erupted with new fighting. But the government, struggling for its life, paid no attention.

Inquiries made by foreign adoption agencies were apparently filed in trash baskets or otherwise ignored. The effect of this nonpolicy of neglect was often dreadful. One U.S. adoption agency, Welcome House of Pennsylvania, had finally received permission, after many months of trying, to process sixty infants for adoption in America. Between the time the agency located the babies, however, and Saigon's tardy acquiescence, fifty-two of the sixty had died of disease or malnutrition.

With the help of private donations from abroad, Rosemary Taylor managed to open the four homes around Saigon for refugee children. She established contacts with adoption agencies in the United States, including Friends, but their combined efforts could scarcely keep pace with the growing magnitude of the problem. The orphans flooded the streets of the city.

Those hardy enough to have survived the war, sickness, and hunger were still impoverished. With no money, their inevitable futures were bleak. Prostitution or menial domestic work for the girls, and cycle driving, petty hustling, or the army for the boys, was as much as they could reasonably expect.

In 1971 Rosemary wrote to the Grants, telling them of a six-month-old girl named Lara, who was available for adoption. With the urging of their older children, they had already decided to open their own home to as many Vietnamese children as they possibly could. They quickly wrote back, urging Rosemary to expedite the application, then prepared for the newest addition to their family.

With the unavoidable paperwork completed, and just two weeks before Lara was scheduled to come to America, they received another letter from Rosemary Taylor. A doctor at Lara's orphanage had discovered she had polio. The prognosis was she'd never be able to walk. In Rosemary's letter the subtle suggestion was made that perhaps the Grants would like to reconsider their decision.

With tens of thousands to choose from, there were thousands of perfectly healthy children available. The Grants cabled an immediate two-word reply: "Send Lara."

One of the impediments to a sufficiently large-scale adoption program was always the sensitivity of the adopting parents. Most Americans, after deciding to adopt a Vietnamese child, insisted on a healthy infant, usually a girl. Generally the commitment stopped short of embracing children who were psychologically or physically damaged.

While the feelings are understandable, the results were regrettable. Many of the orphans fell into the dead-end category of unadoptables. If the Grants weren't so extraordinary, Lara might have been one of them.

She was brought to the United States and given a series of remedial operations. Lara responded beautifully and made remarkable progress. With that positive experience, the Grants again wrote Rosemary Taylor and specifically asked for a handicapped child. They figured they had space for another, and wanted to help a child who wouldn't otherwise get help.

Rosemary had been told of the pretty child in Sister Sylvie's orphanage. The fighting had temporarily eased off, but civilian travel by road to Soc Trang was still impossible; Rosemary had helicoptered out to meet Tia. She saw how lovely and well-behaved she was, but despaired of ever finding the child a home because she was so severely handicapped.

That letter from the Grants made Rosemary hopeful. She replied, sending along a picture of Tia. As soon as the family received it, they decided Tia was going to be "their" child.

Although both of the other girls, Diahan and Lara, had been sent to America by themselves, the Grants decided that either Duane or Wendy should go over and bring Tia home. Rosemary had told them how much the child had suffered already, and they wanted to prevent the exodus to the United States from becoming another ordeal for her.

By the time Wendy arrived in Vietnam in late 1972, road travel had opened, temporarily, between Soc Trang and Saigon. Tia had by then been in Sister Sylvie's orphanage for two years. After breakfast one morning, Tia was helped to get ready for the first leg of her long trip home. Even though she still refused to acknowledge publicly that she was finally being adopted, she feverishly prepared for her meeting in Saigon with her "visitor" from America.

With her long, straight black hair carefully combed, and wearing an ao dai, the traditional silk dress of the women of Vietnam, made for her by one of the sisters, Tia tearfully said good-bye to her friends at the orphanage.

From Soc Trang, that isolated, war-torn hamlet on the edge of the tropical forest, Tia was driven by truck over miles of dirt roads, until finally they arrived in Saigon. It was the start of a dazzling but difficult trip for her. She had never been in a motor vehicle, and had certainly never been more than a kilometer or two from town. They tried to make her as comfortable as possible, but each bump was another painful milestone.

She was brought to the Allambie Orphanage in the city. It was the first time Tia had seen big buildings, traffic, or great crowds of people. She was quiet and very frightened.

Once inside, Tia was brought into the large central courtyard, to await her first meeting with Wendy.

"It was like looking out over a sea of hopeful little faces," Mrs. Grant said, remembering. "I was holding a photograph of Tia, and looking around for the face that matched it, but I couldn't find her."

"Mama?" Wendy finally looked down, attracted by the small voice of a child crawling toward her, almost at her feet. When Wendy saw Tia dragging herself across the dirt floor like a puppy whose hind legs had been broken, she started to cry. She put her hands on the child's delicate face and told her she had come to take her home. Later, Tia asked if Wendy was crying because she was disappointed in the way Tia looked. Wendy, with one of the staff interpreting, explained gently that she was crying because she had met the beautiful daughter she'd been waiting a long time to see.

Boulder, Colorado, is as different as any city can possibly be from Ba Xuyen province in the jungle of the Mekong Delta. The university town, twenty-five miles northwest of Denver, rests in the cool beauty of the foothills, surrounded by the snowcapped Rocky Mountains.

When Wendy and Tia were home with Duane and the other kids, it was decided that the child's first operation should be put off for about six months. The doctors in Colorado, after examining Tia, had told the family that she'd need at least three major operations before her legs would be straightened enough to allow her to walk with braces. The Grants thought it best to allow her some time to adjust to her new home and family. She'd already been through so much, including traveling from the other side of the world and from a medieval life-style to the twentieth century.

The assimilation into the family was an easy, carefree time for Tia. Caressed by loving parents, it was a learning time for her. She wasn't ready for school in the formal sense, but for several hours each day Wendy and the children would act as Tia's guides and instructors. With everyone helping, they began teaching Tia to speak, read, and write English. It was a family affair, and it had the highest priority in the Grant household.

The informal classes would take place around the kitchen table during the days and around the big living-room fireplace in the evenings. Nobody forced her.

Even the younger children were sensitive to how much she'd been through. But despite their leisurely pace, her progress was remarkable. Her vocabulary grew from a handful of words to passable conversational English in just a few months. Soon she was teaching the other children some Vietnamese.

Her progress wasn't limited to fluency in language; there was also a more subtle change in her personality. She began shedding an inner tension. Tia was unwinding. For the first time in her life, the eight-year-old was living away from the destruction and sounds of war. She could go to sleep without being blasted awake by explosions or the screams of low-flying jet bombers.

Her infectious laughter filled the house every day. The other children also loved the experience, because Tia was so obviously delighted in things they had been taking for granted. The family has two Shetland ponies, Papoose and Niña, and Loren and Walter would spend, hours teaching Tia to ride. Loren would lead the pony, while Walter walked alongside, holding Tia firmly in the saddle. Later, after the successful completion of her operations, Tia would be able to ride by herself.

Winter and the snow it brought to the Rocky Mountain foothills was another learning experience for Tia. The closest thing to snow in Soc Trang had been the occasional ice-cream cone one of the sisters brought her at the orphange.

When the time finally came for her first operation, Wendy and Duane justifiably felt they had done everything they could to prepare Tia. They'd spent hours explaining that the end result of the pain and discomfort was that Tia would be able to walk again. But when they drove her to the hospital, she became withdrawn and unnaturally quiet.

Her mood was unchanged when they brought her up to her room, so the Grants stayed with her for several hours, trying to break Tia out of the shell she was drawing around herself. Finally Wendy had to explain that it was time for them to leave her. They promised they'd be back to visit in the morning but that they had to go home now and look after the other children.

As Wendy stood up to go, the impassive mask on the eight-year-old's face fell apart. She started crying, then screaming uncontrollably. Tia was terrified and seized with panic. She grabbed Wendy by the arms. "My mother took me to Soc Trang!"

"What do you mean, sweetheart? Tell me. I don't understand."

Wendy was speaking softly, trying to calm her down. She looked at Duane; both were worried and confused.

Still holding tightly to Wendy's arms, Tia said again, "My mother took me to Sister Sylvie . . . not my grandfather!" It had come almost as a shriek, forced out through her tears.

"She took me and left me . . . she said she was going to buy candy, but she never came back! She lied!"

Tia released her grip on Wendy's arms and collapsed back on her hospital bed. Her already twisted body curled more tightly in what looked like fetal anguish. Her confession made, she was sobbing more quietly.

The operation had been an abstract concept, which didn't frighten the child who had suffered so many real privations. Her panic had come from the belief that her new mother, like her mother in Vietnam, was using a subterfuge to abandon her.

"Tia, sweetie," Wendy started to explain to the pitifully frightened little girl, "your daddy and I aren't going to leave you here. We love you. We just want you to be well. The people here are nice people who are going to make your legs better . . . so you'll be able to play with Lara and Lisa and Diahan and the boys."

Wendy was sitting alongside her on the bed. Duane was standing nearby, caressing the disbelieving and petrified child's hair, trying to reassure her.

"You're ours now, honey. And you'll always be ours."

But during the months Tia spent in the hospital, she never quite got over her fear of being abandoned. The Grants would sense the tension in the little girl whenever it came time for them to leave, and every morning when they arrived to visit her, they saw the burst of joy and relief on her pretty face.

Wendy is afraid that the fear of rejection will be with Tia for a long time. It is, so far, the one indelible scar of a wretched childhood spent in the middle of a terrible war.

"She was lied to and given away by her mother when she was only four or five years old. She's a brave little girl, but it will take her some time to overcome something as awful as that. We only hope it'll be someday soon."

Tia's had some other flashbacks to her life in Vietnam, but none have been as sad or serious as her fear of rejection and abandonment. Shortly after she and Tia had arrived from Vietnam, Wendy came down with a serious case of hepatitis. Since she was confined to bed, the children all pitched in to do the housework. Since Tia still couldn't walk, she'd sit endlessly near her mother's bed, sponging her forehead and pinching her wherever it hurt.

After Tia's third operation, she was ready for her braces. The big event came on Christmas Day 1973. The whole family gathered to watch her take her first faltering steps. She had been brave; now she was triumphant.

She'll always need a brace on at least one leg, but she's no longer the little crab who crawled along the clay floor of the orphanage in Soc Trang.

"Tia's a child with every reason to resent life, but she doesn't at all," explains Wendy. "She's survived war, a crippling disease, and the loss of her parents. To be able to go through all that and still retain character, love, joy, and trust in people is really remarkable."

Tia had progressed far enough by February 1974 to be able to walk unassisted down one of the long corridors at the Denver airport. There, with her mother and the other kids, she watched through the big glass windows one afternoon as her father stepped off an airplane. With Duane was an eight-year-old Vietnamese boy named Vinh, another war orphan.

Both his parents had been killed in the fighting in the Mekong Delta. Alone, Vinh had been forced to make his way north to the capital. He was taken in by a Vietnamese family, but was used by them as an indentured servant. After several months Vinh was hit by a recklessly driven motorcycle while walking across the street one day in Saigon on an errand.

With his leg broken, Vinh was useless to his foster parents, so he was dumped back on the streets. Luckily, the eight-year-old was picked up by missionaries in Saigon and taken south to the orphanage in Soc Trang.

Duane had originally made the trip to Vietnam on a fact-finding mission for the Friends for All Children. He had no intention of adopting another child, until he spotted Vinh peeking at him from behind a tree within the walled orphanage compound.

When the always exhausting formalities had been completed, Duane and Vinh had come home. The eight-year-old walked nervously off the plane, shyly and uncertainly approaching his new family. Tia came boldly forward, put her arm around Vinh, and said softly in Vietnamese, "My brother, don't be afraid. Everything will be all right."

When, a year later, Wendy came home from her last trip to Southeast Asia, Duane met her at the airport and drove her to Boulder, where all seven children gave her a rousing welcome. For the last several weeks they had been watching the television news reports of the collapse of Cambodia and then South Vietnam, and all had agonized over the fate of their mother, who they knew was over there on still another rescue mission.

Then there was the terrible Galaxy crash, and the uncertainty over whether she had been on board. Even after Wendy had arrived safely in San Francisco and telephoned, there was another week's delay while she and her colleagues worked to ensure that all the children had been properly placed. Now she was home, and her children were overflowing with happiness and relief.

They also made a beautifully tremendous fuss over the twins she'd brought home with her from Phnom Penh. Both girls were already asleep on the couch, with an attentive audience that included Duane and all seven Grant children. Walter and Loren finally went out to the car to bring in their mother's suitcases.

It was a tradition in the house, after either Duane or Wendy had come home from one of these long trips abroad, that they distribute presents to the children, souvenirs of the trip. But this trip had been so different from the rest that Wendy had no time to shop, and in any case, in Saigon there had been no stores left open to shop in.

Wendy had an idea, though. She gave each of the two youngest girls, Tia and Diahan, one of the twins to look after. The twin assigned to Diahan was named Aino Naomi. Tia's charge was named Aili Margaret, after Margaret Moses, the Australian woman who had died in the crash of the Galaxy.

Hawthorne Avenue is a sleazy rat hole of a street running up a long, nameless hill that squats in the middle of the South Ward ghetto of Newark, New Jersey's largest and blackest and one of the nation's poorest cities. The sagging three- and four-story tenements that line both sides of that cratered street are built of wood and look as if they predated the Civil War. The buildings are dry, cracked, and combustible, and seem constructed of kindling, ready for the torch. Heated in the winter with coal, they are firetraps.

Eight-year-old Erwin Ponder lived in one of them, indistinguishable from the rest, about midway up the hill. From the sidewalk in front of his building he could look down and take small comfort in the fact that the houses at the bottom of the hill were even shabbier and more vulnerable than his own. Of course, his building served the same relative function for the people, slightly better off, who lived higher up the hill, above him.

The main landmarks around Erwin's block were an over-priced grocery store and two gin mills, Dave's Long Bar and Wolf's Bar. Both places were known in the neighborhood as notorious "buckets of blood." That's an expression the locals use to describe the kind of establishment where, when somebody is knifed or otherwise badly hurt or killed in a brawl, the total response from the proprietors is to drag the carcass out to the sidewalk, far enough away so that it no longer represents a potential threat to their liquor license.

The street is barren of any trees and is actually devoid of any features even remotely pleasing to the eye. The predominant color of the area is dirty gray, except for the sloppy splashes of more brightly colored garbage piled in and around the woefully inadequate trashcans that partially blockade the sidewalk at intervals of about fifty feet.

The narrow alleyways to either side of Erwin's building were used as convenient receptacles for the tremendous overflow of garbage. That wasn't too bad in the winter, when the cold kept the wet refuse at least partially iced, but in the hot days of summer, Hawthorne Avenue stank and served effectively as a great breeding ground for huge swarms of flies and mosquitoes.

Sitting on the building stoops, too shabby and down-and-out even for the greasy corner bars, were the semiconscious winos who frightened the smaller children, but who took the brunt of the ruthless mischief and the petty assaults of the older kids. Hawthorne Avenue was the pits, a fitting rival for Dacca or Calcutta, near the top of the list of obscenely unfit places for people to live.

In the backyards of the buildings, it was a different world. Not good, but better. The predominant feature back there was the clotheslines, hung heavily with long rows of multicolored laundry that flapped in the breeze over the brown dirt of the yards. There were no gardens, but at least the weeds added an aspect of green that was alien to the street side of the buildings.

For years the huge courtyard formed by the square block of laundry-filled backyards measured the limits of young Erwin's world. His apartment was on the second floor of a four-story wooden tenement building that only recently has fulfilled its obvious destiny and burned down. There was a rickety, termite-rotted old stairway that led directly from the apartment kitchen down into the yard, and Erwin and the cousins who lived with him would spend their afternoons playing on the concrete landing at the foot of the steps.

Erwin was just a couple of years old when his father abandoned their home. The man was a characterless drunk, not mean, but weak, and he had left home rather than endure the wretched difficulties of trying to raise a family out of a dead-end existence.

So Erwin was brought up by his mother and grandmother. Both were from that rare breed of tireless ghetto women who managed, through a heroic combination of tenacity and impossibly hard work, to provide their children with an opportunity to escape the inevitability of their inherited station in life.

They were intensely religious, in the way that now only the very poor and oppressed can be religious—strictly, fundamentally, and unquestioningly. They were also stern disciplinarians, totally committed to protecting Erwin from the mean streets of Newark.

For as long as the family lived on Hawthorne Avenue, on the fringes of civilization, Erwin was told to come directly home from school. Usually one of the women would be waiting out in front of the house. They were there to escort the child past the leering, drunken zombies who cluttered the stoops, and both ladies were ready to lash bravely out at any wino who bothered or threatened to bother Erwin or the other children.

Even when he was playing in the relative safety of the yard, Erwin and his cousins were watched over carefully by either his mother or grandmother. There was a kitchen window overlooking the yard, and the women frequently checked to make sure the kids didn't stray. They were permitted only as far as the abandoned factory behind their building. It had once manufactured paint, and the children passed most of the time playing in a little shed behind that main building. It was their "fort," filled with tall stacks of entertainingly empty former paint cans.

Eleven people lived in Ponders' five-room apartment. Besides Erwin, his mom, and his grandmother, there were Elese, his retarded sister; two uncles, George and Jimmy; and five cousins, Adrienne, Laschelle, Dorothy, Andy, and James. Uncle George had once been a barber, Uncle Jimmy an occasional painter of signs, but neither man made any regular or continuing contribution to the operating expenses of the house. Like the children, the friendly, harmless old men were also dependents, supported by the sweat of the women.

Aside from the cleaning and feeding of her own

family, Grandma worked as a domestic for rich people on the other side of the city. Erwin's mother also worked constantly during the day as the head of the household, then, at night, as a nurse's aide at Beth Israel Medical Center, a large complex located up at the top of the Hawthorne Avenue hill.

Each evening after putting all the kids to bed, she would make the long, grueling walk up the hill to the hospital. She always dressed up for work in the baggy black-cotton dress she'd purchased at the discount store. It was shiny from repeated ironings. She had a matching pillbox hat, made of cardboard, and her nylon stockings were rolled up over her calves so they wouldn't fall down.

Mrs. Ponder could have taken the Hawthorne Avenue bus, but she never wanted to spend money on herself. So all year long, regardless of the weather, she made that walk up the hill. When she walked, her shoulders sagged in the way they do when somebody has become prematurely old from too much hard work too soon.

"It just seemed to me," Erwin remembers, "that Mom was always working. In all the time we lived on Hawthorne Avenue, I can't remember her actually sitting down to eat the dinner she'd made for the rest of us, and I can't remember being awake when my mother was asleep." He shakes his head, as if only just able fully to comprehend the magnitude of her contribution. "She did it for us . . . she pulled us through that shit by herself."

There were neither enough bedrooms nor beds for the eleven of them. Everybody doubled or tripled up. Uncle Jimmy and his sons, Andy and James, all slept on a big bed that took up most of the tiny room set aside for them. Grandma slept on a folding bed in the alcove with Elese, who was never permitted to leave the apartment because of her affliction and vulnerability. Uncle George, who was out most nights, used their bed during the daytime. Cousins Adrienne, Dorothy, and Laschelle all slept together in the same room where Erwin shared a bed with his mother. Eleven people, four beds, one bathroom.

The miraculous thing about the unbelievably crowded condition of the apartment was that Mama and Grandma always contrived to keep the place clean. It may have been dilapidated, but it was also spotless. The filth of Hawthorne Avenue was not permitted inside the Ponder home.

Despite the protectiveness of his mother and grandmother—and perhaps, at least, partially because of it—Erwin's early years in school and on the street were almost impossibly difficult. He looked like a pansy, and because of that he was cruelly victimized by some of the older kids. He was smaller than most kids his age, and he looked different from them. For instance, the fashion for boys in those pre-Afro days was closely cropped hair. Because they thought it was prettier, the ladies had styled Erwin's hair long and straightened. They also dressed him in cute Buster Brown shorts.

That fashion, combined with his fair skin and unusually full pink lips, caused him to bear the brunt of every teenage bully's unreasoned passion "to punch out the little faggot."

So he fought them, because the chubby eight-year-old, in his sissy short pants, had spunk. Sometimes his antagonists were several years older than he was, and he usually lost, but he never ran away. Head bent, ramlike, arms flailing ineffectually about, Erwin would hopelessly charge the bigger boy, only to be knocked down and laughed at some more.

Finally, when he was almost nine years old, his mother tired of the hysteria of watching him stagger home with blood on his shirt. Mrs. Ponder decided two things. First, they would have to move out of this godawful neighborhood, because no matter how hard she tried, there was no way to insulate her children from its dangers. Second, she would do something she had thought she'd never do again. Mrs. Ponder decided to get married.

She had met a gentle and adoring man named William Thomas during her work at the medical center. He had been involved in a terrible hit-and-run automobile accident four years earlier, in 1958. The tragic accident had cost him both legs, so he had been resolutely undergoing continuing rehabilitation at Beth Israel. Confined to a wheelchair, Mr. Thomas could never pay the Ponder family a visit, because their second-floor walkup apartment was frustratingly inaccessible to him. So Mrs. Ponder, the nurse's aide, and Mr. Thomas, the patient, had conducted most of their friendly courtship on the grounds of the medical center.

When they were married, they applied for and were finally granted public housing. Shortly afterward, the family moved into the Dayton Street projects, about a mile from Hawthorne Avenue.

Like most of Newark's public housing, Dayton Street was a vertical ghetto. Still in the heart of the South Ward, still a slum by objective criteria, it was at least elevator-equipped. The complex consisted of nine eight-story buildings arranged in a semicircle and facing a large central courtyard. Whatever its intended purpose, the courtyard had become a collecting place for scattered broken glass and the abandoned hulks of cannibalized automobiles by the time Erwin and his family moved in there. Still, it was a significant step up from the total desperation of Hawthorne Avenue.

There were three small bedrooms in the new apartment, and certainly not enough room for all twelve of them. So the structure of the Ponders' extended family began to change when they made the move into city housing. First off, uncles George and Jimmy and cousins Adrienne and James moved out to find a place of their own. Then Grandma left. She went back home to Pittsburgh to live with an older sister who needed her more than her now happily married daughter.

Dayton Street was junkie heaven. Unlike the old winos laid out along Hawthorne Avenue, the street people around the projects were younger and more heavily into dope. They were also tougher, more violent, and more wantonly reckless than the pitiful old drunks had been. The junkies weren't panhandlers; they were predators, not asking, taking.

For a funny-looking, short, fat kid, it became a matter of survival. His grandmother had gone, and his mom, now married to Bill Thomas, didn't have as much time to supervise her son's life as closely as she had previously done. In any case, she couldn't have been with Erwin everywhere he went, and he wouldn't have wanted her to be anyway. He was getting older and more independent, and in the projects the maturing process is condensed and accelerated. Humanity and the harsh realities of urban life are more concentrated there.

For three grim years Erwin took his lumps. Not admitting it to his mother and stepfather, he finally came to the inescapable conclusion that if he was to survive his own adolescence, he needed help. Help was a street gang called the Aztecs.

At the time, the Aztecs were the dominant force in the South Ward. With about 150 members, ranging in age from ten to twenty, they were a society within a society. The older and stronger kids provided the muscle, advice, and protection in exchange for the adoration and loyalty of those less able to take care of themselves. That was Erwin at first, but as he got older and bigger, he became more self-confident and more hostile to people outside the clique.

When he first joined the Aztecs, Erwin went through a period of probation. One of his tests was to steal some fruit from the freight yard behind the A&P.

He met Tommy and Merrick, two other Aztec rookies, at about six o'clock in front of the store. It was a summer Sunday, and the supermarket was barred and shuttered in a way that is typical in slum neighborhoods. Erwin was scared.

"Hey, man . . . I don't want to go back there," he confessed to the others as he looked cautiously around the corner of the building, trying to spot the freight-yard guard.

"C'mon, Erwin . . . we got to!" complained Merrick, fidgetingly standing behind him. Merrick was a lot more nervous about going back to the Aztecs empty-handed than he was about the possibility of their being discovered by the guard.

"Whatta ya see?" demanded Tommy. He didn't like just standing there out in front of the store, visible to the street.

"Well . . ." Erwin hesitated. "I don't see nobody," he finally admitted.

"Then c'mon!" ordered Tommy, as he stepped boldly out from behind the wall and began running for the freight cars parked about one hundred yards away. Merrick followed quickly behind him. Erwin took a deep breath, then trotted after them, bringing up the rear.

The yard had been raided that morning by some of the older guys, so the padlock on the door of the fruit car had already been forced open. When the three novices got alongside it, there was a brief argument over who would be the first to climb inside. Much to his dismay, and only over his stenuous objections, Erwin was selected by a hurried vote of two to one.

"I ain't goin' in there—no way."

"Get your ass in there, Erwin!"

"Oh, shit," he replied finally, reluctantly climbing on a crate and into the car, because at that point it was easier to go in that it would have been to punk out.

He'd been inside for only about thirty seconds when his redoubtable colleagues began getting squeamish.

"Hey, Erwin . . . what's goin' on in there?"

"Fruit, man!" he answered, now swaggeringly, as he pried open one crate after another, finding a gold mine of cantaloupe and watermelon. "Lots of fruit."

The three young perpetrators of the great train robbery spent the next five minutes sampling their spoils, oblivious to the possibility of being spotted. It was only after a watermelon-seed-spitting contest that they decided it was time to make good their getaway. Which, coincidentally, is when they were spotted by the slumberous guard, who'd been spending his afternoon dozing in the shade under another freight car.

"Halt!" he called out halfheartedly as he rambled after them.

"Halt, shit," Erwin took time to reply as he and his friends, even burdened by the watermelons they were carrying, easily outdistanced the huffing, puffing, still not very interested watchman.

With his success in the "Great Watermelon Raid" and similar escapades, Erwin's standing with his Aztec brothers grew impressively. The growth of his reputation, not surprisingly, also closely paralleled the growth of his body. He wasn't a little pansy anymore. He shed the baby fat, cut the long, straightened hair, and burned all his short pants. He quickly became one of the antagonistic and openly hostile ghetto punks who so shock and outrage outsiders with their belligerent "don't-mess-with-me" attitude.

By the time he was fourteen years old, Erwin had almost completed the downward spiral of a kid headed nowhere. Spending more and more time on the streets, passing the day with the petty thievery and casual violence that characterize the South Ward, he had become a school dropout by the time he reached the eighth grade. School had become irrelevant to him. Erwin had already decided on what he wanted to do when he grew up. He was going to become a pimp.

On Saturday mornings Erwin would make a special effort to get up early. By eight-thirty he was up and out, sitting on one of the broken benches in front of the projects. He was waiting for his hero, Brother Rob. Robert was the resident pimp of Dayton Street, and he was usually getting in at about the same time Erwin was getting out.

The fourteen-year-old would watch the Cadillac gliding smoothly up the long driveway into the project parking lot. It was, Erwin thought at the time, a beautiful car. Long, shiny, it had the full complement of gaudy accessories that are de rigueur in pimpdom. The whitewalls were wide, the mud flaps had reflectors on them, everything possible had been chromed, and the interior of the fire-engine-red coupé was done up in white rabbit.

"That Caddy gleamed like a gold tooth," Erwin remembers.

Robert dressed to match his car. He was tall, about six-foot-two, and he looked even taller because he was skinny and always wore a wide-brimmed hat flamboyantly topped with a dyed ostrich plume. To Erwin, Robert was a black macho prince, the epitome of polish and good taste.

One Saturday morning in May, near the end of what should have been Erwin's eighth-grade year in the Dayton Street Junior High School, he watched the familiar red Caddy pulling up in front of the projects. Instead of its usual glidingly elegant entrance, however, the big coupé came rushing into the parking lot. At the last possible moment, Rob slammed on the brakes and brought the car to a swerving, screeching stop, narrowly missing some small children playing hopscotch.

Erwin held his breath as the kids scattered, then speechlessly watched as Rob kicked open his door, scrambled around to the other side of the car, and tore open the door on the passenger side. He roughly pulled the woman who'd been sitting there out of the car, straightened her up, then punched her in the face.

"You whore!" the pimp screamed at the fallen girl, whose nose was bleeding. "You ever hold out on me again, I'll kill your ass!"

"I wasn't holding out, Robby," she protested pitifully. She was young, not much older than Erwin, and she was wearing a flimsy red-silk dress that matched Rob's Cadillac and that was now up around her backside. "I was gonna give you all the money, honey . . . I swear I was!"

"Don't give me that 'honey' shit," he muttered contemptuously. Then he kicked her. "Now, get your ass inside, bitch!"

The girl scrambled to her feet and started running into the building that Rob lived in. On her way, she ran, frightened and whimpering, her nose still bleeding, past Erwin's bench.

He didn't say a word. Erwin just watched Rob get back into his car and park it in his assigned spot in the

lot. He drove the Caddy carefully now, overly so, as if
apologizing to it for the uncharacteristically rough way
he had driven it earlier.

As the pimp walked toward Erwin's bench, the
fourteen-year-old shyly waved at him, afraid that Rob
was still in a fury.

"Hey! What's happenin', Earl?" Rob asked. The
pimp never got Erwin's name right.

"Not too much, Brother Rob. . . . Not too
much," Erwin repeated nervously.

"How's school, little brother?" Rob was smiling, as
if nothing unusual had happened.

"I ain't goin' to school no more," Erwin said
proudly.

"What chu mean you ain't going to school?" answered Rob, sincerely annoyed. "Then what chu gonna
do for a livin'?"

"I wanna be just like you, Rob."

"Like me, shit," the pimp retorted. "You don't
wanna be like me no way, little brother. You get your
ass back in school."

With that, Rob walked into the building. Although
he saw Erwin many times after that, he never spoke
with the fourteen-year-old again.

In keeping with the unwritten but widespread policy of educational expediency, Erwin was promoted out
of the eighth grade even though he had effectively
dropped out. He was too young to quit school and too
old to be left behind.

He personified the failure of inner-city school sys-
tems throughout the nation. At the age of fourteen, his
achievement scores in reading, math, and English com-
prehension all fell around second- and third-grade levels. He had always been an inattentive student, but his
performance the previous year in the eighth grade had
been disastrous.

Desperate with the feeling that she had lost control
and that Erwin would never make it through his first
year of high school, his mother (now Mrs. Thomas)
found out about a special remedial program from the
guidance counselor at Dayton Street School. Called High

School Head Start, it was a six-week summer program designed to supplement the dreary, haphazard, and inadequate grad-school educations that had been received by ghetto youngsters about to enter high school.

The program was run by Dr. Albert Reiners for students who were the lost causes, the failures of the failing system, students like Erwin.

After contacting Dr. Reiners, Mrs. Thomas managed, after a considerable struggle, to convince her very unhappy son that he had to attend summer school.

Because the program funding was limited, Dr. Reiners had inexpensively rented space in the old Queen of Angels School on Belmont Avenue, not far from the projects in the South Ward. At least a century old, the ancient parochial school was dilapidated, incurably obsolete, and on this first scorching day of summer classes, not air-conditioned.

As he would do every year, Dr. Reiners began the six week session with an assembly of students and teachers. It was held in the stuffy gymnasium, the only room in the building large enough to hold them all. Once the chattering died down, and everyone had been seated in the shaky, graffiti-scarred, movable bleachers, the professor began his speech.

He told the children to have confidence in themselves and their teachers. Forget about past school performance, he urged, and concentrate on this new opportunity. This school is different, he said. Here, all we care about is you kids making it.

Erwin was late to the first day of classes and walked into the gymnasium in the middle of Dr. Reiners' address.

"Hello, son. Come in. I'm Dr. Reiners," the professor greeted Erwin as the fouteen-year-old sauntered noisily and disdainfully into the gym.

"That's good . . ." Erwin's reply brought embarrassed amusement to the students who had arrived before him, and suppressed groans of "problem child" from the assembled faculty. Erwin continued, "What do you want, a medal?"

Dr. Reiners smiled patiently, waited for the quiet

chuckles to dry up, then explained how he just wanted to know Erwin's name.

Reluctant to compromise his dramatic entrance, Erwin ignored the professor's entreaty and sat down next to the only familiar person in the room, Leroy Wilson.

"You're Deke, ain't chu?" Erwin asked. Leroy was called that because his father had once been a deacon in the church.

"Yeah . . . and you're Itch." (The origin of Erwin's nickname is unknown.)

"That's me." Erwin smiled, pleased that the guys around the neighborhood knew his street name. He and Leroy had seen each other around, but had never really met before today.

Ostentatiously ignoring what was officially going on, they consoled each other on the mutual misfortune of enforced summer school.

"This summer's gonna be a drag," Deke lamented as he looked around the hot, crowded gymnasium.

"You said it, brother . . . you said it," Itch replied.

The basic problem with trying to save "lost causes" is that they're sometimes too far gone even for remedial action. Dr. Reiners knew that he had taken on a tough job trying to educate the victims of years of educational incompetence, lack of facilities, and administrative neglect. Absolutely the last thing he or the program needed was a couple of sarcastic and disruptive wise guys.

At the end of that long, hot first day of school, Dr. Reiners called out to Erwin as he and Leroy were walking past his office.

"Hey, Itch! Can I talk to you for a minute?"

"How'd you know my nickname?" demanded Erwin, surprised and vaguely embarrassed at having a teacher speak so familiarly to him in front of Leroy.

"Your mother told me when she signed you up for this program," the professor explained, moving away from his office door and casually sitting down on top of his desk. "Now, can I talk to you for a second?"

"I guess so," Erwin answered as he walked into the office. Leroy followed him inside. "What you got to say?"

"Both you boys"—the professor looked first at one, then the other—"both you boys can use some help with your schoolwork. You know, and I know, that high school is not going to be easy. And I don't think either of you is going to make it past the ninth grade in South Side High unless you get some help."

He went on to explain to Erwin and Leroy that he understood how uncomfortable it was to go to summer school. How much he had disliked the idea of it when he was their age, but how much it could help a student who wanted to be helped.

"Well, that's my speech for today," he said as he stood up. "I'll see you both tomorrow."

"Not if we see you first," replied Erwin, laughing. He extended his hand to Leroy, who slapped him "five." Together they ran into the corridor and out of the building.

As they raced toward Dayton Street, Leroy asked Erwin if, perhaps, the teacher had been talking sensibly about their educational needs. "What does he know?" was the essence of Erwin's reply.

Throughout the first three weeks of the program, it was business as usual for Erwin. Viewing the program as merely an inconvenient interruption of his normal summer schedule, he was always either late to class or absent without leave. While Dr. Reiners never said so to the fourteen-year-old, he had become almost convinced that Erwin's hard-core hostility was impenetrable and that he would be one of the program's failures.

Despite Erwin's unacceptable attitude and conduct, however, his instructors remained relatively patient and up front with him, and gradually he began to see them, if not as friends, then at least not as enemies.

If there was a definite turning point, it came during his art class. The instructor was a young, hip black man named Gordon Mays. A father figure to most of the other boys, he was tolerable to Erwin.

Erwin began the class, as he usually did, segregating himself from the mainstream of classroom activity.

Bored, he began drawing on the black piece of paper in front of him. The instructor at one point walked over to him, attracted, no doubt, by his unusually quiet demeanor. Much to Mr. Mays' surprise, Erwin was actually doing quite well.

"You know something, my friend?" Gordon said, pointing to Erwin's sketch. "That ain't half bad."

With a lifetime of negative school experience behind him, Erwin was not easily convinced. "Go on . . ." he said, looking more closely at his own work, "you're jivin' me."

"No, I'm not. This shows me plenty." Gordon was going out of his way to assure the skeptical street kid, but the attention Erwin's work was receiving had by this time attracted the notice of the rest of the class. Erwin felt a rush of embarrassment.

"You know something?" he said defensively. "I don't even like doin' this crap." Erwin got roughly out of his chair, walked over to where Deke was sitting, and told him they'd get together after school. With that, he left for the day.

Later in the afternoon, after he'd been joined by Leroy, Erwin was asked by his friend what had made him so angry.

"Aw . . . that Oreo was puttin' me on."

But he wasn't, Leroy answered back, Mr. Mays had meant what he'd said about Erwin's drawing. He even told the class that it was pretty good.

It was legitimate praise, and Erwin didn't know how to deal with it. He put it out of his mind for the rest of the afternoon, but the next morning, he was on time for all his classes. All the teachers noticed it, but pretended not to.

During art class, Gordon Mays again walked over, looked at his work, and again told him that it wasn't half bad. This time Erwin was more willing to believe him.

"You mean that?"

"Of course I mean it," Gordon answered, gesturing to the new day's sketch, a roughly drawn but still gracious swan. "And you know something else?"

"What?"

"You could be good at a whole lot of things if you tried."

Erwin figured immediately that the teacher was giving him a lecture.

"You talkin' about school things?" he said, angrily resuming the old mask of belligerence and hostility.

"My friend, I'm talkin' about life. . . ." Mr. Mays sighed as he turned away. "Think about that, little brother."

Summer school became a catalyst for Erwin, setting off an evolutionary process in the tough guy. Buoyed by the sincere interest and helpfulness of the program staff, he began to mellow. They appreciated his work, so he started appreciating it.

As he became more involved with his classwork, his interest in rough-and-tumble street life began to decline. With the help of Gordon Mays and an English teacher named Vera Thompson, Erwin's basic academic skills were rapidly improving. He discovered also that he could find pleasure and gain a measure of self-respect in reading, painting, and other nonviolent activities. But summer was ending.

One of the favorite neighborhood hangouts was Weequaic Park, not far from the Dayton Street projects. Late one afternoon, Erwin, Leroy, and about two dozen other guys, most of them members of the Aztecs, were there. They were just sitting around talking, or skipping rocks across the surface of the park pond. It was the day before the summer program was to close, and the subject was on Erwin's mind. He admitted privately to Leroy that he had been mistaken about it and that the school hadn't turned out as badly as he had thought it would. He even suggested that he was going to miss it.

"Miss it? Wow!" said Leroy, shaking his head and laughing. It was a heretical thought, given Erwin's historical opposition to school.

"But this one's different," Erwin quickly explained. "They really care about where you're comin' from."

Embarrassed by his own change of mind, Erwin

abruptly changed the subject, suggesting that he and Leroy take a walk. Eventually, however, the subject turned again to school. What was really bothering Erwin was that September meant the beginning of high school, and for both boys that meant South Side High.

Grade school for kids from the inner city is bad enough. Facilities are substandard, teaching staffs inadequate, and buildings too often hugely overcrowded. But ghetto high schools, particularly in a place like Newark, are a much more intense experience. It's impossible to maintain a scholarly and detached atmosphere, because the realities of the streets don't stop at the schoolhouse door.

South Side High in the middle 1960's reflected the community it purported to serve. Filled with children who, by necessity and experience, had become adults before they were out of their mid-teens, it was equipped with the least and worst of whatever was available. Since drug addiction raged unchecked in the South Ward, it ran rampant in the high school, and since violence was a way of life on the street, it also echoed through the corridors of South Side.

The high school was built in 1913, and although it's been condemned by the city's buildings department since 1957, it's still open. South Side is a three-story brick building that occupies an entire square block right in the heart of the South Ward. Built to hold a thousand students, it has an average enrollment of nearly twice that. Typically, only about half the entering freshmen end up graduating. Of them, twenty percent go on to college, but only a handful of that lucky group stick with it and earn a college degree—perhaps fifty of the original two thousand.

"You know what I'm bothered about, Deke?" Erwin asked as he and Leroy walked away from the others in the park.

"What's that?"

"South Side's gonna be a whole lot different than summer school."

In most high schools, the role of the instructors is to teach. In South Side, the primary job is trying to maintain order. It's a holding action from the beginning bell of the classroom period until the ending bell, signifying a shift of policing responsibility to the next teacher in the next class.

For the students, the most enjoyable diversion is making the hapless instructor's life as miserable as possible. It's chaos, but in the midst of it there are students trying conscientiously to learn.

They are heroes. Erwin wasn't one of them.

Back in an environment where disorder was the norm, he reverted to the old style. He'd been in school less than a week when he was suspended for the first of what would be three times during his freshman year. Not surprisingly, it was for fighting.

He was sitting with some friends in the school cafeteria. It was in the basement, a roughly finished mammoth room, dimly lit and filled with long tables and benches. The cavernous lunchroom doubled as a "study hall," where students were assigned when they had no classes scheduled during a particular period. Erwin had been sketching and talking to the kids around him when an older student came up to him.

"Ain't you Erwin Ponder?" It sounded both like an insult and a challenge.

"Who wants to know?" answered Erwin, never easily intimidated.

"George, from Hawthorne Avenue . . . that's who." He was bigger than Erwin, and he had clearly come over to start a fight. "And I knew you when you was nothing but a little faggot."

With that, George snatched up some change that was on the table in front of Erwin.

"Give me back that money!" Erwin yelled, knocking over the bench he was sitting on, as he got abruptly to his feet and grabbed for George's hand.

The kids who'd been sitting around him had already moved several feet away, and a large crowd was gathering in anticipation of the fight.

When Erwin reached out for his money, George dodged him and grabbed Erwin's backside.

"Sure, sweetie!" he said derisively.

That was it. There was no longer any way Erwin could salvage his honor without fighting. He tackled George and brought him to the floor. Ignoring the bigger guy's punches, Erwin got one hand on George's throat and started punching him in the face with the other.

In ghetto schools, instructors are often hired not so much for their academic backgrounds as for their physical prowess. The two men who supervised the study hall were hulking giants. Attracted by the roars of the crowd, who'd been urging either Erwin or George on to victory, the teachers ran over and, as roughly as possible, pried the two boys apart.

"Both your asses are getting thrown out of school!" one of the teachers warned as Erwin and George went at each other again, after having been pulled apart.

When calm was finally restored after several minutes, and both boys were being escorted to the principal's office, all Erwin could think of was his mother finding out that he'd been suspended.

"My Mom's gonna kill me!" Dealing with the fight was easy, and Erwin was used to it. Disappointing his mother was a much more serious matter.

The principal suspended both of them on the spot, telling the boys not to come back unless and until they brought their parents with them. George couldn't have cared less; he didn't live with his parents, and in any case, was looking for an excuse to leave school. He decided to join the military.

For Erwin, however, it was a catastrophe. After the principal's announcement, he went wandering in Weequaic Park. He stayed there all day and didn't go to his apartment until late in the afternoon, timing it so it would look like he was just getting home from school.

For the next three days he didn't tell his mother what had happened. Every morning he would dress for school and leave at the usual time, then stay away until late afternoon. She found out about the suspension only when a truant officer came to the projects to question her about Erwin's behavior.

Mrs. Thomas didn't yell at Erwin. That would have let him off far too easily. Instead, she cried and let her almost-fifteen-year-old son know how terribly he had hurt her. Erwin stammered around, awkward and defenseless; then, finally, out of desperation, to stop her crying, he agreed to apologize to whomever he had to apologize to, and go back to school if they'd take him— a resolution that lasted until the end of the first quarter's grading period.

Early one evening, after receiving Erwin's first report card, his mother and stepfather spoke to him as he walked into the apartment.

Although Bill Thomas had come into his life relatively recently, Erwin had tremendous respect for his mother's husband. Despite his handicap, Mr. Thomas always tried hard to be independent and productive, and loved his new family. Even when Erwin strayed miserably, his stepfather never lost confidence that his son would turn out all right.

To Erwin, his father "is a loving and beautiful man. Even after everyone else lost faith in me, he kept his. He always knew I could do it, and that made *me* feel like I could do it. No matter what, he was always in my corner."

This evening was no exception.

Mr. Thomas spoke to him first, telling Erwin that his mother and he were very concerned about his schoolwork. Erwin's grades, his stepfather explained as gently as he could, were terrible. It looked, he continued, as if Erwin were going to fail everything.

At first Erwin reacted bitterly. "You don't understand. . . . I can't learn nothin' in a place like that." As he said that, he turned to go into the bedroom. He was stopped in mid-stride when his mother called out his name "Erwin!"

Mrs. Thomas was generally a hard-working, softspoken woman who suffered in silence. Unless she got very angry. On those rare occasions, she could not be denied, and when she used that strong tone of voice, Erwin knew it was an inflexible order. In this case, to turn around and come back into the living room.

He hesitated for a second, but then, realizing that he had no choice, Erwin turned around and walked sheepishly back into the living room. Exaggerating how depressed he was at the world's lack of understanding of him, he flopped onto the couch next to his mother, heaving a deep sigh in the process. His father wheeled over next to them.

"Son," the older man started, "you have to get an education—that is, unless you want to be shining shoes your whole life," he added matter-of-factly, alluding to Erwin's weekend job shining shoes outside the Port Authority Bus Terminal.

"Shoeshine boy," his mother echoed, to emphasize how serious the situation was. But Erwin pretended not to hear. Although he had abandoned pimping as a chosen career after getting the cold shoulder from Brother Rob, he was still confident that somehow things would turn out all right.

"If you think you're so good," his father finally exploded out of exasperation, "why don't you do somethin' to prove it?"

It was the kind of challenge that was calculated to have a dramatic effect on a proud kid like Erwin. For the first time, he looked up and started listening.

His mother suggested a transfer to another school, if it could be arranged. Erwin was skeptical, but he was also curious, wondering if some positive action was possible. His mother, heartened that he was showing at least some interest, suggested Arts High School.

"Aw . . . that's a fag school," he complained.

"Erwin!" His fundamentalist mother was shocked. "Don't be talkin' that way!"

His father, accustomed to street language, responded more pragmatically. "Didn't you tell us once how much you enjoyed paintin' and writin' poems and such . . . when you were at the summer school?"

"Yeah, but that was different."

"What's the matter?" His father knew how to motivate him. "You afraid they're gonna call you names or somethin'?"

Finally, to get his father off his back, Erwin told his parents that he'd accept the transfer if it could be arranged, which he doubted. That reassured his mother, because she had already decided to inquire about a possible transfer to Arts High. She was certain she had heard encouraging things about the school. It wasn't supposed to be great, just better than South Side.

During the time the transfer application was being processed, Erwin was back at South Side. It really was the kind of blackboard jungle they used to talk about in the 1950's. The "in" drug was heroin. Most of the kids didn't shoot it, however; they snorted it. Heroin is just as addictive that way, but it can be taken without all the bulky apparatus needed by mainliners.

Taken by snorting, heroin often causes a running nose and vomiting, especially among the inexperienced. By late afternoon, the boys' rooms at the high school stank of puke, and the attendance rate in classes fell disastrously.

If the school was tough on boys like Erwin, it was worse for the girls. Few remained maidens much past their fourteenth birthday, and one of the most common offenses leading to suspension was to be caught making love in the auditorium balcony or in the basement corridors.

Those were the days before the pill, and a girl having to leave school because of pregnancy was an almost daily occurrence. Unlike the situation in a more bourgeois area, however, there were very few shotgun weddings, and the girl would be back in school shortly after the baby was born. The child would have been either put up for adoption or incorporated into the family of the girl-mother. So many girls became pregnant that there was little social stigma attached to it.

According to Erwin, "going to school was just something kids did to keep their parents and the law off their backs. Nobody got uptight if a girl got knocked up or if some kid became a junkie. It happened on the street every day. There was no big difference if it happened inside the school; it was all the same place."

Before the Christmas holidays, Erwin and his family received word that his requested transfer to Arts High had been approved. For the fifteen-year-old, it was a time for decision-making and change. He and Leroy had already signed up for a second summer in the Head Start program, and he was looking forward to going to a new school in the fall. He was sure, though, that he wouldn't have a chance of success unless he changed a whole lot of things about his life.

The thing that needed the most immediate attention was his membership in the Aztecs. The group's predilection for petty larceny and adolescent extortion just didn't fit into his parents' hopes and his own plans for a personal renaissance.

Erwin's resignation from the street gang was probably the most classically heroic act of his early life. If anything, leaving a gang is more fraught with potential danger and uncertainty than joining one. No irrevocable contract is signed, no blood oath sworn to, but the unspoken understanding is, "Once an Aztec, always an Aztec."

There are, of course, legitimate and generally accepted reasons for leaving. If a member moves out of the neighborhood or gets too old or marries, he is usually elevated to an emeritus position. But what is unacceptable and virtually without precedent is to resign voluntarily, simply as a matter of personal preference.

Erwin chose a day in early spring to break the news. It was a sunny day, about a dozen Aztecs were hanging out, as they usually did, in the playground in the middle of the projects.

Erwin called out to the leader, motioning for him to come over where Erwin could speak with him for a minute privately.

"Yeah, Itch . . . " the older kid answered threateningly as he squared off with Erwin. "I been meanin' to talk to you, anyway."

"What about?"

"What's this we hear about you changin' schools

and all?" He was standing so close to Erwin now that the fifteen-year-old could smell the booze on his breath. "You tryin' to be some kind of sissy-ass artist or something?"

By this time Erwin had grown into a well-proportioned semi-man who could take care of himself if he had to. He called the bluff. "I don't know about that . . . but I'll tell you, I'm leavin' I'm leavin' South Side, and I'm leavin' the Aztecs." He said it coldly, like it didn't make a damn bit of difference to him if it meant he had to fight.

"You're what!" The leader wasn't used to having his authority questioned.

"You heard me." The fifteen-year-old's eyes were locked solidly on the now flinching leader's. It was as if Erwin were growing and the other guy shrinking. "Take it easy, man," Erwin finally said. He was smiling as he turned to walk away. "I got to get to school."

During his second summer in the Head Start program, Erwin did exceptionally well. He consistently surprised both his instructors and his fellow students with his dramatic change in attitude and priorities. He worked hard, went on all the school outings, and just generally found out things about himself. As he says now, "I really liked what I found."

"He was a new man," says Dr. Reiners proudly. "The low image of himself that Erwin brought to the program was completely gone." The mask of hostility and belligerence was disappearing.

One of his most creative outlets was the school newspaper. Erwin was a frequent contributor of articles and poems, at last having a place where he could tell people how he felt about things. Many of his works were on the beauty and bitterness of life in the South Ward.

One poem, "Reveal Unto Me," asks for " . . . a word of harmony. A world where the races have no conflict. A world where black people are proud of being black, and where an atmosphere of unity exists among all brothers."

The most important field trip during the summer

session was the annual picnic. It was held on the green suburban campus of Seton Hall University, about ten miles from downtown Newark. The setting of the picnic was designed to broaden the horizons of the students and let them know that even college was an accessible goal.

After lunch, Erwin and Leroy walked away from the main picnic area and started touring the campus.

"You know something, Deke?" Erwin said to his friend.

"What's that?"

"I dig this place . . . college, I mean."

"So?"

"So I'm gonna try to go to college!"

"Shit, Erwin. You ain't even halfway through high school."

Erwin's sophomore year, his first in Arts High, went very well. He was strongly motivated for the first time in his life, and his grades and conduct were better than even his parents' most optimistic hopes. In addition to doing well in his classwork, he also discovered other positive aspects of school life. Using the time he had previously squandered on the streets, Erwin tried out for and became one of the stars of the high school's basketball and track teams. He continued his writing, as well, and became one of the editors of the literary magazine. As his first year in the new school was ending, Erwin's announced intention of going on to college was sounding increasingly less improbable.

His third summer in the Head Start program began in a flourish of optimism, but then almost ended in tragedy.

On one of those suffocatingly hot nights in the South Ward, a black taxi driver named John W. Smith was arrested for tailgating a police car. The police car stopped, the two officers walked back to Smith's cab, took him roughly out, and allegedy smacked him around.

The street population on a summer night in a place like the South Ward is always vastly larger than it is at any other time. There are no air-conditioners, and the heavy, humid air lies oppressively on the tenement buildings. Seeking at least a little relief, everybody is on the streets late into the night. Fire hydrants are commandeered for use as cooling fountains, and whole families eat dinners, drink, socialize, and listen to music sitting outside their buildings.

When the two cops grabbed Smith, a large crowd quickly coalesced. Some of them had seen how the man was treated and were angry. Most, however, had nothing else to do and were angry only at being so poor and so wretchedly uncomfortable.

One kid turned a hydrant on the police car, while others started throwing cans and bottles at the officers. The crowd was closing its ring around the police car when the cops hurried inside and drove their prisoner away.

Smith was taken to the Fourth Precinct, but on the way, according to the word on the street, he was worked over again. The crowd swelled even more as it followed the police car, and by the time it reached the precinct, had become a near-mob, seething and ready for trouble.

Outside the precinct, ad-hoc community leaders began denouncing the violent arrogance of the Newark Police Department. Release John Smith, they demanded. For an hour they negotiated with the cops, but then the would-be leaders lost control of the younger, more impatient in the crowd. The kids started throwing pieces of slate torn up from the street at the building, and windows were broken.

Finally, the cops inside the police station, abundantly supported by cars converging on the Fourth Precinct from the rest of the city, charged into the crowd. It was the beginning of one of the bloodiest urban riots in the nation's history.

For the next several days, Newark was in flames, and the South Ward was ravaged by looting, arson, and death. City and state police, joined within twenty-four hours by National Guardsmen, battled roving gangs of young people armed with rocks, and later on, Molotov cocktails.

Eventually the soldiers and policemen began

shooting looters on sight. The death toll would reach forty-seven men, women, and children.

Dr. Reiners decided to keep the school open if possible. The program was only six weeks long, and any time lost would have been irretrievable; but there was another, more important reason. Most of his students weren't far removed from the rough-and-tumble street life, and he feared they'd get caught up in the violence if the school was closed.

Even with the classes that kept him off the street during the day, Erwin still had plenty of chances to get involved. Walking the few blocks between his apartment in the Dayton Street projects and the Queen of Angels School, he was roughly searched, sometimes two or three times each day, by National Guardsmen.

"Okay, boy. That's far enough!" the shorter of two guardsmen called out to him one afternoon as Erwin rounded a corner on his way home from school. Both of the men had their M-I rifles leveled at the sixteen-year-old's belly. He was carrying his books in his right hand, but didn't want to drop them because he was afraid the nervous citizen-soldiers would misinterpret the sudden move. So Erwin kept his tight grip on the books and raised his left hand.

"Drop the books, nigger!" the shorter man ordered. "Let's see what you got hidden in there."

"There's nothing in there!" protested Erwin, getting hot with resentment.

"You better do what he said, sonny," said the taller soldier, just as menacing, but slightly more polite.

Erwin had a sudden urge to break and run. His head darted around, looking for cover. There was none. It would have been impossible and foolish to try. Humiliated and afraid, he threw the books against the sidewalk.

"Here!" he said angrily. "See for yourself."

"Just back against that wall, sonny," the taller soldier ordered, as he and his partner kept their rifles trained on Erwin.

"Put your hands against the wall and spread your legs."

As Erwin started to move, the short man spoke again. "Try any smart stuff, and you're dead, nigger."

The tall one searched him. Finding nothing, he turned to the books, scattering papers randomly all over the street, until he was satisfied.

"Okay, he's clean," he said to his partner.

"They're never clean," joked the short one as he slung his rifle and started walking up the block. Laughing, the taller man stood, handed Erwin some of his books, then marched after his companion.

It still wasn't over.

That evening Erwin had dinner at the apartment of a friend named Myra Franklin. She and her family lived right across the "courtyard" in the projects. It had already been decided that Erwin would be staying the night, because it was nine-fifteen. The curfew was rigidly set at nine P.M., and the military had let it be known that they'd shoot anybody on the street on sight after that.

Myra and Erwin were looking out her living-room window, down at the incredible scene being acted out on Dayton Street. From that window they could see armored personnel carriers rumbling past burned-out police cars, trash fires, and acres of broken glass.

Helmeted policemen and soldiers, carrying rifles, were everywhere, and the air was filled with gunfire and the sirens of fire engines responding to one of the hundreds of emergencies.

They also saw an eight-year-old girl run out from one of the project's buildings. She ran about twenty feet out on the walkway that runs between the buildings, hesitated uncertainly, then continued her little dash to another building across the courtyard. Like Erwin, she'd stayed too late at a friend's house, but unlike him, she had decided to go home. The noises were frightening her, and she wanted to be with her mother.

As Myra and Erwin watched, the child was shot in the head. For several minutes she lay about midway between her building and her friend's. Finally a group of soldiers cautiously approached in combat formation. Rifles held at the ready, they crouched as they ran, always looking up at the building windows facing them.

When they discovered that their victim had been a child, the commanding officer quickly sent a runner for an ambulance. His men formed a circle, rifles facing outward, around her body.

Erwin never figured out if the soldiers thought they were protecting the little girl or themselves. In any case, she was already dead.

The next evening, he was watching the dreadful spectacle again, this time from his own window. It was past curfew, and a guardsman on the street saw Erwin's silhouette in the window. The sixteen-year-old saw him at the same instant, and ducked. A bullet whistled past Erwin's head, smashing into the living room wall behind him.

Despite the provocation, Erwin managed not to involve himself in the rioting. He had come too far to revert to lawlessness, so he watched with desperate sadness as the flames that tortured his neighborhood burned down and died out.

The grim weeks following the Newark riots passed, with the South Ward community too numb even to be outraged at its losses. Parts of the neighborhood looked like Dresden after the fire-bombing.

Most of the rest of the summer sessions were used discussing and writing about what had happened. Dr. Reiners continually urged his students to be positively involved in the profoundly difficult process of cleaning up and rebuilding their neighborhood, a task they all accepted.

Despite the terrible time leading up to it, Erwin's junior year at Arts High was even more successful than the first year had been. He finished with honors, and later, when he had completed his fourth and final semester in summer school, it was with the conviction that he'd definitely be going on to college.

"Hurry up, Erwin, or we'll be late."

The staff of the summer program staged a mini-graduation for their first-ever graduating class. The ceremony was held in the same stuffy gymnasium where the program had started four years ago.

"You have the invitation, Mama?"

"Yes, I do. Now, you get going, Erwin. Your father and I will meet you there."

They did. Arriving a few minutes before the ceremony began, Mr. Thomas was sitting up proudly in his wheelchair, his wife standing quietly, with the same feeling of pride, beside him.

Dr. Reiners was the principal speaker, as he had been four years before. He spoke to the twenty-five young men and women, and let them know how tremendously proud he was of his first graduating class and their remarkable accomplishments, achieved despite awesome odds. Four years before this, he reminded his class, most people would have thought that this day would never come. It was because of the students' dedication and hard work that the graduation had become a reality.

They had done very well, he told them again, but he urged them not to stop at this intermediate point. Finishing the program was only half success. "I want all of you to think about college. I know that Erwin Ponder, Leroy Wilson, and some of the others have applied to Seton Hall University. Well, they'll probably be accepted. All of you should think in those same terms. Don't stop now. Keep trying, and keep growing."

He paused for emphasis, looked straight at Erwin, and said jokingly, "If Erwin Ponder can win a college scholarship, then there is no telling what the rest of you can do!"

After the friendly laughter had quieted, Dr. Reiners asked Erwin if he would like to say a few words. Erwin hesitated, slightly awkward and embarrassed, but completely in the spirit of what was going on.

"I'd just like to thank you and the other instructors. You believed in us, and by doing that, you gave us a chance to believe in ourselves."

Everybody applauded, and most of the assembled mothers, including Erwin's, cried.

In his senior year at Penn State, John Cappelletti had his greatest football season. The All-America tailback gained more than 1,522 yards rushing and scored seventeen touchdowns. In December 1973 Big John and the rest of his family were the guests of honor at the Downtown Athletic Club's annual banquet, held in the grand ballroom of the Hilton Hotel in New York.

It had just been announced that John had won the club's coveted Heisman Trophy, symbolic of preeminence as the best college football player in the country.

The huge, gaudy ballroom was filled to capacity. After a battalion of waiters had noisily cleared away plates still littered with uninspired roast beef, almost four thousand happily chattering, semi-rowdy football fans and friends were drinking robust toasts to John's impressive achievements.

On the dais, he nervously sat through his long, praise-laden introduction, clearly more at home on the field than with the club's corps of Scotch-drinking armchair quarterbacks. He looked briefly toward his family's table for reassurance. They were all there—his mom and dad; his sister, Jean; and all three of his brothers, Martin, Michael, and Joey.

All were formally attired, Mr. Cappelletti feeling vaguely uncomfortable in his rented tuxedo. It was the first time he'd had to put one on since he and Mrs. Cappelletti had been married twenty-eight years before.

Eleven-year-old Joey was a surprise guest at the gala celebration. Youngest in the family, he had been very ill and bedridden up until this morning, when his mother had told him that John had won the award. Once he heard the good news, it was impossible to keep

Joey in bed. He had insisted on coming up to New York from their home, just outside of Philadelphia. If outward appearances were any indication, he was feeling fine.

Joey tugged excitedly on the sleeve of his father's tuxedo as the introduction finally ended and John stood to acknowledge the huge wave of applause that swept back and forth through the big room. It took two men to hand John the Heisman Trophy, a fifty-five-pound bronze statue of a football player. Then, after the pictures were taken and the official photographer had made his inevitable "one more for the West Coast" joke, it was time for John's acceptance speech.

He adjusted the microphone, cleared his throat, and started. He had prepared a formal speech, but at the last minute decided against using it.

There was still a noisy undercurrent of joking, rustling, and the small clatterings of empty dessert dishes coming from the hundreds of tables crowded into the ballroom, but it lasted only for the first few sentences of the speech. As soon as everyone realized the tone and content of what John was saying, the mood in the room changed abruptly to thoughtful silence.

"I'd like to dedicate this trophy to a lot of people I've been around, and especially to the youngest member of my family, Joseph, who is very ill."

As he mentioned his brother, John looked down at the family's table. All of them were sitting up proudly, conscious that as John looked at them, so did many of the people sitting around them. Joey tugged on his father's arm again as his big brother's eyes met and held his for a second. Then John turned away and continued, first thanking his parents; his coach, Joe Paterno; and his mates on the great 1973 Penn State team. Then he talked about Joey again.

"He has leukemia," John quietly explained. "And if I could dedicate this trophy to him tonight and give him a few days of happiness, it'd mean everything to him. For me, it's a battle only on the field and only in the fall. For Joseph, it's all year round." The mood in the audience was a mixture of sorrow, sympathy, and the empty, uncomfortable feeling we get when someone tells us something private and terrible.

"I think this trophy is more his than mine," John continued to his hushed audience, "because he's been such an inspiration to me."

By the time he had finished his acceptance speech, almost everyone in the suddenly sober room, including the jocks, was either teary-eyed or crying outright. John had trouble saying the last few words, which were almost whispered. "I'd just like to thank you for putting up with me tonight."

He turned toward his seat at the right of the podium and sat down heavily. There was a moment of eerie and almost absolute silence in the ballroom; then, like a thunderclap, the ovation broke and continued as the audience stood and shouted bravos and smiled through their tears.

Like the rest of the people in the ballroom, the other Cappellettis were standing and applauding. Joey was thrilled, but prudent. He asked his father for reassurance.

"You mean he gave the trophy to me?" he asked incredulously. "But that's his trophy. He won it."

Mr. Cappelletti put his rough, callused, construction-worker hands gently on his youngest son's shoulders.

"Your brother wants you to have it, Joseph."

Archbishop Fulton J. Sheen was the next speaker. He'd been scheduled to give the benediction, but if he had written one, he also abandoned the prepared text.

"For maybe the first time in your life"—the archbishop dramatically held out his arms as he spoke to the audience in his booming, intense voice—"you have heard a real speech from the heart and not from the lips. . . . Part of John's triumph was made possible by Joseph's inspiration. You don't need a blessing. God has already blessed you in John and his brother Joseph."

It had been scheduled as John's night, the culmination and greatest triumph of his college football career. He generously gave the night and the trophy to

Joey, who deserved both brotherly love and generous-
ity.

They say we all start dying the day we're born.
For Joey, it's more literally true than it is for most. In
his case, the process has been accelerated by leukemia
and encephalitis, a frequently fatal brain disease. The
encephalitis came first, following a bout with what
looked like just a sore throat and chickenpox.

When he was seven years old, he lived through the
first of dozens of major medical crises. The encephalitis
had temporarily blinded him; his head swelled to three
times its normal size and his temperature stayed around
106.

He was packed in an ice bath, while doctors struggled for an entire summer to save his life. When the
crisis was apparently over, they discovered he had leukemia.

On the advice of their family doctor, his parents
took Joey to Children's Hospital in Philadelphia, a
world-famous institution for the care and treatment of
pediatric cancer. With a large group of other children,
he began the long, painful treatment process. Five years
later, he was still going for the weekly visits. But of the
original group of thirty-nine boys and girls who began
the treatments with him, he was the only survivor.

"Have you ever been to Hawaii?" his friend Mark
asked him, immediately conjuring up dreamy images of
hula girls, palm trees, and impossibly blue water. He
and Joey were sitting, as they usually did, on the highly
polished floor of the bright white hospital corridor.
Waiting to go in themselves, they'd talk like this for
hours outside the treatment rooms. They were familiar
fixtures at the hospital, oblivious to and undisturbed by
the nurses and aides who hurried up and down carrying
trays of equipment or food for the patients. The boys
would almost always be talking about places they'd seen
or wanted to see.

"No, but I've been to Florida," Joey offered. A
year older than Mark, he was definitely more worldly.
". . . when John played there in the Orange Bowl."

Because the mortality rate was so nearly universal,

Joey never had the chance to make many friends among the other children in his treatment group. Nine-year-old Mark, also the hardy veteran of several years of visits to Children's Hospital, was an exception. He came from a poor family in Philadelphia, and like Joey, he was at the hospital every Monday morning, treatment day for the relentlessly shrinking group.

"Did you go to Disney World?" Mark asked, almost breathlessly waiting for Joey's reply.

"Yep," answered his friend casually.

"You did!" Excitedly, Mark demanded that Joey relate every detail of his trip.

When he was finished telling his story of the many splendors waiting in the Disney resort in Florida, Joey urged Mark to go and see it all for himself.

"Aw . . ." Mark hesitated, because he was embarrassed. Finally he confessed, "My folks could never afford to send me there."

When the day and the painful treatments were finished, Joey and Mark said good-bye. Riding back to their home in Upper Darby with his mother, Joey told her what he and his friend had talked about. Unlike her son, who at the time was ten years old, Mrs. Cappelletti knew that Mark was no longer keeping ahead of the disease. She had watched the conditions of dozens of others in the group deteriorate before, and by now she was an expert. She knew Mark was dying.

When Joey's father got home from work later in the afternoon, Mrs. Cappelletti told Joey to tell him about Mark.

After he had finished, Joey asked his father, "Can't we help him, Dad?"

Even with some help from his older children, Mr. Cappelletti's construction-worker salary and the family savings could barely keep pace with the incredible medical expenses incurred caring for Joey. Helping another child was a luxury far beyond their means.

"Maybe we could take up a collection!" Joey enthusiastically suggested. Mr. Cappelletti, whose first name is John, thought about it for a while.

"Maybe we could, at that."

Well known to many of the community groups around Upper Darby, Mr. and Mrs. Cappelletti were able to organize a Send Mark to Disney World campaign. They also made the first contribution, donating twenty-five dollars.

Mark visited his fantasy land shortly before he died in 1973.

With his friend gone, Joey's trips to the hospital became more grim and lonely. Because the most immediate danger from leukemia comes when rampaging white blood cells travel up the spine to the brain, painful spinal taps are part of his basic treatment.

When they wake up on Mondays, both he and his mother steel themselves against that inevitability. Then, for the next six or eight hours, Joey endures the pinching, prodding, and sticking necessary to keep the white-blood-cell count in his body at a manageable level.

His day is filled with severe physical pain. His mother's suffering is different. For her, the most painful thing is watching the new cases being registered at the hospital's admissions office. The parents and their children are so frightened—the kids put off by the awesome size and pace of the big hospital, their parents afraid of something more awful.

"When we get a new case in the hospital, I just shiver." Mrs. Cappelletti is a small, loving, considerate woman; because she has suffered through so much with Joey, the emotion that shows through most clearly is sadness. "By now I know what's ahead for them and what they have to go through."

Besides the pain, the disease itself and the powerful anti-cancer drugs have taken a terrible physical toll on Joey. Most of his hair has fallen out, and the twelve-year-old, embarrassed by that, almost always wears a woolen seaman's cap pulled down low over the back of his head. He's about average size for a kid his age, but his bones have been so weakened by the disease that his 118-pound frame droops from time to time.

"I'm not afraid of the hospital," Joey still says with bluster and bravado. Despite the cumulative unpleasantness of the weekly visits, he takes them, if not happily, then at least philosophically. "I just say, 'hurry up, Doc, get it over with!' "

There are days, however, when the pain is unbearable.

"That's one of the worst things about this disease," his mother says. "There are so many complications. Like the time he had trouble with his spleen. For five days and nights he was bent over in pain. It was like he had an attack of appendicitis that lasted for a week."

The Cappellettis live in a modest brick house on South Madison Avenue, a tree-lined street in Upper Darby, a working-class suburb just outside the Philadelphia city line. Joey's brother John learned to play football on that narrow street in front of their home.

John plays now for the Los Angeles Rams, but even though he's living on the West Coast, he still sees Joey frequently. Before he would sign his contract with the Rams, John insisted on the insertion of an unusual clause. It provides that two of the Cappelletti family will be supplied airplane and stadium tickets to all Rams home games.

John is a big, zestful guy, but melancholy creeps over him when he talks about his kid brother. "He's gone through so much, and he always takes it so well. He's an inspiration to me and to the rest of the family. He's brave, you know, and his courage has brought the whole family closer together. If there's some hidden purpose to all he's suffered, it must be to make the lives of the people he touches more meaningful."

Joey is unquestionably brave. With leukemia, though, there are so many demands and drains on his reserve. Aside from the inevitable emergencies, there are the unrelenting Mondays.

"For a long time, the hardest thing for Joseph to accept," his mother says, "was that even though he was going to the hospital and getting all those terrible treatments, he wasn't getting any better."

Being sick is, for him, a way of life, but children are tremendously adaptable, and Joey has tried to adjust even to this ultimate misfortune.

"Every day he's not in the hospital is a special day, and we try to make the most of it."

In spite of his handicaps, Joey has been unwilling to leave the world of sports exclusively to his big brothers. Whenever he's well enough, he quarterbacks for one of the pickup teams who play two-hand touch football on South Madison Avenue.

Whenever the weather is good, he impatiently passes the day waiting for the other children to get home from school. Usually, from about two o'clock on, which is at least an hour too early, he sits waiting under one of the big oak trees in front of his house. Already wearing his helmet and shoulder pads, he casually tosses his football up and down, while telling Governor, his dog and constant companion, how well he's going to do when the game finally gets started.

Affected by Joey's enthusiasm to get the game under way, the school kids generally don't even go home to change. They just dump their books on one of the parked cars and impatiently choose up sides. Joey's popularity on the block ensures that he'll be one of the captains, and because he can't run very much, he's always one of the quarterbacks. None of the kids talk about Joey being sick. It's something that's been going on for so long, it's just one of the conditions of the game, like the weather or the parked cars.

Then, right up until dinnertime, the two teams fight it out, charging up and down South Madison Avenue. Only the occasional traffic and their parents calling them into the house interrupt the heady feeling that if they do well in the big game, they'll all be strong contenders for next year's Heisman Trophy.

"How do you feel today, son?" his father asked him one morning. As he struggled to pull himself out of bed, it was obvious that Joey was weak and sick.

"Where's my uniform?" Joey's question was his answer. He was determined to go to the game.

"Are you sure, Joseph?" In the summer of 1973, Mr. Cappelletti was the coach of a Little League baseball team called the Pee Wee Cardinals. Joey had joined the team and because of his great spirit, made it to every game and practice.

"I'm okay, Dad," he said, holding on to his dresser to steady himself. Joey's bedroom is like a big trophy case. The walls are lined with pennants, and the handmade shelves sag from the weight of all the awards tracing the high-school and college sports careers of his older brothers. Joey always wanted to be part of that, so despite feeling feeble and weak from the effects of either the disease or the medicine, he would drag his uniform on.

"I probably should have stopped him," his mother says, "but he wanted to play so much. Even on the days he didn't actually get into the game because he wasn't strong enough to swing a bat or stand out in the field, he still wanted to be there in his uniform."

"Cappelletti, pinch-hit for Harris!" During one ballgame, when his father looked down the bench in the dugout and saw Joey looking unusually spry, he sent him in. Swinging his bat around to warm up, then using it to knock some nonexistent dirt out of his spikes, Joey stepped up to the plate.

He adjusted his cap, eyed the pitcher intensely, and took a mighty cut at the ball. The first pitch was strike one—Joey had missed, swinging so hard that he almost knocked himself over. But if it looked funny, nobody laughed. Spectators for both teams were rooting for Joey.

He swung at and missed the second pitch also, but he connected with the third. He hit a ground ball that skipped between the first and second basemen for a single.

It took a great deal of self-control for Mr. Cappelletti not to leap for joy at his son's success. He sent a runner in for Joey, then all the Pee Wee Cardinals on the bench applauded as Joey trotted back toward the dugout, tipping his cap and grinning widely.

His parents were relieved when the season finally ended, but they were also extremely proud of Joseph.

"He's a fighter," his father says, eloquently summing it all up.

As is usual, the league held an awards dinner. Between five and six hundred ballplayers, their managers, coaches, and parents filled the Alpine Inn, a Bavarian restaurant in the area that has a large hall frequently used to cater important local events.

It was a special night for the kids, the kind during which everyone got his name called and a trophy to take home just for playing. After dinner, and after the long process of handing a statuette to each ballplayer in the league was over, the special awards were announced for best batting average, best pitching record, most valuable player, and so on.

When that was done, the Pee Wee Cardinals announced that they had one more award to present. One of the businessmen who sponsored the team stood up.

"The Cardinals would like to present this trophy"—he held it up so everybody in the room could see it—"which read, 'To the most courageous player on the Pee Wee Cardinals, 1973,' to our pitch-hitting ace . . . Joey Cappelletti!"

Joey was stunned. He truly never expected anything like it. He sat at the table with his mouth opened in astonishment, looking around at his parents. His father patted him on the back, his mother urged him to go up and get it.

"Go ahead, Joseph. You have to accept it!"

He finally got out of his seat and meandered through the crowded tables to the head of the room. Joey has a way of tossing his head back and forth when he's embarrassed. He was doing that when he shyly took the award, his eyes solidly fixed on the floor, and started to walk away.

"Aren't you going to make a speech, Joey?" the businessman asked.

Joey slowly turned and with tremendous effort came back to the microphone. "Thanks. This is neat." It took him about two seconds to say it, and about another five to hurry back to his table, blushing grandly. Everybody applauded. There aren't many ten-year-olds who can boast of having won both the Pee Wee Cardinals' courage award and the Heisman Trophy in the same year. Both are now conspicuously displayed, occupying central space on the mantelpiece in the living room.

Partly because of what they've endured, helplessly watching Joey fight an unbeatable disease, the Cappelletti family is very closely knit. Michael, Martin, and John, all in their early twenties, are virtually inseparable when they're home, and are always catering to their little brother. John took two weeks off during the summer when Joey turned twelve to spend with him down at the New Jersey shore.

Because John is such a well-known and admired football player in the New Jersey–Pennsylvania area, hordes of young fans would follow the boys whenever they walked down the beach. When John was asked for his autograph, he would turn and ask Joey kiddingly if he should give it to them. Joey never said no, but he understandably enjoyed a great amount of prestige that vacation.

Joey's older sister, Jean, is a student at Archbishop Prendergast High School in Upper Darby. She wants to be a professional nurse. It's something she never would have chosen, except for her brother's experience. She's always been queasy about blood and the other sad realities of sickness. Now she wants to care for children, like Joey, who are terminally ill, making whatever life they have left as bearable as possible.

Joseph's illness also played a major role in John's original decision to attend Penn State. After a great sports career at Monsignor Bonner High Schoool, he had received dozens of offers of athletic scholarships from colleges across the country. Midway through his senior year, with the choice of colleges still undecided, John's classmates scheduled a fund-raising benefit night for Joey.

He was seven years old at the time, and had just been diagnosed as a victim of leukemia.

The usual tradition at Monsignor Bonner had been for the graduating class to leave some memento or gift to the school. The class of 1970 unanimously decided, instead, to hold a fundraising student rally to help the

Cappellettis offset the tremendous medical costs confronting them. A thousand students attended, and they raised more than fourteen hundred dollars.

The guest speaker was Joe Paterno, Penn State's legendary coach. At the time, he was also the national chairman of the American Cancer Society.

Paterno spoke about Joey and other children with the same affliction. John was deeply touched by his sincerity and understanding. John already knew that Paterno was a good football coach; that day he also found him to be a man worthy of admiration and respect. John signed with Penn State on March 16, 1970, the same day Joey and his parents first stood in the admissions office of Children's Hospital, nervously waiting to register.

When John was playing for Penn State, the family, including Joey, never missed a game either at home or away. Even if Joseph was feeling very sick, he'd always go. Sometimes his parents would voice a vain protest, as they did when he was playing Little League baseball, but they discovered eventually that the excitement of an upcoming game often acted as a temporary curative.

"If he feels like going anywhere, now we let him go." His mother explains that "he's so determined to act like the other kids, I think that's why he's still here."

One birthday, Joey was invited to Penn State's locker room before their game with the University of West Virginia. The warm-ups were finished, and the hulking ballplayers were making last-minute adjustments to their equipment, getting their hands taped, or slouching on the benches, listening to final instructions from the coaches.

When it was time for them to take the field, the squad gathered in a silent circle as Coach Paterno led them in the traditional prayer.

"Now, let's go!" They clapped once in unison when it was over, and let out a blood-curdling yell. Then the team started filing out, their spikes sounding like a stampede of buffalo on the concrete floor of the locker room. Joey was standing near the exit, slapping the giants on their legs and offering encouragement as they lumbered past on their way to the field.

As John went past, he smiled and offered Joey a special birthday present.

"I'm going to get four for you today, Joey," he promised.

"You mean you're going to score four touchdowns?"

"That's what I mean."

"Wow!"

Four touchdowns in a single football game is a rarely obtained total for any ballplayer. Yet it never occurred to Joey to doubt his brother.

In Penn State's rout of West Virginia that afternoon, John ran for 130 yards and scored four touchdowns before Coach Paterno put in the second string.

"Just like he said he would!" Joey happily told his family, sitting in the stands. "He told me he was going to do it!"

The grateful team later that afternoon awarded Joey the game ball as an additional birthday present for his valuable moral support.

In the five years Joey has been going to Children's Hospital, the family has spent tens of thousands of dollars on nonstop medical expenses. Mr. Cappelletti puts in as many hours of hard-working overtime as he can, but his salary is eaten away by the enormous, endless bills that follow every painful Monday-morning visit Joey makes to Philadelphia.

"It's been with us for such a long time, and it's so expensive . . . it's a very expensive sickness."

Joey's father says it with great reluctance, as if embarrassed to mention the practical aspects of his son's illness.

The family income is supplemented during the summers by their snow-cone and pretzel stand on West Chester Pike, the main thoroughfare near their home. It's just a haphazard homemade plywood thing, near a busy intersection where the cars are moving slowly enough to see it. John actually started the thriving little business during one of his college summer vacations.

His father jokes that John went into business because he was too lazy to get a real job, an allegation his mother energetically denies. The stand is Joey's favorite hangout during the summer months, and being the only kid on the block with an unlimited supply of snow cones doesn't hurt his popularity.

But in colder weather, when school is in session, he's frequently very lonely. All the other children his age are in school. Joey occasionally attends, but he is usually too sick or his condition is too unstable to risk a full day of classes. He has a tutor who comes to the house every day except Mondays.

He's studying between the fifth and sixth-grade levels. His friends used to ask why he didn't go to school, but by now his staying home is accepted as normal. The other children don't know the specific nature of his illness; they just know he'll never be well.

"Who are your best friends, Joey?" I asked him one afternoon in the fall. We were playing catch with a partially deflated football in the small backyard behind his house. In order to get far enough apart to make the game interesting, Joey had placed me precariously close to the windows in the back of the house, while he stood against the back fence in the narrow space between the garage and his mother's clothesline.

"Bugs and Governor," he answered without hesitation, concentrating on getting enough distance and putting a decent spiral on the semiflattened ball.

Having to fight loneliness as well as illness during each school year, Joey has become very attached to Governor, the dog, and Bugs, his rabbit. At one time there had also been a rooster, but he wasn't very popular around the neighborhoood. Upper Darby isn't exactly a farming community, and the area residents had had a hard time adjusting to the rooster's wake-up calls.

Governor is small, skinny, brownish, and of dubious ancestry. He's also friendly, full of energy, and noisy, and as Joey and I tossed the football back and forth, Governor would charge from one to the other, barking in endless, usually fruitless pursuit. But whenever one of us missed the ball, there would be a time-out of several minutes while we tried to corner the sly dog, who was casually chewing the laces and teasingly pretending not to hear us calling him.

"He's a mutt, I guess," Joey explained lovingly. "But he's a great mutt."

When the ball was finally recovered and the game over, Joey, Governor, and I sat leaning against the garage. There was almost no traffic out on South Madison Avenue. It was a quiet afternoon, crisp, cool, and crystal-clear—the kind of day that usually fills people with optimism. The little dog had even settled down and dozed off.

"You know something, Joey?" I looked at him, full of admiration.

"What?"

"I think you're really a brave kid."

"Yeah? Why?"

"Well . . . uh, just because."

"Because why?"

"You're always so happy," I said finally, but his face was still full of questions. Unwilling to explain it anymore than that, I asked another question instead. "Where do you get your courage from?"

"My courage? From *The Wizard of Oz*," he answered matter-of-factly.

"*The Wizard of Oz?*"

"Yeah. Didn't you see it? I saw it three times!"

"Oh. The movie!"

"Yeah. You remember. There was the straw man with no brain. The tin man with no heart. And the lion with no courage." He explained it slowly, the way people do to young children or illiterates.

"Whenever I get afraid," he continued, "I think of the cowardly lion. Then I'm not afraid anymore." He said it as if it were the most obvious proposition in the world.

When he isn't on the street playing football with his friends, or in the backyard with Bugs and Governor, Joey is around the corner at the firehouse. He gets along well with all the guys in Upper Darby's small fire department and has become a fixture at the station.

The fire fighters call him "Trouble," which, of course, he isn't. But it's such a nice, normal nickname for a twelve-year-old who's thinking about becoming a fireman when he grows up, that it's touchingly appropriate.

It's impossible to give a current account of Joey's physical condition, because it will doubtless change several times before it can be printed. In the summer of 1974, for instance, after a long period of relative stability, Joey collapsed totally.

For the first time in the five years she'd been bringing him to Children's Hospital, Mrs. Cappelletti was asked to stay overnight. Joey had been admitted in critical condition, and the staff wanted her there when he died.

"It's something they never do unless they think it's the end." Mrs. Cappelletti is, unfortunately, experienced in the methods of the hospital. For her there are no longer any subtleties. "They feel it's easier on the family if they're right there with them when they go."

But the scrappy fighter, winner of both the Pee Wee Cardinals' courage award and the Heisman Trophy, fought back and recovered temporarily.

As she spoke, his mother was looking out the kitchen window to the backyard. Joey was still back there, tossing a stick for Governor. "There are times when I think about the thirty-nine boys and girls in the original group, and I start to wonder whether he's really the lucky one. I know I shouldn't say it, and most times I don't believe it . . . but is it lucky, really, for a kid to go through all Joey's had to go through?

"He's had such a tough life. It's all he's ever known. Joey knows how sick he is, but he's a brave little man, and even if somebody went up to him and told him he was going to die, he wouldn't believe it. He has more faith and hope than that."

REACH ACROSS
THE GENERATIONS

With books that explore disenchantment and discovery, failure and conquest, and seek to bridge the gap between adolescence and adulthood.

☐	PHOEBE Patricia Dizenzo	2104	$ .95
☐	BONNIE JOE, GO HOME Jeanette Eyerly	2490	$1.25
☐	NOBODY WAVED GOODBYE Elizabeth Haggard	2670	$1.25
☐	THE UPSTAIRS ROOM Johanna Reiss	2858	$1.25
☐	DAVE'S SONG Robert McKay	2893	$1.25
☐	I NEVER LOVED YOUR MIND Paul Zindel	7993	$ .95
☐	THE FRIENDS Rosa Guy	8541	$1.25
☐	OX GOES NORTH John Ney	8658	$1.25
☐	WHERE THE RED FERN GROWS Wilson Rawls	8676	$1.25
☐	RUN SOFTLY, GO FAST Barbara Wersba	8713	$1.25
☐	ELLEN: A SHORT LIFE, LONG REMEMBERED Rose Levit	8729	$1.25
☐	SUMMER OF MY GERMAN SOLDIER Bette Greene	10192	$1.50
☐	HATTER FOX Marilyn Harris	10320	$1.75
☐	THE BELL JAR Sylvia Plath	10370	$1.95
☐	IT'S NOT THE END OF THE WORLD Judy Blume	10559	$1.25
☐	THE MAN WITHOUT A FACE Isabelle Holland	10757	$1.25
☐	I KNOW WHY THE CAGED BIRD SINGS Maya Angelou	10842	$1.75
☐	RICHIE Thomas Thompson	11029	$1.75
☐	MY DARLING, MY HAMBURGER Paul Zindel	11032	$1.50

Buy them at your local bookstore or use this handy coupon for ordering:

Bantam Books, Inc., Dept. EDN, 414 East Golf Road, Des Plaines, Ill. 60016

Please send me the books I have checked above. I am enclosing $_____ (please add 35¢ to cover postage and handling). Send check or money order —no cash or C.O.D.'s please.

Mr/Mrs/Miss_____

Address_____

City_____State/Zip_____

EDN—4/77

Please allow three weeks for delivery. This offer expires 4/78.